INTENT FOR A NATION

MICHAEL BYERS

what is canada for?

INTENT FOR

A NATION

A relentlessly optimistic manifesto
for Canada's role in the world

Douglas & McIntyre
Vancouver / Toronto

For Cameron and Fraser

Douglas & McIntyre Ltd.
2323 Quebec Street, Suite 201
Vancouver, British Columbia
Canada V5T 4S7
www.douglas-mcintyre.com

Library and Archives Canada Cataloguing in Publication
Byers, Michael, 1966–
Intent for a nation : what is Canada for? / Michael Byers.Includes index.

ISBN 978-1-55365-250-2

1. Canada. 2. Canada—Politics and government—21st century.
3. Canada—Relations. I. Title.
FC640.B93 2007   971.07   C2007-901901-3

Editing by Scott Steedman
Copy editing by Wendy Fitzgibbons
Cover design by Peter Cocking
Text design by Jessica Sullivan
Printed and bound in Canada by Friesens
Printed on acid-free paper that is forest friendly (100% post-consumer recycled paper) and has been processed chlorine free.

We gratefully acknowledge the financial support of the Canada Council for the Arts, the British Columbia Arts Council, the Province of British Columbia through the Book Publishing Tax Credit, and the Government of Canada through the Book Publishing Industry Development Program (BPIDP) for our publishing activities.

CONTENTS

— ACKNOWLEDGEMENTS —

M Y THINKING ABOUT Canadian foreign policy
has been influenced by many people, only a
few of whom I can thank here.

I owe a profound debt to my parents, Brigitte and Bob Byers.
Not least, they helped me understand that different Canadians
connect with this country in quite different ways. My mother is
an immigrant, born in Germany, and my father, of older Canadian
stock, has some First Nations blood in his veins.

I am enormously grateful to Katharine, my wife and best friend.
She too immigrated to Canada, just three years ago. Watching her
learn about and adapt to this country has given me a better appreciation of its wonders and eccentricities.

A number of pro-Canadian activists have inspired me, even if
we do not always agree. They include Maude Barlow, Duncan Cameron, Bruce Campbell, Murray Dobbin, Mel Hurtig, Seth Klein,
David Langille, Peggy Mason, Jillian Skeet and Steve Staples.

My understanding of Canadian foreign policy has been enhanced through frank discussions with John Amagoalik, Dawn

Black, Bill Blaikie, Stephen Clarkson, Andrew Cohen, Robert Greenhill, Paul Heinbecker, Rob Huebert, Wade Huntley, George Hynall, Paul Knox, Suzanne Lalonde, Jack Layton, Stephen Lewis, Margaret Macmillan, Alexa McDonough, Frank McKenna, Roy McLaren, Alex Neve, David Orchard, Louis Pauly, John Polanyi, Kent Roach, Colin Robertson, Douglas Ross, Stephen Toope, Wesley Wark, David Welch, Jennifer Welsh and many, many others—including numerous civil servants whose names I will not divulge.

I am also grateful to Gilbert Merkx for initiating the process that took me back home, by asking me, while I was a law professor at Duke, to also direct that university's Center for Canadian Studies. Lloyd Axworthy—a political idol of mine for nearly three decades—helped things along by recruiting me to the University of British Columbia.

I owe a particular debt to Len Finlay of the University of Saskatchewan. Twenty years ago, Len taught me about the wonders of Shakespeare and thus inspired my love of the English language; last year—in an essay published in *English Studies in Canada*—he fortuitously provided the title for this book.

Finally, I am grateful to the many editors who have improved my writings on the topics covered here, including Natasha Hassan, Jerry Johnson, Bob Levin, Patrick Martin, Val Ross and Carl Wilson of the *Globe and Mail*, Jim Atkins of the *Toronto Star*, David Beers of the *Tyee*, Paul Laity and John Sturrock of the *London Review of Books* and especially Scott McIntyre and Scott Steedman of Douglas & McIntyre.

This book benefited from research assistance from Jennifer Breakspear and financial support from the Walter and Duncan Gordon and Pierre Elliott Trudeau foundations. As always, Kathy and Mike Edmunds provided the quiet retreat where most of the writing was done.

MB
VANCOUVER · January 31, 2007

A S A CHILD, I spent my summers on a farm near Stoughton, Saskatchewan. My awareness of international affairs dates from that time. For although southeastern Saskatchewan might seem a long way from anywhere, global politics were ever present. My grandparents' livelihood depended on the price of wheat, and that price was determined by events abroad. I remember my grandfather, with only a Grade 8 education, discussing quotas and subsidies with acumen worthy of an international trade lawyer. At the same time, we saw the contrails of American B-52 bombers high overhead. The planes were flying north to the High Arctic, where they would circle on standby—just like in *Dr. Strangelove*—waiting for the order to fly into the Soviet Union to drop their nuclear bombs. Rural Saskatchewan was smack dab in the middle of the Cold War.

I have spent my life learning, reading, thinking and teaching about Canada's place in the world: first as a high school student in both Ottawa and Lethbridge; then as an English literature and political studies major at the University of Saskatchewan in Saskatoon, and later as a law student at McGill in Montreal. For twelve years—from 1992 to 2004—I lived outside Canada. The first seven years were spent in Britain, studying and teaching international law at Cambridge and Oxford universities. The next five years were spent in Durham, North Carolina, as a professor of law and director of Canadian Studies at Duke University. It was then time to return to Canada to teach political science at the University of British Columbia (UBC).

It is a strange experience, returning to one's country after an extended period abroad. Everything is familiar, yet so much has changed. Things you had once been attached to—Peter Gzowski and *Morningside*—exist no longer. Things you had forgotten—the almost spiritual role that hockey occupies in the Canadian psyche—suddenly reappear.

Returning from an extended absence can improve your understanding of where you come from, since you have seen how things are done differently elsewhere. One of the reasons Canadians support universal public health care so passionately is that so many of us have lived in countries without it. Canada's strict limits on the financing of political parties are possible because so many of us have seen how badly wealth distorts politics elsewhere.

Returning from a long absence can also help you see changes that, because they have occurred slowly, are less visible to those who have stayed at home. For me, the most shocking change was the dramatic increase in the number of homeless people on the streets of our cities, in this, one of the wealthiest countries on Earth. I still find it disturbing that many of my fellow citizens are so desperate for a few pennies that they are willing to sort through the Dumpster behind my house at 6:00 AM.

Of course, I have noticed positive changes too, most notably the incredibly socially conscious and internationally oriented character of the current generation of Canadian youth. I am privileged to teach hundreds of young Canadians each year, not just at UBC but also—thanks to the tradition of the "guest lecture"—at universities across Canada and around the world. Their optimism and idealism, their faith in how progressive views can improve the world, is inspiring and a little humbling. And a contrast to what I encountered in both Britain and the United States!

In much the same way, returning after a long absence can help you to see that widely accepted assumptions have become outdated, or that national debates have—for reasons of bias or lack of information—diverged or fallen behind debates on the same issues elsewhere. The Canadian debate about climate change is the best contemporary example of this. In September 2004, British prime minister Tony Blair stated that climate change could be "so far-reaching in its impact and irreversible in its destructive power that it alters radically human existence." Blair's assessment was generally accepted in Europe: the debate there now concerns how to reduce carbon dioxide emissions by 60 per cent or more within the next few decades. But anyone taking the same position in Canada is dismissed as a member of an alarmist fringe group.

I have now been back in Canada for three years. My eyes are still fresh, but my understandings are better grounded. I have used my time to reconnect with my country and its people, travelling from Halifax, Nova Scotia, to Tofino, British Columbia. I have even sailed the Northwest Passage on the Canadian Coast Guard icebreaker *Amundsen*, spending two weeks living, learning, and speaking French with its Québécois crew. And I have involved myself in national debates on issues from transboundary water to missile defence, Afghanistan and the Middle East. I see this place as it is now, in all its messy reality, rather than how, in my absence, I dreamed it to be.

But my time outside Canada has also made me far more optimistic about this country's future than the majority of Canadian academics, journalists and policymakers, many of whom believe that Canada is destined to be a minor actor on the world stage.

Even the most optimistic doubt that this country can play more than a modest role, by generating some new ideas, mediating the occasional conflict and, above all, by riding the coattails of more powerful states. They see the glass as half empty.

I see the glass as half full, for Canada is a potentially influential country. Consider the facts: Geographically, we are the second-largest country in the world. We have a population of nearly 33 million well-educated, globally connected people, many of them immigrants or the children of immigrants, speaking two official languages and dozens of other ancestral tongues and coexisting in remarkable harmony. We have one of the highest standards of living, good public services and a strong infrastructure. Our abundant resources are becoming ever more valuable, and we have vast tracts of rich agricultural land. Our location, halfway between Asia and Europe and contiguous with the United States, places us close to the world's largest markets, at a time when advances in transport and communications are further reducing the cost and time involved in engaging with other countries. We have the eighth-largest economy on the planet and are the only G8 country (apart from oil and gas-rich Russia) with balanced books. We are a member of the Organization for Economic Co-operation and Development, the North Atlantic Treaty Organization, the Commonwealth, the Francophonie and the Arctic Council. We have no sworn enemies and are still well regarded for our contributions—mostly during the 1950s, '60s and '70s—to multilateral diplomacy, international law and United Nations peacekeeping. We are, believe it or not, the envy of the world. We are—take a deep breath and don't laugh—a powerful country.

Yet successive Canadian governments have failed to exercise leadership internationally. They have failed to push for real and positive change. They have underplayed Canada's potential, content to stand in the shadows or—worse yet—to meekly follow the lead of a powerful but uneasy neighbour, the USA.

It is time to seize upon the vast potential of this great country, including the goodwill, expertise and ability of so many Canadians.

It is time to assert our historical independence and take progressive action on the challenges facing Canada and the world today. Canada should, as a country, be asserting itself as a "global citizen," shaping the international agenda and using its influence to secure positive, progressive change. As Canadians, we should dare to dream great dreams. As Canadians, we should dare to make them happen.

UN CANADIEN ERRANT:

Why I Gave Up My
U.S. Green Card

"THIS IS THE FIRST time I've met someone who wanted to do that."

The U.S. immigration officer's southern drawl, so out of place in the Vancouver airport, was accentuated by incredulity.

A "green card," which is actually off-white in colour and called a Permanent Resident Card, provides full rights to enter, live and work in the world's most powerful country. It conveys most of the advantages of U.S. citizenship, so much so that it can be traded in for an American passport after just five years. Yet there I was, four and a half years after I had acquired it, asking for my green card to be taken away.

Acquiring U.S. permanent residency is an arduous process, involving blood tests, chest X-rays and numerous documents, including police certificates attesting to a crime-free past. Even with a prominent sponsor, Duke University, it had taken me three years to get my green card.

Apart from the 50,000 "diversity immigrants" selected by lottery each year, the 50,000 refugees and the roughly 140,000 who, like me, are targeted for universities and high-tech jobs, most of those who aspire to live and work in the United States have no chance of legally settling there. Still, millions flock to the country, like moths to a flame.

I was on my way to a conference in San Diego when I surrendered my green card. The next morning, out for an early run, I saw scores of Mexican men tending lawns and flower beds. Later, a woman from Guatemala cleaned my hotel room. I remembered one of my graduate students at Duke, now a law professor in Mexico City, explaining that most such labourers hold forged social-security cards that are convincing enough to protect their employers from the police, while providing no protections for the workers.

Some illegal immigrants do have decent jobs. In North Carolina, my colleagues and I frequented an upscale restaurant where one waiter, "Mark," spoke fondly of his family in Calgary while admitting, with evident regret, that he had not been home for ten years. I wondered why not—an arrest warrant, perhaps?—but I knew that Mark was working solely for tips and probably not filing taxes in either the United States or Canada. This, in itself, was likely reason enough for him not to approach the border.

In 2000, *Globe and Mail* columnist Jeffrey Simpson estimated that 660,000 Canadians were living and working illegally in the United States. Most Canadians blend easily into U.S. society. The lack of a "foreign" accent helps, as does our fluency with American pop culture. It is also true that many Americans assume that Canada, like Puerto Rico, is very nearly part of their country.

Immigration papers acquired greater significance after September 11, 2001, as concerns about security escalated into hysteria and fear replaced curiosity as the standard response to things unknown. Before 9/11, my wife's English accent often generated a friendly response, including the comment, "You sound just like Princess Diana." After the attacks, the warm chatter gave way to a strained silence.

At least my princess had a green card and was, therefore, on the legally advantageous side of the divide between "us" and "them." Thousands of men of Arab ethnicity were rounded up and either detained or deported without charge or access to lawyers. Significantly, none of them were citizens or permanent residents of the United States.

Of course, even U.S. citizenship does not provide the protections it once did. In 2002, the Bush administration jailed two Americans without charge or access to lawyers, in direct denial of habeas corpus, a common-law principle that dates back to the Magna Carta. And then there is the secret, unconstitutional wire-tapping program.

"Are you sure you want to do this?" the immigration officer whispered as she ushered me towards the secondary-screening room.

"Yes," I replied. "I don't want to lie to you. I no longer live in the United States."

Under U.S. law, permanent residents lose that status if they leave the country for more than one year. Yet many green-card holders flout this law, returning to the United States periodically to "keep their options open." Many maintain U.S. addresses, sometimes with family or friends but often with commercial providers, to sustain the fiction that they reside in the United States. Some companies even rent street addresses, as opposed to box numbers, and will automatically ship mail onward to a designated foreign address.

Absentee green-card holders in the past often used their driver's licences to cross the border, or they relied on new passports that were free of stamps that might alert an attentive immigration officer to their dubious status. If asked, they denied having a connection with the United States.

Such ploys are becoming riskier as the computer systems of different U.S. government departments, and different national governments, are linked together as part of the post-9/11 drive to improve security. At particular risk are green-card holders who have failed to file U.S. tax returns, as all those with permanent resident status are required to do.

As of January 2007, anyone entering the United States by air or sea has been required to have a passport. From June 2009, the same requirement will apply to all those who enter at land crossings. The Canadian government has lobbied against this move because of concerns that it will deter millions of Americans—less than one-quarter of whom currently have passports—from visiting Canada. The cruise ship and conference industries are particularly vulnerable, along with the 2010 Winter Olympics to be held in Vancouver. The new requirement will also make it more difficult for green-card holders living in Canada, and Canadians living illegally in the United States, to move freely between the two countries.

At the secondary screening, I was greeted by an immigration officer whose name tag, features and accent suggested Vietnamese origins.

"Which form should I use?" he asked his supervisor. The supervisor, a stout man with a Midwestern accent, gave a world-weary sigh: "Voluntaries get the short form."

It took forty-five minutes to complete the short form. It was an entirely businesslike procedure: no small talk, no smiles. At one point, I commented on the complexity of the process. The immigration officer replied, "Well, this is a big deal. It's like getting married."

More like getting divorced, I thought.

My wife and I had moved to North Carolina in 1999. The stock market was booming, most Americans felt prosperous and secure and Bill Clinton—despite Whitewater and Lewinsky—was still capably in charge. It seemed obvious that one of two smart, experienced, open-minded internationalists, Al Gore or John McCain, would follow in January 2001.

But then we were amused, perplexed and finally appalled at the dirty tricks deployed in the 2000 election campaign, first to defeat McCain and then to steal victory from Gore. And we felt nothing but horror as the Twin Towers collapsed, knowing not only that thousands of lives had been lost, but also that George W. Bush's neo-conservative advisers would seize their chance to plot a militaristic course.

My instinctive response was to put words to paper. Five days later, on September 16, 2001, my article "The hawks are hovering. Prepare for more bombs" appeared in London's *Independent on Sunday*. I continued to write about the Bush administration, almost exclusively for British papers, chastising it for its violations of human rights and international law, its hostility towards multilateral institutions and its destabilizing doctrine of pre-emption.

Needless to say, my opinions attracted considerable hostility, all the more so because I was expressing them from within a conservative law school at a conservative university in the very conservative South. I stood my ground, but it was not easy. And then it occurred to me: the United States was not my country; it was not a place for which I wanted to fight. My thoughts drifted northward, to the place where my values had been forged.

The immigration officer worked his way through a series of questions designed to confirm my identity and soundness of mind. The last question was the toughest: "Why do you wish to surrender your permanent resident card?"

How do you explain to an American—especially one with a flag on his shoulder and a gun on his hip—that you no longer wish to live in his country?

I thought about the man across the counter, how he might have fled the postwar chaos and poverty of Vietnam, how he might have been plucked off a rickety boat by the U.S. Navy and perhaps gravitated towards the immigration service out of gratitude to his new homeland.

At the same time, I thought about how I might be replicating his experience in one small but important respect. My principal motivation in surrendering my green card was not to avoid problems at the border. I was seeking to commit—without hesitation or qualification—to my own special place.

You see, as someone who was born in Canada, I never had to affirm my citizenship. I never had to demonstrate my deep love for this country, with its vast and spectacular landscapes and diverse yet tolerant peoples, its distinct and complex history, values and institutions and its oh-so-promising future. Unlike the millions of Canadians who were born outside Canada, I had never made my choice.

The moment was upon me. My heart bursting with pride, I looked the immigration officer in the eye and said, as simply and non-judgementally as possible: "I have chosen to live permanently in Canada."

"Permanently?" he asked.

"Yes," I said. "Of course."

INTENT FOR A NATION

When Stephen Harper was asked whether he loved Canada, he hesitated, pursed his lips and replied, "Canada is a great country."

The Canadian political philosopher George Grant would not have been surprised. He wrote about people like Harper four decades ago in his influential 1965 book, *Lament for a Nation: The Defeat of Canadian Nationalism*: "In its simplest form, continentalism is the view of those who do not see what all the fuss is about. The purpose of life is consumption, and therefore the border is an anachronism." Grant pronounced that Canada had effectively ceased to exist, since the distinctive aspects of Canadian society and politics could not withstand the integrating forces of continental capitalism and universal modernism radiating from the United States.

Was he right?

Grant said foreign policy would be first to succumb: "A branch-plant society could not possibly show independence over an issue on which the American government was seriously determined." He thought that the defence crisis of 1963 proved his point: when the U.S. State Department publicly rebuked John Diefenbaker for refusing to allow nuclear-armed missiles on Canadian soil, Canadians did not rally around their embattled prime minister; they voted him out of office.

I was born in 1966, one year after *Lament for a Nation* was published, and I have lived with Grant's thesis ever since. As a student at McGill, I remember one of my professors arguing that the 1988 "free-trade election" confirmed Grant's prediction. Canadians had given Prime Minister Brian Mulroney a clear mandate to eliminate tariffs on U.S. exports and thus the need for U.S. corporations to maintain subsidiaries here. They also endorsed Mulroney's acceptance that U.S. domestic law would apply to disputes between Canada and the United States over "dumping"—a technical term for the export of products, such as softwood lumber, at less than their alleged cost of production.

Around the same time, another young man was falling under the influence of a group of neo-conservative professors at the University of Calgary whose policy prescriptions would have made Canada almost indistinguishable from the United States. Although Stephen Harper ran against the Mulroney government in 1988 under the Reform Party banner, he supported the free trade agreement unequivocally.

Four years later, when I left Canada, I was convinced that the country was finished. My conviction deepened in 1994 when Jean Chrétien broke an election promise and ratified the North American Free Trade Agreement. The expanded pact shielded U.S. investors from Canadian environmental, health and safety regulations while mandating U.S. access to our energy supplies.

Chrétien's decision to stay out of the 2003 Iraq War was momentous. Forty years after Diefenbaker's downfall, a Canadian prime minister had declined to participate in a major U.S. military action. It seemed that, after all, economic sovereignty was not a prerequisite for independence in the foreign-policy domain.

Grant's thesis was tested again in 2005. George W. Bush had

deemed missile defence essential to U.S. national security and requested Canadian participation. But with polls indicating that most Canadians were against it, Paul Martin swallowed hard and said no.

Around the same time, pollsters discovered that the values of Canadians and Americans were diverging. Canadians had become more secular, tolerant of diversity and questioning of authority, while Americans were moving in the opposite direction. In Canada, these changes manifested themselves in the legalization of same-sex marriage and near-decriminalization of marijuana. In September 2003, the cover of the *Economist* was a moose in shades, under the banner "Canada is 'cool'."

Political scientists question whether individuals—as opposed to economic and political structures—have much influence on history. Yet it is difficult to explain Canada's continued independence without referring to Tommy Douglas, Lester B. Pearson and Pierre Elliott Trudeau. Douglas held the balance of power in the two minority parliaments that followed Diefenbaker's defeat. Together, he and Pearson introduced universal public health care and the Canada Pension Plan and kept Canada out of the Vietnam War. Trudeau then introduced the Official Languages Act, the Foreign Investment Review Agency, wage and price controls, and the national energy program. None of these leaders exhibited the all-encompassing, small-l liberalism and subservience to Washington that Grant had predicted of all subsequent Canadian governments. Diefenbaker was gone, but remnants of a socially conscious Canadian nationalism remained.

During the 1990s, Canada drifted towards the United States under the influence of free trade, a burgeoning U.S. economy and the charismatic moderation of Bill Clinton. So did many other countries. The relative peace and prosperity of the post–Cold War period—and the apparent victory of the liberal democratic capitalist model—prompted the economist Francis Fukuyama to announce the "end of history."

Were it not for George W. Bush, Canada might be on its way to becoming the fifty-first American state. But the U.S. president's bellicose rhetoric and overt religiosity made many Canadians nervous, while his administration's regressive cuts to taxes and social programs and massive increases in defence spending transformed the United States into a more unequal, fearful and militaristic place. Canada might still be moving in the direction of the United States, but since the year 2000, the United States has been moving away much faster.

Grant's thesis extended beyond the absorption of Canada into the United States. He believed that all countries would eventually unite into a "universal and homogeneous state" founded on a U.S.-centred modernism. Again, this prediction looks less likely today that it did in 2000, when the United States still seemed in ascendancy.

Bush's advisers squandered "soft power" through their evident contempt for international law and the opinions of other countries, while running up a national debt that has given foreign creditors—most notably the Chinese government—a stranglehold over the U.S. economy. At the same time, they became locked in a nihilistic struggle with radical Islam, creating chasms in international society that are more reminiscent of Samuel Huntington's "clash of civilizations" than they are of Fukuyama's—or Grant's—transnational blending of differences into a worldwide version of the United States.

Today, China is not the only country that is gaining power and influence relative to the United States. India, with a population of 1.1 billion and an economic growth rate of 8 per cent, is poised to become a great power. Europe is now a single economy that is larger than that of the U.S. Russia, which made the ruble a fully convertible currency in 2006, is returning to geopolitical relevance on the back of high prices for oil and gas. Instead of hegemony or homogeneity, we seem to be witnessing the emergence of a multipolar world made up of interdependent—though still fiercely independent—nation-states.

Canada's influence should be growing too, for all the reasons identified above and more: our geographic size and location; our well-educated, globally connected population; our high standard of living, strong public services and infrastructure; our abundant resources, large economy and firm fiscal foundations; our membership in international organizations and reputation for moderation and progressive thinking. Moreover, Canada has demonstrated the ability to achieve great things. We have done so internationally, for example, with the 1997 Landmines Convention. We have done so domestically, with universal public health care and our diverse, harmonious and livable cities. If Canadians have an inferiority complex, it is only because we became accustomed to living in the shadow of the world's most powerful state.

All of which made Stephen Harper a strange choice for prime minister in January 2006. Harper had wanted Canada to join the Iraq War in 2003. As he explained to the House of Commons: "In an increasingly globalized and borderless world, the relationship between Canada and the United States is essential to our prosperity, to our democracy and to our future." He also thought Canada should join the U.S. in missile defence. As early as May 2002, he criticized opponents of missile defence for offering "knee-jerk resistance ... despite the fact that Canada is confronted by the same threats from rogue nations equipped with ballistic missiles and weapons of mass destruction as is the United States."

Being elected prime minister changed neither Harper's views nor those of his rebranded Conservative Party. Although the quest for a majority government temporarily modulated their domestic policies, in foreign affairs their continentalism remained starkly evident. In just one year, the Harper government extended our involvement in a U.S.-led war in Asia, gave the Pentagon access to maritime surveillance over our coastal waters, followed the lead of the Bush administration on climate change and the Middle East and took surreptitious steps towards participating in missile defence.

Harper and his colleagues have always believed that Canadians would just as happily be Americans, and they have done their best to make us so. Fortunately, George Grant was wrong. Our distinctiveness—our love of country—is rooted in the non-economic compartments of our national psyche.

It remains to be seen whether Stéphane Dion is all that different. Is the new Liberal leader up to the task of withstanding the inexorable pressures of continentalism while providing meaningful leadership at the global level? Certainly, when it comes to Dion's signature issue of climate change (the focus of Chapter 6 of this book), his record as former federal environment minister is not encouraging.

At this point in Canadian history, we need vision and action, not just a "safe pair of hands." As Grant pointed out: "But a nation does not remain a nation only because it has roots in the past. Memory is never enough to guarantee that a nation can articulate itself in the present. There must be a thrust of intention into the future."

Canadians are confronted with great challenges, ranging from our deep economic, cultural and military exposure to the United States to climate change and nuclear proliferation. We need a vision to light the way, something more inspiring than keeping the U.S. border open to trade. This country is not a shadow of someone else's destiny; we have a greater purpose. Let's find that thrust of intention. Let's decide—by ourselves—what Canada is for.

— 1 —

TERRORISM:

Get a Grip

"I HOPE THEY CATCH the sods who did it," said the workman who was installing a new floor in my mother-in-law's kitchen near London, England. It was July 7, 2005, just five short minutes after the first radio report of explosions on Underground railway trains, and he was already back to work. Fifty-two people were killed and around seven hundred injured in the attacks. But the response of the British public was calm and measured. Later that day, my sister-in-law received a phone call from friends who, unable to find a train home after work, had repaired to a pub instead. The next day, I received an e-mail confirming a lunch meeting a few days later near Tavistock Square, where one of the suicide bombers had destroyed a double-decker bus.

The reaction of the British government was also measured. The army was not called in. The police described their work as a criminal investigation. A G8 summit meeting continued at Gleneagles, Scotland, with Prime Minister Tony Blair back at the negotiating table after a quick trip home to London.

The British had been bombed before. At the height of the Blitz in September 1940, German aircraft dropped more than five thousand tons of explosives on London in just one month. Later that year, Coventry was hit by nearly nine hundred incendiary bombs during a single night. For three decades, the Irish Republican Army (IRA) maintained a terrorist campaign against London, claiming more than one hundred lives. In 1973 alone, thirty-six bombs were detonated in the British capital. I remember taking the Underground on February 9, 1996, the day that a truck bomb exploded at Canary Wharf, killing two people and destroying a six-storey building. Yet the foundations of British democracy remained unshaken. Catholics or people of Irish ancestry were not collectively blamed. The IRA taught the British an all-important lesson: if you are fighting to defend your way of life, you must not give up your way of life.

In contrast, our American neighbours had little experience with terrorism prior to September 11, 2001. Many aspects of their response were excessive. They detained U.S. citizens without charge or access to lawyers, conducted a widespread and illegal electronic surveillance program, produced spurious legal opinions justifying torture, then invaded an uninvolved sovereign country on the basis of trumped-up evidence. Much of the response was counterproductive, as George W. Bush finally admitted in May 2006. At the same time, the president expressed regret at his own choice of language—including the memorable "wanted dead or alive"—in the immediate aftermath of the attacks on the World Trade Center and the Pentagon.

In June 2006, almost five years after 9/11, the Canadian police and intelligence services arrested seventeen men and youths in Toronto who they alleged were conspiring to commit terrorist acts. In the public sphere, the response was a strange mix of American hysteria and British coolness. Right-wing commentators immediately began chortling "we told you so." For them, the arrests were proof positive that radical Islamic terrorists were targeting all Western democracies, a situation that demanded unwavering support for U.S. foreign policy, stronger anti-terrorism laws and tighter security, including much closer scrutiny of Canadian Muslims. The following excerpt from a *National Post* column by Andrew Coyne is typical of what many said and wrote that week:

> The Canadian Security and Intelligence Service currently has on its watchlist at least 50 other terrorist cells in Canada, similar to the one alleged in the present case: young Muslim men who subscribe to an extreme interpretation of Islam, coupled with an even more extreme agenda of apocalyptic mayhem. For every cell the security forces know about, they estimate there are another 10 they do not know about.
>
> Everyone is talking about how this case is a "wake-up call." But if we are led to believe that, because this particular (alleged) attack was thwarted, the danger is past—or that it is possible to prevent all future attacks—we are little further ahead. The chances that the authorities can detect every last one of these plots in time to defuse them are remote. We can "harden the targets," we can lengthen the odds, but the likelihood approaches certainty that some time, somewhere, one of them will break through.
>
> What then? Rather ask: What now? We are about to undergo one of the greatest tests our society has yet had to endure—that is, whether we can remain a coherent society, different social groups sheltering under the same broad set of beliefs, in the face of an existential threat originating from within one particular group.

For a week or so, it seemed as if I were living in the United States again, with Canadian media outlets having morphed into imitations of Fox News, the *Washington Times* and freerepublic.com. Fortunately, the Canadian people exhibited considerably more restraint. In one poll conducted by Ipsos-Reid for CanWest Global just ten days after the arrests, 66 per cent of Canadians said they lacked sufficient information to tell whether the suspects were guilty or not. It seemed as if, having watched Americans overreact to 9/11, most Canadians were not about to jump to conclusions. The foiled plot was disturbing, but there was as much reason to feel secure as there was to worry; after all, the police and intelligence services had done their jobs. Prime Minister Stephen Harper, who undoubtedly reads the polls, wisely chose not to exploit the arrests as the basis for a major speech or policy change.

There is no disputing that terrorism—commonly defined as any action intended to cause death or serious injury to civilians in order to intimidate a population or compel its government to act—is a bad thing. The police and intelligence services deserve our thanks for having identified and arrested the alleged plotters before they posed a danger to anyone. Moreover, Coyne is correct to assert that Canada will likely suffer a terrorist attack at some point. Eighty-eight Australians died in October 2002 when a car bomb blew up outside a nightclub in Bali, Indonesia. Nearly two hundred Spaniards died in March 2004 when bombs exploded on four commuter trains in Madrid. The attacks on the London Underground followed one year later. It would be surprising if Australian, Spanish and British involvement in the U.S.-led invasion of Iraq was not a factor contributing to the attacks. Today, with more than two thousand troops engaged in a war in Afghanistan, Canada is almost certainly on a target list somewhere.

Yet terrorism is not new to Canadians. In 1970, Pierre Trudeau invoked the War Measures Act to counter what he called "an armed, revolutionary movement that is bent on destroying the very basis of our freedom." Fortunately, the threat was not as serious as the prime minister thought: only one person died during the October Crisis and most of the nearly 500 people detained were soon released without charge.

In June 1985, Air India Flight 182 was blown out of the sky over the Irish Sea. The bomb had been placed aboard in Vancouver and

280 of the 329 people who died were Canadian citizens. The October Crisis and the Air India bombing demonstrate that terrorism can arise from internal grievances or from grievances carried here by immigrants who feel no particular animosity towards Canada or other Canadians. Islamic fundamentalists do not have a monopoly on terrorism. And eventually, like all previous waves of terrorism, the current wave of Islamic terrorism will gradually fade away.

Most Canadians know this. Millions of us have roots in countries that have been subject to terrorist attacks. Vancouver's Punjabi community, which bore the brunt of the Air India bombing, was already scarred by terrorism in Kashmir. Toronto's Singhalese and Tamil communities are haunted by the continuing violence in Sri Lanka. Montreal's Jewish and Arab communities cringe every time a bomb explodes in the Middle East. Just about every immigrant community in Canada has been marked by terrorism in some way. This sad heritage does work to Canada's benefit in one respect: thanks to one of the highest rates of immigration in the world, this country has acquired a built-in sense of perspective and resilience concerning terrorism.

Those of us who call for cool heads are not naive. In addition to my time in Britain, I have visited Egypt and Israel during periods when both countries were subject to terrorist attacks. I taught in the United States during September 11, 2001, and its aftermath. An aunt and uncle of mine live five kilometres from the Bali nightclub where the October 2002 bombing occurred. Another of my aunts lost her boss, the CEO of the Deutsche Bank, when the Red Army Faction blew up his car outside Frankfurt, Germany, in 1989. Many other Canadians have more painful stories to tell.

Keeping calm after the Toronto arrests was made easier by the fact that the putative terrorists were amateurs. They had been tracked for two years and only acquired a (supposed) capacity to act when the police sold them bogus ammonium nitrate. Their apparent leader spoke openly about his violent intent, in one instance to a member of Parliament. The Hells Angels are much more professional and probably more dangerous.

Some commentators tried to provoke fear by focussing on reports that the conspirators had been inspired to violence by Web sites that celebrate the activities and ideology of Al-Qaeda. But why should this come as a surprise? Violence is constantly celebrated in our society—in music and movies, on TV and on countless Web sites, most of which are not Islamic. Violent acts are committed every day in our schools, streets and homes, usually by non-Muslims. Any focus on Islamic Web sites is unfair, even dangerously selective.

More recently, there have been calls for racial profiling to facilitate the detection of terrorists. At Duke Law School, my African American students called it "driving while black." Statistically, a black man in an expensive car is more likely to have committed a crime than a white man in a similar car, mostly because of the substantial economic disparities that still exist between those groups. And so my students, who had graduated at the top of their classes in some of the United States' best colleges and already had jobs lined up at prestigious New York and Washington law firms, were regularly pulled over and searched, sometimes at gunpoint.

Racial profiling fails on numerous counts. First, statistics are rarely applied consistently. If we wanted to be statistical about risk, we would save far more lives by prohibiting all young men from driving cars than we would save by racially profiling for terrorist suspects. Indeed, the number of roadway deaths caused by aggressive young male drivers *each year* greatly exceeds that which has *ever* been caused by terrorists. Second, racial profiling is unfair to the vast majority of people within the targeted group, who have done absolutely nothing wrong and who may—like my Duke law students—be seriously inconvenienced or even put at risk as a result of being profiled. Third, consider the negative impact that racial profiling has on the members of the group being targeted. Harassment and aggression breed resentment, not co-operation. Someone who feels harassed by the authorities just for being Arab or Muslim would be less inclined to inform those same authorities about a group of young men behaving suspiciously at the local mosque.

Like it or not, some small subset of people in any society will always feel aggrieved. Only a small number will seriously contemplate violence, and even fewer will actually act. Terrorism is part of a timeless phenomenon that can never be eradicated. It can only be reduced and managed. The challenge is to do so without engendering even more discontent.

After 9/11, Canada followed the United States in dramatically increasing funding for border guards, the police, and intelligence services. Those same authorities were given unprecedented powers of surveillance, detention and interrogation, with Canadians paying a significant price in terms of our civil liberties. Yes, Canada may be a safer place as a result, since it is now more likely that we will detect and apprehend any angry and amateurish young men and perhaps women who gather to plot a terrorist attack. But what are the chances of any surveillance system detecting truly professional terrorists? What airline security system can stop eight or ten physically fit young men with martial arts training from taking over a passenger plane without the use of weapons? Above all, what assurance do we have that a security-driven, war-fighting approach to terrorism will actually make the world a safer place?

As the Canadian major general Andrew Leslie said in August 2005: "Every time you kill an angry young man overseas, you're creating fifteen more who will come after you." A security-focussed, militarized approach is not necessarily the best way to reduce and manage terrorism. In the past, some countries have addressed the root causes of anger by adopting policies that foster inclusion and understanding, including by providing the right to vote in democratic elections along with laws and procedures that guard against the arbitrary exercise of power by the state. They have developed means of policing and intelligence gathering that are focussed and efficient, that guard against violence without provoking more of it. They have learned—sometimes through a painful process of trial and error—that terrorism succeeds only if societies and governments allow themselves to be terrorized. They have recognized that negotiating with terrorists is often a necessary prelude to a reduction in violence and, eventually, peace. The British successfully negotiated with the IRA, and Israel in the past has repeatedly secured the release of captured soldiers by, again, negotiating.

In this context, a comparison with crime is not out of place. The United States has the death penalty, a huge prison population and much higher rates of violent crime than Canada. Is a process of cause and effect operating here? When we lived in North Carolina, my wife and I were repeatedly struck by the large amounts of money that were evidently being spent on police and prisons—the county jail is the largest and most modern building in downtown Durham—instead of on good public schools and a public health care system.

Some countries have also understood that overreacting to terrorism can itself be dangerous. When we obsess about terrorism, we lose sight of other, perhaps more serious risks. For example, former U.S. vice president Al Gore maintains that climate change is a far greater global threat than terrorism. You might reasonably conclude that the terrorist threat has provided some governments, most notably the Bush administration, with a smokescreen for their failure to address this other, very dangerous phenomenon.

There is no denying that terrorism is a serious problem. But our society faces a plethora of serious and complex problems. A sense of perspective is always required, along with cool heads. Remember, the terrorists win only if we allow ourselves to be terrorized.

So take a deep breath. Exhale. Relax.

THE LAWS OF WAR

The image of a hooded man standing on a box, with electrical wires dangling from his outstretched hands, is seared into our collective memory. It scars the psyche almost as deeply as the image of two skyscrapers collapsing in Manhattan. This is partly because the atrocities at Abu Ghraib were committed by soldiers from an advanced Western democracy that long served as a beacon of hope for the world's oppressed and abused. And it is partly because the American soldiers involved, and their superiors, should have known better: they were, after all, members of a highly professional military that has long prided itself on adhering to the laws of war.

The laws of war are often referred to as "international humanitarian law," since these rules are designed to prevent unnecessary suffering during armed conflicts. They are paralleled, in times of peace, by international human rights. And they include the prohibition on the use of chemical or biological weapons, the prohibition on the intentional targeting of civilians and the prohibition on torture and cruel or inhuman treatment or punishment.

For decades, individual Canadians have been at the forefront of efforts to protect human beings during times of both peace and war. In 1948, McGill law professor John Humphrey helped draft the Universal Declaration of Human Rights. In 1956, then foreign minister Lester B. Pearson pioneered the concept of United Nations peacekeeping—and won the Nobel Peace Prize in 1957. In 1994, then lieutenant general Roméo Dallaire served as force commander of the UN peacekeeping mission in Rwanda and strove valiantly to persuade the member states of the UN Security Council to enforce the prohibition on genocide. In the late 1990s, then foreign minister Lloyd Axworthy threw his weight first behind a new multilateral treaty banning anti-personnel landmines and then behind the creation of the permanent International Criminal Court. Today another Canadian, Philippe Kirsch, serves as the first president of that judicial body.

Another Canadian, Louise Arbour, is the UN high commissioner for human rights. She has distinguished herself in that office through a willingness to speak truth to power and, in December 2005, she issued the following public warning: "The absolute ban on torture, a cornerstone of the international human rights edifice, is under attack. The principle we once believed to be unassailable—the inherent right to physical integrity and dignity of the person—is becoming a casualty of the so-called war on terror."

For decades, Canadian governments took human rights and international humanitarian law seriously. In 1976, Canada was one of the first countries to ratify the Optional Protocol to the International Covenant on Civil and Political Rights. In 1977, Sandra Lovelace, a Maliseet woman from New Brunswick, used the protocol to file a complaint with the UN Human Rights Committee. She alleged that the Canadian government had violated international law when it stripped her of her status and rights under the Indian Act after she married a non-Native man. The Human Rights Committee upheld her complaint, and the Canadian government responded by doing the right thing: amending the Indian Act to make it consistent with international standards. Today, Sandra Lovelace Nicholas sits as a senator in the Canadian Parliament.

In 1993, members of the Canadian Airborne Regiment tortured and killed a teenager during a peacekeeping mission in Somalia. Their actions were violations of international humanitarian law and the Canadian government responded accordingly. Several paratroopers were court martialled for their role in the atrocity; one served five years in jail. And, in a move that signalled just how serious the offences were considered, the entire Canadian Airborne Regiment was disbanded.

Canada also took the protection of civilians seriously when it came to the selection of military targets. During the 1999 Kosovo War, Canadian CF-18 fighter pilots, who train with their American counterparts, were never assigned as wingmen to them. Canada has ratified the First Addition Protocol to the 1949 Geneva Conventions, whereas the United States has not, and for this reason our pilots are subject to more stringent requirements concerning the protection of civilians. Accordingly, in Kosovo they could not be counted on to respond to some threats, such as anti-aircraft fire coming from a school or hospital, in the same way that an American pilot would. Where the American pilot would attack the source of the anti-aircraft fire, the Canadian pilot would—quite properly—turn his plane on its tail and leave.

Unfortunately, there was a discernible change of approach on the part of the Canadian government to these and other rules after September 11, 2001.

In 2002, Canadian soldiers in Afghanistan were ordered by their American commander to lay anti-personnel landmines around their camp. When the Canadians refused—citing our obligations under the 1997 Ottawa Landmines Convention—American soldiers, whose government has not ratified the convention and who are thus not subject to the same restrictions, laid the mines for them. More recently, Canadian forces in Kabul and Kandahar have benefited from the protection provided by anti-personnel landmines laid by Soviet forces during the 1980s. The Canadian government argues that the Landmines Convention has not been violated, since the prohibition on the "use" of anti-personnel mines does not extend to reliance on mines laid by others. As I explain in Chapter 5, this strained interpretation hardly reinforces our claim to be the leading proponent of the total elimination of these viciously indiscriminate devices, which have killed more than one million people over the past three decades.

Yet this compromise on landmines is less serious than the manner in which we have shirked our responsibilities concerning suspected Taliban or Al-Qaeda fighters captured by Canadian soldiers in Afghanistan. For here we have been complicit in the erosion of the prohibition on torture, the very erosion that Louise Arbour condemned.

TRANSFERRING TO TORTURE

In 1998 and 1999, I met dozens of torture victims as I worked with a coalition of London-based human rights groups trying to have former Chilean president Augusto Pinochet extradited from Britain to Spain to face criminal charges. The next year, when I arrived at Duke University, my new secretary was a former special-forces soldier who had been tortured by a Colombian drug cartel; fifteen years later, the scars from cigarette burns were still visible on his arms. More recently, I've had the honour of meeting Maher Arar, a Canadian who was wrongfully arrested in the United States in 2002 and forcibly handed over to Syria, where he was tortured while imprisoned for a year without charge.

On each occasion, the first thing that struck me about these torture victims was the deadness in their eyes. Torture—the deliberate infliction of severe pain—is a despicable and inhumane practice. That's why it is absolutely prohibited by a wide range of treaties. That's why every civilized country has committed itself to preventing torture and punishing it wherever it's found. That's also why, whenever we transfer individuals into the custody of another country, we should do what we can to protect against the possibility of their being tortured after they leave our hands.

Canadian soldiers in Afghanistan took their first prisoners in January 2002 and promptly transferred them to U.S. custody. They handed the men over despite the fact that then U.S. defence secretary Donald Rumsfeld had publicly refused to convene the "status determination tribunals" required by the Third Geneva Convention to investigate whether individuals captured on the battlefield are "prisoners of war," a legal term referring to a category of prisoners entitled to special treatment. Canada, by choosing to hand over the prisoners in these circumstances, also violated the Third Geneva Convention. But the transfers did not undermine the prohibition on torture, since there was, at that time, no reason to believe that U.S. forces would mistreat the men.

Today we know better. The photographs from Abu Ghraib were only the first pieces of a growing body of evidence indicating that, at best, the U.S. military has failed to educate its soldiers about international humanitarian law. At worst, the revelations—including a series of leaked legal memoranda that seek to justify torture—suggest a policy of law breaking that extended all the way up the chain of command, to Rumsfeld and perhaps the commander-in-chief himself.

It's in this context that we must assess the announcement, in September 2005, that Canadian soldiers in Afghanistan had again transferred prisoners to U.S. custody. The full scope of the Third Geneva Convention no longer applies to Canada's operations in Afghanistan, because our soldiers are there with the full consent of the sovereign government in Kabul. But Canada is still bound by a provision, Common Article 3, that applies to armed conflicts that are "not of an international character." Common Article 3 specifies that a number of acts "are and shall remain absolutely prohibited at any time and in any place whatsoever," including "cruel treatment and torture" and "outrages upon personal dignity, in particular, humiliating and degrading treatment." Canada, by transferring prisoners to a foreign military that has recently committed violations of precisely this kind, has been risking complicity in breaches of the Geneva Conventions.

We have also been taking chances with the 1984 Torture Convention, which decrees that "no state party shall expel, return or extradite a person to another state where there are substantial grounds for believing that he would be in danger of being subjected to torture." Given what we now know about practices at U.S. military detention centres at Abu Ghraib, Guantanamo Bay Naval Base in Cuba, Bagram Air Base in Afghanistan and elsewhere, the possibility that our prisoners will be tortured in U.S. custody is real. It does not suffice, as the Department of National Defence has argued, that Canada has received assurances from the United States that any detainees received by it will be treated properly. Torturing governments always deny and seek to conceal their actions; what matters is their track record.

Transferring prisoners to Afghan instead of U.S. custody cannot relieve Canada of responsibility, since Kabul may be expected to comply with a U.S. request for a further, onward transfer. Yet this is precisely what Canada has been doing since December 2005, when Chief of the Defence Staff Rick Hillier signed a detainee-transfer "arrangement" with the defence minister of Afghanistan. Under it, Afghanistan promised to treat humanely any individuals received and to allow representatives of the International Committee of the Red Cross (ICRC) to visit the detainee. Yet the Afghan government is hardly a beacon of humanitarian law: according to the UN-funded Afghanistan Research and Evaluation Unit, nineteen of Afghanistan's newly elected members of Parliament are suspected war criminals. Moreover, the Afghan government is very susceptible to being influenced by the United States, which still has nineteen thousand troops in the country, eight thousand of them operating independently from the NATO-led international security assistance force.

Indeed, the Canada-Afghanistan arrangement explicitly envisages that some prisoners will be transferred onward to the custody of a third country, but it does nothing to guard against that country being one where prisoners are at risk of being tortured or otherwise abused. Amir Attaran of the University of Ottawa has accurately described the document as a "detainee laundering agreement," for it enables Canada to move its prisoners indirectly into U.S. custody without the scrutiny involved in direct transfers.

The limitations of the Canada-Afghanistan arrangement become even more evident when compared with a Memorandum of Understanding concluded several months earlier between the Netherlands and Afghanistan. That memorandum provides Dutch officials with a right of access to any of their transferred prisoners; the Canadian arrangement does not. The Dutch memorandum provides for a right of access for "relevant human rights institutions within the UN system"; the Canadian arrangement does not. Instead, the Canadian arrangement relies solely on the ICRC, an organization that normally does not tell other countries about any evidence of abuses it discovers. In September 2006, Canadian foreign affairs minister Peter MacKay acknowledged this reality:

In all of its activities, in particular visits to prisoners, the ICRC's relations with its contacts and detaining authorities are based on a policy of discretion... In cases where the ICRC visits detainees we have transferred to Afghanistan, we are confident the ICRC would advise the Afghan authorities, as the current detaining authorities, if the ICRC had any concerns about a particular detainee or the conditions of detention.

MacKay was careful *not* to suggest that the ICRC would inform the Canadian authorities.

Amazingly, Canada did not even secure the right—as the Dutch did—to be notified by the Afghan authorities before they send one of our transferred prisoners onwards to a third country.

In February 2007, the *Globe and Mail* reported allegations that at least one Afghan was beaten while in the custody of Canadian soldiers. The allegations are serious—and must be subject to a rigorous criminal investigation—but just as serious was the revelation that the Canadian Forces cannot account for the location or condition of the forty prisoners they captured prior to April 2006 or the several dozen taken since then. All we know is what General Hillier has said: "We hand them over to either the Afghan national police or the Afghan national army. We're trying to help build a country; you've got to help build their rule of law, a justice system, which includes a prison system."

But surely the fact that Afghanistan is a broken-down country is a reason for caution rather than blind trust. Afghanistan's military, police, judicial and correctional institutions are undergoing a far-reaching transformation that is far from complete. Corruption and human rights violations remain commonplace. By relying solely on the ICRC to oversee transferred prisoners, and by failing to secure a right of notification as to any change in their location or condition, the Canadian government is washing its hands of them in a situation where their human rights—and our obligations—are clearly at risk.

We also need to worry about our soldiers, who have been placed at legal risk as a result of the transfer arrangement. The Torture Convention requires countries to "ensure that all acts of torture are offences under its criminal law. The same shall apply to an attempt to commit torture and to an act by any person which constitutes complicity or participation in torture." The convention thus affirms a basic principle of criminal law: those who aid or abet a crime are criminals themselves. Complicity in torture is subject to the universal jurisdiction of national courts, making it possible for a Canadian soldier to be tried in the courts of any other country for transferring a prisoner into a situation where there is an apparent risk of such abuse. Indeed, in some circumstances, complicity in torture could even be considered a war crime subject to the Rome Statute of the International Criminal Court. Canada ratified the Rome Statute in 2000; as a result, any Canadian solider who aids, abets or otherwise assists in torture could end up being prosecuted in The Hague.

The situation is clearly unacceptable. So, where do we go from here? The Canada-Afghanistan arrangement should be renegotiated to include all the protections provided in the Dutch memorandum. As the Dutch are demonstrating in southern Afghanistan today, these protections have no detrimental operational consequences. Nor is there any reason to believe that the Afghan authorities would object to a renegotiation, since they have already agreed to the terms of the Dutch memorandum. Nor, indeed, would these protections interfere with efforts to improve the Afghan police, prison and judicial systems; if anything, they are likely to enhance them. And there is one more protection that we should insist on including: a right of veto over any proposed transfer to a third country. For without a right of veto, the right to be notified would be deprived of any real effect.

In November 2005, then defence minister Bill Graham gave a lecture to one of my classes at the University of British Columbia. The former professor of international law told the students that

Canada had no choice but to transfer prisoners to U.S. or Afghan custody, because we lacked the facilities to hold them and building such facilities would be impracticable. One of the students challenged this assertion, arguing that expediency is no excuse for violating fundamental human rights. Indeed, if compliance required building our own detention facilities, so be it; as the eighth-largest economy in the world, this is something we could afford.

Finally, there is the additional issue of how our actions are perceived in Afghanistan, not just by the local authorities, but by ordinary people. In that increasingly hostile region, those who risk complicity in torture risk losing the most important battle—the battle for hearts and minds.

EXTRAORDINARY RENDITION

Just six days after the September 2001 terrorist attacks on New York and Washington, George W. Bush signed a "presidential finding" that provided the Central Intelligence Agency (CIA) with broad authorization to disrupt terrorist activity, including by killing, capturing or detaining Al-Qaeda members anywhere in the world. On this basis, the CIA began secretly transferring suspects, either to the intelligence services of countries notorious for torture or to clandestine prisons located outside the United States and, therefore, beyond the reach—or at least the scrutiny—of U.S. courts.

This practice, which the Americans refer to as "extraordinary rendition," has directly affected a number of Canadians. In September 2002, Maher Arar—a Canadian who is also Syrian by virtue of that country's refusal to accept renunciations of citizenship—was arrested while transiting through New York's JFK Airport. After twelve days of questioning, he was taken to Syria, where he was imprisoned.

Stephen Toope, an independent fact-finder appointed by a Canadian judicial inquiry, determined conclusively that Arar was tortured while in Syrian custody, including by being beaten on the palms and wrists with an electrical cable and being confined for ten months to a cell some two metres long, one metre wide and slightly more than two metres high. Toope concluded:

> The effects of that experience, and of consequent events and experiences in Canada, have been profoundly negative for Mr. Arar and his family. Although there have been few lasting physical effects, Mr. Arar's psychological state was seriously damaged and he remains fragile. His relationships with members of his immediate family have been significantly impaired. Economically, the family has been devastated.

Toope then added, with reference to Arar's battle to clear his name: "Mr. Arar strikes me as a person with what one might describe as moral courage."

For more than three months, the Canadian government resisted pressure to establish an inquiry into possible involvement by the RCMP or Canadian Security Intelligence Service in the rendition and torture of Maher Arar. However, we now know some of what happened.

In September 2004, an internal RCMP investigation revealed that at least one of its officers learned of U.S. plans to deport Arar before Arar was flown to the Middle East but did not immediately convey this information to other officers. The same investigation concluded that, after Arar's arrest, RCMP officers decided not to travel to New York City to question him, because no RCMP aircraft was available and commercial flights were supposedly too expensive.

Finally, in testimony before the commission of inquiry that eventually was established, the senior officer in the investigation into Arar said the RCMP suspected that he was being tortured in Syria but nevertheless decided to share with the Syrians dubious information the force had about him.

In September 2006, the inquiry commissioner, Justice Dennis O'Connor, concluded that the decision to remove Arar to Syria was "very likely" based on inaccurate and misleading information from the RCMP. He also refuted any doubts about Arar's innocence: "I am able to say categorically that there is no evidence to indicate that Mr. Arar has committed any offence or that his activities constituted a threat to the security of Canada."

Along with the renditions, the United States was, and maybe still is, operating clandestine prisons. In November 2005, the *Washington Post* reported that the CIA ran a series of covert prisons, so-called black sites, in a number of foreign countries, including in Eastern Europe. According to the *Post*, "Virtually nothing is known about who is kept in the facilities, what interrogation methods are employed with them, or how decisions are made about whether they should be detained or for how long." The parallels to these secret prisons—such as the Soviet Gulag and Latin American "disappearances"—are obvious, as is their international illegality. Secret prisons contravene the prohibition on arbitrary arrest or detention set out in the Universal Declaration of Human Rights and numerous multilateral treaties. In September 2006, after months of denials, George W. Bush finally admitted the existence of the secret prisons—and declared that they had been closed.

At the same time, the *Post* reported that "CIA interrogators in the overseas sites are permitted to use the CIA's approved 'Enhanced Interrogation Techniques,' some of which are prohibited by the U.N. convention [on torture] and by U.S. military law." The techniques include "waterboarding," whereby a detainee is repeatedly submerged under water and made to believe that he or she will be drowned. In October 2006, a radio interviewer asked U.S. vice president Dick Cheney: "Would you agree a dunk in water is a no-brainer if it can save lives?" The vice president replied, "Well, it's a no-brainer for me."

Unfortunately, it appears that there has been a degree of Canadian complicity in the practice of extraordinary rendition, above and beyond the Arar affair. In December 2005, it was reported that seven airplanes linked to the CIA had recently used Canadian airports more than fifty-five times, including for refuelling stops in Newfoundland and Nunavut. Many more CIA flights have presumably crossed Canadian airspace, given that the shortest flight lines from the United States to Europe or the Middle East cross this country's vast territory.

When asked about the matter, then prime minister Paul Martin said that he had "checked with the deputy prime minister, checked with the officials in charge, and there are absolutely no indications that anything of that kind is occurring." For her part, the then deputy prime minister, Anne McLellan, said she was investigating the questionable flights. But she also asked for patience: "We are now in the process of following up on what we know about any of those, but as you can imagine, 55, it takes time to determine whether there's anything unusual in relation to any of those named flights."

It is likely that Martin and McLellan were simply trying to punt an embarrassing story past the federal election campaign that was then taking place. But it is also possible that they or their officials knew—or chose not to know—that the CIA flights were occurring, and that individuals on board were being involuntarily transferred to secret prisons or foreign intelligence agencies notorious for torture. If so, the politicians' evasive language could be rooted in concern for their personal responsibility, not just under Canadian law, but also in foreign courts or even the International Criminal Court. For such actions would, again, constitute complicity in torture. Now that Martin and McLellan have ceased to be ministers and no longer benefit from the immunities attached to high office, they might think about avoiding foreign travel, at least to human-rights-respecting states.

I do not want to overstate the legal situation; these are only possibilities. At the same time, it is disturbing that such possibilities have been allowed to arise. There were—and still are—two simple and entirely appropriate responses to the U.S. practice of using extraordinary rendition and secret prisons: refusing to share intelligence that might be used for such purposes, and denying CIA planes permission to use Canadian airports or airspace until the matter has been properly investigated and resolved.

STANDING UP FOR HUMAN RIGHTS

There is no question that Canadians abhor torture. The deliberate infliction of severe pain and suffering is a particularly heinous crime. Indeed, the prohibition on torture, along with other fundamental human rights and rules of international humanitarian law, was established by a generation that knew all about pain and suffering. They had lived through two world wars, the rise and fall of fascism in Germany, Italy and Japan, and the Holocaust. Their commitment to preventing human suffering finds expression in the first three stanzas of the UN Charter of 1945:

> We the peoples of the United Nations determined to succeeding generations from the scourge of war, which twice in our lifetime has brought untold sorrow to mankind, and to reaffirm faith in fundamental human rights, in the dignity and worth of the human person, in the equal rights of men and women and of nations large and small, and to establish conditions under which justice and respect for the obligations arising from treaties and other sources of international law can be maintained...

Today, one of the key questions facing Canadians concerns whether we still stand by that commitment, at a time when our superpower neighbour has been torturing people and outsourcing torture to other states. Was our commitment to prevent human suffering meant only for good times, not for those times when the going gets rough?

In December 2004, George W. Bush visited Ottawa and Halifax. Shortly afterwards, I had the opportunity to chat with a senior Canadian bureaucrat who had been involved in the trip.

"In his private meetings with the president, did Paul Martin raise the issue of torture and extraordinary rendition?" I asked.

"Are you kidding?" my contact laughed. "With 86 per cent of our exports going to the United States?"

I had heard the argument before, usually coupled with an assertion that the Americans will do what they want regardless of what
we say. In the upper levels of the federal bureaucracy, it has become
fashionable to be "realistic" about Canada's inferiority vis-à-vis
the United States. Yet fashion can get in the way of careful thinking—thinking that constantly re-evaluates its assumptions and
analyses recent developments, such as Canada's decision to stay out
of the 2003 Iraq War. Personally, I am not convinced that Canada
has much to lose by opposing those U.S. policies that diverge significantly from international opinion and violate international law.
Indeed, we might have something to gain.

Canada is an influential country. Our influence is augmented
by our middle-power tradition of multilateral leadership, which
has always included promoting peace, defending human rights and
championing international humanitarian law. Moreover, when
we stand up to the United States, we rarely incur a penalty. We
only gained by staying out of the Iraq War: saving Canadian lives,
avoiding the ensuing quagmire and signalling to other countries
that Canada remains an independent country—open, among other
things, to its own diplomatic and trading relations. We might even
have gained some kudos in Washington—a city dominated by bare-
knuckle politics rather than quiet, Canadian-style consensus—by
demonstrating that Canada is a grown-up country, that our support must be earned and never assumed.

When it comes to fundamental human protections, the recent
pattern of law breaking by the United States creates an opportunity for Canada. For decades, Americans provided global leadership with regard to human rights and international humanitarian
law. Since September 2001, they have abdicated that role, leaving
space for an experienced, well-minded middle power such as Canada. But if we are to lead the way on this or any other international
issue, it is essential that we remain on our best behaviour and not
let standards slip in the way they have next door.

Finally, Canada's record on human rights and international
humanitarian law matters because we are a democracy. If our sol-

diers and politicians are complicit in torture, we, in a sense, are all torturers. Human rights require constant vigilance to defend against those who seek to violate or undermine them, or who simply take the easy way out by acquiescing to violations committed by others. Democracy, the most reliable mechanism for maintaining individual human rights, and the very essence of our society, also requires constant defending. At root, our respect for human rights and international humanitarian law should not be based on our relationship with the United States. It should be determined by who we—as Canadians—are, and what we intend to be.

— 2 —

WARFIGHTERS OR PEACEKEEPERS?

Afghanistan,
Mission Impossible

A PHOTOGRAPH of Canadian commandos shepherding Afghan prisoners out of a helicopter appeared on the front page of the *Globe and Mail* on January 22, 2002. The caption identified the soldiers as Americans, but the photograph ended up embarrassing then prime minister Jean Chrétien. Six days later, still believing the soldiers were American, he told the House of Commons that the issue of Canadian soldiers capturing prisoners in Afghanistan was "hypothetical."

Ironically, Chrétien's unintentional misleading of Parliament came to light partly as a consequence of his own government's severe cutbacks to defence spending. For on seeing the photograph, military experts realized that the soldiers were not Americans because the latter, being relatively well equipped, would hardly be wearing jungle-green camouflage in one of the driest and most barren countries on Earth! It later emerged that Defence Minister Art Eggleton was told about the prisoners on the day they were captured but failed to pass that information to Chrétien. Some months later, Eggleton was removed from his cabinet post.

The commandos were from Joint Task Force 2, Canada's highly secretive special-forces unit. They were among the first soldiers to arrive in Afghanistan after the terrorist attacks of September 11, 2001, and have been active there ever since, fighting under American or British operational control in "counter-insurgency" search-and-destroy missions. We know that JTF-2 soldiers participated in an attack on an Al-Qaeda cave complex at Tora Bora in Afghanistan in December 2002, and they handed prisoners over to U.S. forces during the summer of 2005.

The first regular Canadian soldiers arrived in Afghanistan at about the same time as the *Globe* photograph was taken. In January 2002, 750 members of the Princess Patricia's Canadian Light Infantry regiment were sent to Kandahar, in southern Afghanistan, as part of an U.S. Army counter-insurgency task force. Four of those soldiers were killed, and eight others injured, in a "friendly fire" incident involving a trigger-happy U.S. fighter pilot in April 2002. The remaining soldiers returned to Canada three months later.

Then, over a two-year period from August 2003 to October 2005, some six thousand Canadian soldiers were rotated through Kabul, in northeastern Afghanistan, as part of a UN-authorized, NATO-led "international security assistance force" made up of troops from some thirty-five countries. The role of this force, providing security and stability for Afghanistan's new government, was consistent with an evolving conception of "peacekeeping." Only three Canadian soldiers were killed during this assignment.

In late 2005, the focus of Canada's military effort reverted to the counter-insurgency mission in Kandahar. Reportedly, Prime Minister Paul Martin volunteered our troops for this new mission because it was the most dangerous available and therefore best suited for amending damage caused to the Canada-U.S. relationship by our refusal to participate in the Iraq War and missile defence. The U.S. government, bogged down in Iraq and with midterm congressional elections just one year away, was keen to reduce its troop levels in Afghanistan. NATO—an organization that has always been heavily influenced by the United States—responded by scaling up its presence from nine thousand to about twenty thousand soldiers, with most of the new troops coming from Britain, Canada, Denmark and the Netherlands.

But not all of the remaining nineteen thousand U.S. soldiers were placed under NATO command. They continued to fight alongside Canadian and other NATO forces but were subject to different lines of "operational control"—a situation likely to increase the risk of friendly fire incidents. Sure enough, in September 2006, two American A-10 Warthog ground-attack aircraft accidentally strafed a group of Canadian soldiers, killing one—former Olympic sprinter Mark Anthony Graham—and seriously wounding five others.

Originally, the plan had been to expand NATO's responsibilities to include southern Afghanistan, and the non-U.S. forces already there, by early 2006. But the transition was delayed by concerns, in Paris, Berlin and elsewhere, over the tactics employed in the counter-insurgency mission. For the better part of a year Canada's soldiers operated as part of the U.S.-led Operation Enduring Freedom, in which, despite being placed in charge of ground operations in Kandahar, they essentially remained under U.S. operational control—in part because of their dependency on U.S. air support. In the end, the French and Germans refused to deploy into the south.

Kandahar Province is the stronghold of Taliban fighters, the nearby mountains bordering Pakistan provide a refuge for Al-Qaeda members, and the agricultural lowlands are dominated by drug barons. Canada's soldiers face ever-increasing risks as these various forces copy the insurgents in Iraq by using roadside explosives and suicide car bombs while, at the same time, coalescing into organized and more effective groups of guerrilla fighters. To some extent, the risks have been exacerbated by heavy-handed U.S.-led tactics, especially the use of air power against villages when the Americans believe Taliban or Al-Qaeda members are present. Hundreds, perhaps thousands of innocent civilians have died in such strikes, prompting angry family members and friends to join the insurgency. Yet Canada's response to the escalating dangers has been to assign more rather than less soldiers and equipment to the counter-insurgency mission. Before it was voted out of office, Paul Martin's government almost doubled the size of the "battle group" being deployed to Kandahar, from 1,250 to 2,300 soldiers.

Still, the Martin government continued to sell the deployment to Canadians as primarily a reconstruction exercise, as the following excerpt from a speech delivered by Defence Minister Bill Graham in October 2005 makes clear:

> [T]he Government of Canada's "3-D Approach," which integrates defence, diplomacy and development assistance in our international operations, is tailor made to a policy emphasis on failed and failing states. This holistic and integrative approach gives Canada comparative strength in achieving objectives on the ground, whether that is security and stabilization, humanitarian relief, institution building or economic development.
>
> And the troubled country of Afghanistan, where the Canadian Forces has been deployed consistently since 2002 in varying numbers and missions, is a quintessential example of where we can effectively bring these assets to bear.

In March 2006, just five weeks after he became prime minister, Stephen Harper flew to Kandahar. In a photo op that could have been scripted by Karl Rove, George W. Bush's chief political adviser, he told our troops that Canadians were subject to the same terrorist threat as Americans. He implied that anyone who questioned the militaristic approach would be emboldening the terrorists and putting Canadian lives at risk. The prime minister sounded remarkably like Bush when he said, "Canadians don't cut and run at the first sign of trouble."

Yes, indeed. But surely we're beyond the "first sign of trouble" now?

As I write, at least forty-four Canadian soldiers have lost their lives in Afghanistan, along with one diplomat. There have likely been additional losses among our special forces, who operate behind a veil of secrecy that extends to the reporting of casualties. Then there are the hundreds of seriously wounded Canadian soldiers, with lost limbs, blindness, brain damage or other forms of severe psychological harm. Hundreds more deaths and injuries are likely in the months and years ahead.

In the immediate aftermath of 9/11, Canadians might have tolerated such losses. The Bush administration had not yet shifted its attention from Afghanistan to Iraq, nor squandered sympathy by bombing villages and mistreating prisoners. The limitations of the counter-insurgency approach had not yet been driven home, notwithstanding the abundance of historical precedents, ranging from the American Revolution to Vietnam and the previous British and Soviet occupations of Afghanistan.

But let us be honest: whatever our political inclination, we all have a tipping point at which we'd call for Canada's troops to be brought home. Nobody is willing to argue that the counter-insurgency mission in Afghanistan would be worth the lives of a thousand Canadian soldiers. On that basis, it is essential that we engage in a hard-nosed assessment of where our national tipping point should be. I will begin by considering the arguments in favour of the mission.

First, it is argued that the mission is necessary to protect Canadians from the threat posed by the Taliban and Al-Qaeda. This is a serious argument, but it can be exaggerated. The Taliban do not pose a threat to the existence of Canada. They are not about to invade. Nor are they developing weapons of mass destruction or missiles capable of reaching North America. The Al-Qaeda elements sheltering behind the Taliban do not pose an existential threat to Canada either. They certainly provide moral and perhaps technical support to aspiring terrorists elsewhere. But if the threat had been truly serious, Washington would not have shifted its focus to removing Saddam Hussein from power in Baghdad. Nor would Pakistan's unelected president, General Pervez Musharraf, be allowed to conclude deals with pro-Taliban militants along the border of Afghanistan, while denying NATO forces access to that region.

Clearly, we do have a national interest in containing Al-Qaeda. Yet even if that interest were worth more Canadian soldiers' lives, it is not clear that the counter-insurgency mission is making progress towards that goal. After five years of efforts by American, British and Canadian troops, southern Afghanistan has become significantly more dangerous.

Second, it is argued that the counter-insurgency mission is needed to restrict the production of opium. Illegal narcotics are certainly a concern. But despite the presence of Canadian troops, opium production has increased dramatically. In September 2006, the Senlis Council, an international policy think-tank with offices in Kabul, London, Paris and Brussels, reported that:

[D]espite all counter-narcotics and alternative development funds, the opium crisis in Afghanistan is worse than ever, and entrenched in almost all facets of Afghan society. Five years of flawed counter-narcotics priorities have brought no positive change in Afghanistan. They have only served to undermine government legitimacy, stability, security and development, whilst farmers have lost confidence in the current Karzai administration. Ultimately, this loss of confidence has ultimately aided insurgents. Five years ago, the total area of cultivated hectares of poppy was less than half of the current total.

Third, it is argued that the counter-insurgency mission is needed to protect the Afghan people. But, again, are we actually achieving this goal? In September 2006, I met Malalai Joya, a diminutive but fiercely courageous woman who, at 27 years old, was the youngest member of the Afghan National Assembly. Joya drew my attention to the appalling conditions in which most Afghans live. Five years after the U.S.-led intervention began, they have an average life expectancy of less than forty-five years (compared with eighty years in Canada), and 1,600 mothers out of 100,000 die during childbirth (compared with 6 out of 100,000 in Canada). Joya also identified the presence of many former warlords in the National Assembly, most of them accused of heinous crimes. She called the election that brought them to power "a sham" and decried the corruption that was siphoning off billions of dollars of much-needed foreign aid. She concluded: "I think that no nation can donate liberation to another nation. Liberation should be achieved in a country by the people themselves."

If protecting the Afghan people is our goal, we need to do a better job of ensuring that Canada's overseas development assistance reaches those who need it most. In October 2006, Amir Attaran explained in the *Toronto Star* that almost all of the money provided by the Canadian International Development Agency to Afghanistan "is channelled through international middlemen, such as the World Bank or the UN Development Program," who "commingle CIDA's money with that of other countries." When they do this, "CIDA refuses to divulge any monitoring, evaluation or audit reports without the agreement of those other countries" even though "nothing in the Access to Information Act obliges CIDA to consult so widely or to withhold project results."

Attaran concluded:

A possible reason for CIDA's secrecy is that the prognosis for Afghanistan's development is lousy.

Nearly five years after the Taliban's ouster, even Kabul, the capital city, goes without full-time electricity. This year's Afghan heroin trade will net a street value of more than $50 billion U.S. Compare that to Afghanistan's current development aid from all countries: only $1.8 billion U.S.

If Afghans follow the money then Afghanistan is not likely to develop as Canada wants.

It is also time to talk with the Taliban. In August 2006, New Democratic Party leader Jack Layton called for the withdrawal of Canadian troops from the counter-insurgency mission "as soon as possible—working with our international partners to ensure a safe and smooth transition—but with a view to having it complete by February 2007." At the same time, he indicated the need for a comprehensive peace process that would, necessarily, include elements of the Taliban.

Layton's position was derided by the Harper government and large segments of the media, but it resonated with many Canadians. This was demonstrated by an online poll on the *Globe and Mail* Web site the next day. Not only did 62 per cent of respondents support the proposition that "Taliban fighters should be included in a comprehensive peace process in Afghanistan," the number of votes cast—43,039—far exceeded the usual numbers of votes in *Globe* online polls. The NDP leader's suggestion was hardly radical, for as Winston Churchill once said, "To jaw-jaw is always better than to war-war." Even former U.S. defence secretary Donald Rumsfeld and former U.S. Senate majority leader Bill Frist have mused openly about the need to negotiate with at least some of the Taliban.

Fourth, it is argued that NATO's credibility is at stake. But if that is the case, why have so many NATO members refused to step up to the plate? There are twenty-six NATO countries, and Canada—with our relatively small population and military—has made the fourth-largest contribution of troops to the counter-insurgency mission and suffered one-quarter of the casualties.

And how much does NATO's credibility matter? Fifteen years after the collapse of the Soviet Union—the raison d'être of the North Atlantic alliance—NATO is simply a collection of countries that may or may not choose to co-operate in any given situation. When the United States intervened in Afghanistan in 2001, it chose not to call on NATO for help.

Fifth, it is argued that Canada's credibility would suffer if we withdrew from the counter-insurgency mission. It is certainly true that, within NATO circles, we would be expected to provide reasonable notice. And so we should. But does anyone regard France or Germany as less credible because they refused to deploy into southern Afghanistan? Does anyone regard Spain or Italy as less credible because they chose to withdraw from Iraq? As Senator Roméo Dallaire has explained, the biggest blow to Canada's credibility today is occurring elsewhere, as we sit on the sidelines while a genocide takes place in the Darfur region of western Sudan.

Sixth, it is argued that Canada's credibility in Washington would suffer. This is a serious argument. But it's also the same argument that was advanced by those who thought Canada should join in the Vietnam War. It's the same argument that was advanced by those who thought Canada should join in the 2003 Iraq War. All of which goes to show that Canadians are better judges of the Canadian national interest than Americans. As long as we provide reasonable notice, Washington has no reason to complain.

If these are the arguments in favour of the counter-insurgency mission, what about the arguments against? What are the costs—above and beyond the all-important cost in lost and shattered young Canadian lives?

First, there are financial costs. In May 2006, the Polaris Institute estimated "that the cost of Canada's operations in the current fiscal year (2006–7) will exceed $1 billion, perhaps substantially, and will continue at that level as long as the Canadian mission lasts." This $1 billion *per year* compares to the $1 billion *over ten years* that Canada is providing for reconstruction and development in Afghanistan, which works out to $100 million per year—or 10 per cent of what we are spending on the military mission.

Second, these financial costs constitute opportunity costs. One billion dollars per year could provide a great deal of development and humanitarian assistance, and not just in Afghanistan. Wisely spent, this money could save millions of lives, especially in disease- and famine-ridden sub-Saharan Africa.

Third, another form of opportunity cost concerns the other missions that the Canadian Forces cannot fulfill because of their current engagement. Later in this chapter, I will explain how Canada is missing two significant opportunities—in Lebanon and Darfur—to participate in, and even lead, UN peacekeeping operations in areas where Canada has a substantial national interest.

Now, some people might decry the opportunities in Lebanon and Darfur as unsuitable for Canadian troops because they constitute "mere" peacekeeping. For almost a decade, Canada's generals, along with a growing collection of politicians and pundits, have asserted that peacekeeping is passé and counter-insurgency wars are the new reality. Yet the turn away from peacekeeping has been a choice rather than a necessity. In January 2002, the *Globe and Mail* reported that "Canada decided to send its troops into a combat mission under U.S. control in Afghanistan rather than participate in the British-led multinational force because it is 'tired' of acting as mere peacekeepers, according to a senior British defence official."

Since when have the generations of Canadian soldiers who risked their lives patrolling the world's conflict zones become "mere" peacekeepers? Yes, peacekeeping requires diplomacy and restraint, but it also takes considerable courage. Colonel Pierre Leblanc, the retired commander of Canadian Forces Northern Area, has told me how, when he was a young peacekeeper, there were nights when Canadian soldiers in Cyprus took fire from—and shot back at—both the Greek and Turkish sides of the Green Line.

The myth that "peacekeeping is for wimps" originates in the United States, and it found its ultimate expression in U.S. secretary of state Condoleezza Rice's October 2000 comment, "We don't need to have the 82nd Airborne escorting kids to kindergarten." Every time I read about the death and destruction in Iraq, I think of this comment and wish the world had more properly trained and experienced peacekeepers.

When Canada, as a sovereign country, develops and deploys its military, it should seek to do more than simply duplicate the military capabilities of the United States. If we want to make a real and positive difference, adding a few thousand soldiers to the hundreds of thousands already engaged in aggressive U.S.-led missions is hardly the best strategy. Instead, we should build and use our military for missions—and they will often be peacekeeping missions— that the U.S. military is unable or unwilling to fulfill. Canada's distinct history, our international reputation for independence and objectivity, our highly trained, experienced, diplomatically skilled peacekeepers—all these attributes enable us to punch above our weight, provided that we are not punching in the same place, time and manner as the United States.

Today, there is no shortage of peacekeeping missions where Canadian soldiers could make a valuable contribution. The UN is busier than ever, with more than 65,000 blue-helmeted soldiers from more than one hundred countries deployed in sixteen separate peacekeeping operations: in Congo, Ethiopia and Eritrea, Kosovo, Lebanon, Liberia and elsewhere. At the same time, the Canadian contribution has dropped precipitously, to the point where, as Steve Staples of the Rideau Institute has graphically explained, all of Canada's current UN peacekeepers could fit into a single school bus.

To make matters worse, our declining participation has occurred just as peacekeeping is evolving to suit the strengths of the Canadian Forces even better than before. According to the UN, peacekeeping has become "multidimensional," in that it increasingly takes place within the context of intrastate conflicts and "involves non-military elements to ensure stability." In other words, modern peacekeeping is *exactly* what Bill Graham and the other members of Paul Martin's government committed the Canadian Forces to do in 2005 with their "3-D Approach" integrating defence, diplomacy and development assistance. More broadly, our ongoing disengagement from peacekeeping stands in stark contrast to the development of the concepts of "common security" and, more recently, "human security" as leitmotifs of Canadian foreign policy.

Fourth, and wrapped up in the distinction between peacekeeping and counter-insurgency, is the question of our reputation—most notably the cost to Canada's international reputation for independence and objectivity, and thus our ability to lead and persuade on a wide range of issues. Where would we gain the most: continuing with a failing counter-insurgency mission in Afghanistan or leading a humanitarian intervention to stop the genocide in Darfur?

Fifth, there may even be a security cost to the counter-insurgency mission. Foiled terrorist plots in Toronto and London were reportedly motivated, at least in part, by anger at the presence of Western troops in Afghanistan. Canada's chief of the defence staff, Rick Hillier, has hardly helped matters by publicly characterizing our opponents as "detestable murderers and scumbags." One wonders how Muslims around the world feel when they hear language like this being used on Canada's behalf.

Sixth, General Hillier's language points to another problem. The current mission in Afghanistan could, over time, lead to the development of a Canadian Forces that is focussed almost entirely—in its training, ethos and equipment—on aggressive missions conducted in concert with the United States. The long-term consequences of this would be significant, especially for Canadian foreign policy, since it would diminish our ability to conduct other kinds of missions, especially those not involving the United States.

And let us be clear: our current policy orientation is leading inexorably to a much longer engagement. In August 2005, Canadian major general Andrew Leslie said that helping Afghanistan break out of "a cycle of warlords and tribalism" was a "20-year venture." In March 2006, Rick Hillier said: "From NATO's perspective, they look at this as a 10-year mission, right? Minimum. There's going to be a huge demand for Canada to contribute over the longer period of time."

Seventh, it is possible that Canada's involvement in the counter-insurgency mission is contributing to a decline in this country's commitment to strong rules of international humanitarian law. In the previous chapter, I explained how this is happening, by our soldiers' reliance on landmines laid by other armies and by our transfer of prisoners—directly or via the Afghans—to U.S. custody, where they may well be tortured

Eighth, such bellicose missions challenge the way Canadians think of themselves. We like to imagine that we are "global citizens" uniquely placed to promote a more peaceful, just, inclusive and law-abiding world, but how can participating in search-and-destroy operations in concert with the United States foster this self-identity? Surely stopping genocide would be more consistent with how Canadians have, traditionally, preferred their country to behave?

Stephen Harper sought to cut off these sorts of considerations when, in May 2006, he abruptly called a vote in the House of Commons to extend Canada's participation in the counter-insurgency mission by two more years, from February 2007 to February 2009. The vote also had an obvious political purpose, in that it divided the Opposition Liberal caucus. Twenty-nine members of Parliament from that party voted for the extension, sixty-two voted against and another eleven were conspicuously absent. In the end, the motion passed by the narrow vote of 149–145, with all twenty-nine NDP and most of the Bloc Québécois members voting against. With a smile on his face, the prime minister made a point of shaking hands with Bill Graham, the interim Liberal leader, as well as with Liberal MP Michael Ignatieff, at the time vying to lead the party. The two men, by speaking in support and voting for the extension of the mission, had provided the Conservatives with political cover on the Afghanistan issue for months if not years to come. The new Liberal leader Stéphane Dion, who voted against the extension, now faces the difficult task of repairing a public split within his own party on one of the most important issues facing Canada.

The vote took place just hours after Captain Nichola Goddard had become the first female Canadian soldier ever to die in combat; she was killed by a rocket-propelled grenade during an offensive operation near Kandahar. Yet the flag on the Peace Tower above the House of Commons was not lowered in her honour. As part of its effort to draw attention away from the mounting casualties in

Afghanistan, the Harper government had ordered an end to that practice just a few weeks earlier. It also imitated the Bush administration by banning the media from the airport "ramp ceremonies" at which soldiers' bodies are welcomed home. The moves caused a storm of protest, including from some of the dead soldiers' families. One angry father showed an amateur videotape of returning caskets at his son's funeral, which he had pointedly invited the media to attend.

Canada is in a hole in southern Afghanistan, and it is time to stop digging. Our troops should be withdrawn from the current mission as soon as is reasonably possible. They belong elsewhere, redeployed to other parts of Afghanistan or to places such as Lebanon and Darfur, where they could make a more positive contribution. There is no question that our soldiers want to succeed, and we are proud of them for trying. But it is up to us—and the politicians we elect—to choose missions where success is possible and to change direction when our choices go seriously wrong.

LEBANON: HARPER'S UNMEASURED SUPPORT FOR ISRAEL

In April 2004, I spent a month teaching as a visiting professor at the University of Tel Aviv. It was my first trip to Israel since the start of the "second intifada," and the country was on high alert. The Israeli Defence Forces (IDF) had recently assassinated two Hamas leaders, Sheik Ahmed Ismail Yassin and Abdel Aziz al-Rantissi, and everyone was waiting for the retaliatory suicide attacks. Armed security guards searched everyone entering hotels, shops, restaurants, even the university campus. And it was not only Israelis whose lives were being disrupted: every evening, helicopter gunships thundered down the Mediterranean coast towards Gaza, returning early the following morning.

My Israeli students were among the best I have taught. It helped that the subject matter of the course—the laws of war—was of direct relevance to them. It helped too that they had all served in the military, since Israel has a universal draft. Several were still serving, as the IDF had sent a few of their young lawyers to take my course. Not surprisingly, the students and I disagreed on a number of points, though always in a friendly and respectful manner. One of the most attractive things about Israel is the open and spirited nature of its public debates, even on matters of national security.

The ability to disagree without being disagreeable showed itself again when, on my last full day in Israel, one of the students took me to lunch with his commanding officer, the senior lawyer advising the IDF. A colonel with a Harvard doctorate, she was not one for small talk. After just a few minutes, she cut to the chase:

"There have been a number of missile attacks along our northern border. We're going to respond with air strikes against some Hezbollah installations in southern Lebanon next week. What do you think?"

I was taken aback. Governments do not usually consult foreign academics about their military plans. But I knew that my host was well aware that two bodies of law were in play: the first of them governs the recourse to military force; the second, known as international humanitarian law, limits the way soldiers may behave once a conflict has begun. I began with the former.

"For starters," I said, "any act of self-defence has to be necessary and proportionate. So, in order to stay within international law, you should target only those Hezbollah installations that have been used in the missile attacks."

My host shook her head: "That won't prevent future attacks. We're also acting pre-emptively."

"Well, in that case you're still subject to the criteria from the *Caroline* case," I replied, referring to an incident involving the destruction, by British and Canadian forces, of an American steamboat on the Niagara River in 1837. "The necessity of self-defence must be, quote, 'instant, overwhelming, leaving no choice of means, and no moment of deliberation.' And I'm not sure that your air strikes fit these criteria, since you're not planning on launching them until next week. Where's the imminent threat?"

"It's an ongoing threat," the Israeli lawyer explained. "We have to ensure that Hezbollah's capabilities remain at a manageable level."

"Isn't that the job of the Lebanese government?" I queried. "What you're proposing is, after all, an armed intervention within the territory of a sovereign nation-state."

"The Lebanese government can't control Hezbollah," she scoffed. "If it could, we wouldn't be having this conversation." ·

Although the law of self-defence sometimes permits military action against state sponsors of terrorism, this was a different argument. "You seem to be suggesting that Lebanon, within its southern territories, amounts to a failed state," I said.

"Precisely," the colonel smiled. "We're not violating international law by targeting Hezbollah installations in southern Lebanon because the writ of the Lebanese government doesn't run that far."

The argument was familiar. During my years of teaching in the United States, students had sometimes argued that the UN Charter's prohibition on the use of force against a country's "territorial integrity or political independence" should not extend to countries—such as Somalia—without effective governments. Instead of contesting the point, I pursued its logical conclusion: "If that's the case, you really must limit your strikes to those Hezbollah targets."

The Israeli officer arched an eyebrow: "Why?"

"If you strike other targets, such as roads or airports, you'll make it more difficult for the Lebanese government to do its job. At which point, your argument will become self-fulfilling since you'll be helping to create a failed state."

A nod, followed by an assurance: "You're right. Don't worry. We're focussed on Hezbollah."

At this point I pressed forward, changing the focus to international humanitarian law: "Also, you must never target civilians, or facilities such as water filtration or electrical plants relied upon by civilians."

"Ah, here we disagree!" the colonel exclaimed. "Collateral damage is allowed in situations of military necessity. And dual-use facilities are legitimate targets."

"What constitutes military necessity depends on the relative capabilities of the opposing forces," I countered. "And the dual-use argument is a slippery slope."

The Israeli smiled again: "Perhaps."

"There's a second reason you should do everything possible to protect civilians," I continued. "Israel has to work particularly hard to maintain the moral high ground. Your reputation has suffered because of your treatment of the Palestinians."

"We're completely justified in our treatment of the Palestinians," the IDF lawyer shot back.

I shrugged: "We can disagree on that, for today. But do me a favour, as someone who wants to sympathize with Israel. If you do launch air strikes, please limit yourself to Hezbollah facilities. Leave civilians—and the Lebanese government—alone."

AS IT HAPPENS, the IDF did in fact bomb southern Lebanon the following week, and they restricted themselves to Hezbollah positions. If only they had shown similar restraint two years later when, in July 2006, they responded to the capture of two of their soldiers by Hezbollah militants with a much more extensive bombing campaign. The IDF bombed Beirut's international airport, striking at the heart of Lebanon's tourism-based economy. They bombed arterial roads, bridges, power and gasoline stations and imposed an air and sea blockade. They promised, in the words of their chief of staff, to "turn back the clock in Lebanon by 20 years."

Although Hezbollah does pose a serious threat to Israel, as demonstrated by its ability to reach the Israeli communities of Haifa and Tiberias with missiles, the targeting of non-Hezbollah targets was both unnecessary and disproportionate. It also violated a central principle of international humanitarian law: that individual targets may only be selected if the direct military advantage anticipated from the strike exceeds the expected harm to civilians or civilian objects. Hezbollah's rocket attacks, aimed at the general vicinity of Israeli cities and towns rather than specific military targets, were clearly illegal, but so, too, were some of Israel's attacks.

Of the more than one thousand Lebanese civilians killed, some were struck by Israeli missiles as they followed Israeli instructions to leave their homes and villages. Others were hit because blasted roads, bridges and gasoline stations had made it impossible for them to flee. More civilians died when bombs were dropped in densely populated neighbourhoods where the military advantage could virtually never justify the civilian harm. Others died later as hospitals, water filtration plants and sewage treatment facilities struggled with power shortages.

Attacks on civilians or civilian infrastructure may never be justified by similar violations on the other side. Horrors such as that of the village of Qana, where more than two dozen Lebanese civilians died in a single precision air strike, cannot be balanced by lost Israeli lives.

For all these reasons, I was staggered when Stephen Harper declared that "Israel's response under the circumstances has been measured." The prime minister's position demonstrated an ignorance of international law and a lack of common sense. Even more staggering was Harper's refusal to moderate his stance after eight innocent Canadians, all members of a single family from Montreal, died as the result of an Israeli strike on the Lebanese village of Aitaroun. His later attempt, in October 2006, to label those who questioned Israel's actions as "anti-Israel" was beyond staggering, to the point where he demeaned himself.

Harper's willingness to defend Israel's behaviour can be explained at several levels. He undoubtedly feels sympathy for the past sufferings of the Jewish people, including the Holocaust. He may be influenced by domestic electoral considerations, pro-Israel media moguls and lobbyists. He could be blinded to the complex and evolving nature of the Middle East by a desire to maintain clear distinctions between "right" and "wrong." It is even conceivable that he believes, along with some evangelical Christians, that another war between Israel and its neighbours is a necessary precursor to the second coming of Christ. But most likely the prime minister just wanted to win points in Washington by aligning himself with the unequivocally pro-Israel position of George W. Bush.

In any event, Harper's stance was misguided. By supporting Israel's disproportionate response, he may have helped embolden the Israelis to continue and intensify their attacks—after all, their actions were receiving public support from the leader of a country widely respected for being impartial. By failing to demand that Israel hold back, he might have exacerbated a situation where tens of thousands of Canadians were desperately seeking to flee Lebanon, and the Canadian government was unprepared to help. One thing is certain: Harper has helped to polarize a world already divided over the "war on terrorism" and Iraq. Consider how upset Muslims were, watching the effects of the Israeli onslaught. Consider how upset some of them were by our prime minister's one-sided statement. What impact might this have on our future security at home and our soldiers' efforts to win hearts and minds in Afghanistan?

For decades, Canada took a balanced approach to the conflict in the Middle East. We recognized that Israelis have a right to a secure and viable state at the same time that their neighbours, including the Palestinians and Lebanese, have the same rights. It was our lack of favouritism that enabled us to lead the peacekeeping mission that brought an end to the 1956 Suez Crisis and won Lester Pearson the Nobel Peace Prize.

The balanced approach rests upon the fundamental principles of justice and equality. When Stephen Harper supported Israel's disproportionate response, he devalued the lives of Lebanese citizens. He undermined the laws of war, which exist to prevent unnecessary human suffering without regard to national, religious or ethnic differences. He debased Canada, this wonderfully diverse and tolerant country where Jews, Arabs and people of every other imaginable creed and colour live peacefully side by side. Yes, Israel has a right to defend itself, within recognized and reasonable limits. But in July and early August 2006, those limits were breached. Friends of the Jewish state—Canada among them—should not pretend otherwise.

On August 11, 2006, the UN Security Council finally imposed a ceasefire on both Hezbollah and Israel. The council authorized the expansion of the pre-existing United Nations Interim Force in Lebanon (UNIFL) to a maximum of fifteen thousand soldiers and the deployment of that peacekeeping force throughout the south of the country to monitor the ceasefire and assist the Lebanese Army. It also gave UNIFL a robust mandate by authorizing it to "use all necessary action in areas of deployment of its forces and as it deems within its capabilities, to ensure that its area of operations is not utilized for hostile activities of any kind."

Most of the peacekeepers were provided by Italy (three thousand soldiers), France (two thousand), Bangladesh (two thousand), Indonesia (one thousand), Malaysia (one thousand), Nepal (one thousand) and Spain (one thousand). Smaller contingents were offered by Poland, Finland, Norway and Belgium, with Germany and Denmark providing maritime support. Canada was conspicuously absent. The Department of Foreign Affairs claimed that we were not asked, while the Department of National Defence insisted that all our troops were committed elsewhere. For his part, Prime Minister Harper said it was preferable that the UN force be made up of soldiers from countries closer to the Middle East.

None of the arguments held water. Leadership in international affairs involves stepping up to the plate without having to be asked. The briefing book provided to Defence Minister Gordon O'Connor in February 2006, and subsequently obtained by the NDP through an access-to-information request, clearly stated that Canada had twelve hundred soldiers available for missions above and beyond our commitment in Afghanistan, and indeed, in September 2006, the Department of National Defence had little difficulty finding hundreds more soldiers to send to that country. And, curiously enough, the Middle East is closer and much more accessible to us than Afghanistan.

Canada also has a clear national interest in maintaining the ceasefire between Hezbollah and Israel, since the Middle East conflict has the potential to escalate into a highly destabilizing war with Iran involving attacks on its nuclear facilities. And far more Canadians have personal connections with Israel and Lebanon than with Afghanistan. Last but not least, Canadian soldiers are uniquely suited to peacekeeping in Lebanon. In addition to their considerable experience and training for such missions, they have the necessary language skills to communicate with Israelis (most of whom speak English) and Lebanese (most of whom speak French).

It seemed the Harper government was ideologically opposed to playing a constructive role in the Middle East. This opposition was underlined when, in August 2006, it prohibited any of the six Canadian soldiers serving with the UN Truce Supervision Organization—a body that has operated in the Middle East since 1948—from entering Lebanon. And so, in addition to contributing no soldiers to the expanded UNIFL peacekeeping mission, the government deliberately hampered the UN by imposing constraints on our pre-existing contribution to stabilizing the region. The decision followed the death of a Canadian soldier, Major Paeta Derek Hess-von Kruedener, serving with the Truce Supervision Organization. He and three other UN observers were killed when a precision-guided bomb struck their long-established post, which was located on a barren hilltop and painted white, even after Israeli forces were warned repeatedly that their projectiles were striking perilously close by. Significantly, Prime Minister Harper's first reaction to learning of Major Hess-von Kruedener's death was to question why the observers had been kept in Lebanon "during what is now, more or less, a war." But surely one of the purposes of a "truce supervision organization" is to observe and report on breaches of the peace, thus ensuring political and legal accountability for unnecessary uses of force and other violations of international law? Harper's knee-jerk anti-UN reaction did a grave disservice to a brave Canadian peacekeeper and to generations of others like him.

During a graduate student dinner at Cambridge University in 1992, I boldly, and naively, predicted that three of the world's longstanding conflicts—South Africa, Northern Ireland, and Israel-Palestine—would not be resolved in my lifetime. I was quickly proved wrong. In 1994, Nelson Mandela was elected president in South Africa's first non-racial elections. That same year, the Irish Republican Army declared a ceasefire; four years later, in 1998, the Good Friday Agreement was concluded, bringing a stable peace to Northern Ireland. Given these seismic changes, can we really be so sure that something similar is impossible in the Middle East? And should we not at least try, as best we can, to facilitate that possibility?

DARFUR: WHATEVER HAPPENED TO "NEVER AGAIN"?

Violence-racked Darfur is another place where Canadian peacekeepers could usefully be deployed. Since 2003, more than 200,000 people have been killed, countless women have been raped and several million people have been forced from their homes. But again, the Canadian government says that the mission in Afghanistan precludes any new commitments elsewhere.

The government's position represents a serious moral failure—and is contrary to our national interest in protecting an absolutely fundamental human right. Between 1938 and 1945, some six million Jews and several million other civilians were murdered by the Nazis. It was, in the words of Winston Churchill, the "crime that knew no name." But the crimes of the Holocaust demanded a name, and they soon acquired one: "genocide," defined in the 1948 Genocide Convention as acts "committed with intent to destroy, in whole or in part, a national, ethnical, racial or religious group."

One hundred and thirty-eight countries, including Canada, have ratified that convention. By doing so, they confirmed that "genocide, whether committed in time of peace or in time of war, is a crime under international law which they undertake to prevent and to punish."

We have, on several previous occasions, failed to prevent or stop genocides. Between 1992 and 1995, some 250,000 people were killed, countless women were raped, and millions forced from their homes as genocide consumed Bosnia-Herzegovina. Canada and other members of the UN and NATO were too hesitant, too indecisive to intervene, despite the fact that the horror continued for three long years. In 1994, some 800,000 people were hacked to death in Rwanda. Senator Roméo Dallaire, who was then the commander of the UN Observer Mission in Rwanda, pleaded for 5,000 additional troops, but instead saw his force reduced from 2,500 to 270.

Our failures in Bosnia and Rwanda prompted Canada—along with other NATO countries—to intervene militarily in Kosovo in 1999. We prevented Slobodan Milosevic and his militia from committing genocide there. Then, after the intervention, Foreign Minister Lloyd Axworthy established the International Commission on Intervention and State Sovereignty. The commission, which included among its members Michael Ignatieff, articulated a new concept: the "responsibility to protect." Commonly referred to as "R2P," the concept entails, in extreme cases when states are unable or unwilling to protect their own populations, the broader community of states bearing that responsibility—including, if necessary and feasible, through military intervention.

The agents of the genocide in Darfur have been the Janjaweed, members of nomadic Arab tribes who were armed by the Sudanese government and given the task of suppressing a rebellion by the agrarian people of that western Sudanese province. Sudanese military planes have often bombed villages in advance of Janjaweed attacks, while the government in Khartoum has seized every opportunity to impede a significant international response.

The Janjaweed (who ride camels and horses) and the Sudanese military (which pushes crude barrel bombs out of the back of
cargo planes) would be no match for a well-trained, well-equipped
Western military. Yet they have successfully resisted the limited efforts made so far to curtail their actions. For three years,
the African Union, which includes all of Africa's fifty-four states
except Morocco, tried to stop the carnage while the United Nations
deferred to it, insisting that African problems should be dealt with
by Africans. But the African Union's capacity to intervene was
limited by a lack of peacekeeping experience, training, appropriate
equipment and healthy soldiers (Africa's militaries have been devastated by HIV/AIDS), as well as its own refusal to act in any manner that had not received the consent of the Sudanese government.

In May 2006, African countries recognized that they were not
up to the task. The African Union urged the commencement of a
UN peacekeeping operation in Darfur "at the earliest possible time."
In response, the UN Security Council requested that then UN secretary general Kofi Annan provide recommendations "on all relevant aspects of the mandate of the United Nations operation in
Darfur" including "additional force requirements" and "potential
troop-contributing countries." Annan's office immediately indicated that any force deployed to Darfur would have to include
soldiers from developed countries. As the deputy UN secretary
general, Mark Malloch Brown, said: "We want the rest of the world
to make a higher level of contributions to peacekeeping, involving
more mainstream militaries around the world. It's going to need a
whole new level of investment and logistical support."

Three months later, the Security Council adopted Resolution
1706, formally authorizing the creation of a peacekeeping force for
Darfur. It did hold off deploying the force while last-ditch efforts
were made to obtain Sudanese consent, but let there be no doubt:
Resolution 1706 authorizes a muscular intervention in Darfur
with or without the consent of Khartoum. In the circumstances, a
declared willingness to deploy one or two thousand highly trained

infantry, a few CF-18 fighter aircraft and the Canadian Forces' fleet of Griffin helicopters—which are not being used elsewhere—could be just what is needed to create the political will for the deployment to move forward.

Some have argued that Canada's national interest is not engaged in Darfur, at least not as much as it is in Afghanistan. But the argument overlooks two important points. First, Canada always has an interest in protecting fundamental human rights, and there is no more fundamental right than being protected from genocide. Second, the degree of national interest that we have in any given situation must be balanced against the likely costs, including lost Canadian lives. And as I have said, neither the Janjaweed nor the Sudanese military constitute a serious fighting force.

Moreover, as Senator Dallaire explained in the *Globe and Mail* in September 2006, Khartoum's reluctance to accept a UN peacekeeping force is closely linked to the Canadian government's unwillingness to lead any such mission. According to the former UN peacekeeper, "One of the underlying justifications of Sudan's refusal to accept a UN mission is its professed fear that letting the United Nations in means letting the United States and other major powers into the area." Dallaire then made the exact same point, in relation to Darfur, that this book makes more generally:

It is not only the responsibility of the U.S. and other Security Council members to solve the crisis in Darfur. Their efforts to protect the millions of displaced and menaced people living in Darfur by passing Resolution 1706 have been commendable. It now falls to Canada, as a leader of the world's middle powers, to take charge of the mission, prepare for deployment of Canadian Forces and rally other middle powers—such as Japan, Germany, India, Brazil, and the Scandinavian countries—to commit the resources and troops needed to stop the slaughter.

Canada's reputation as a leading global citizen, earned through diplomacy and our ability to send highly trained soldiers abroad, is at stake. As we decide our next step toward Darfur, we must resolve to prevent disgracing that tradition.

Yes, indeed! Providing leadership and stopping genocide on behalf of the United Nations: what better manifestation of national purpose, of an intent for a nation on the international stage?

— 3 —

MISSILE DEFENCE:

Dr. Strangelove Lives On

IN *DR. STRANGELOVE*, Peter Sellers played a U.S. president trying to stop a crazed American general from launching an unauthorized nuclear strike against the Soviet Union. The Stanley Kubrick film disturbed audiences in 1963 by showing just how close the world was to Armageddon as a result of the hair-trigger procedures necessary for "mutually assured destruction."

The filmgoers of 1963 were acutely aware of the horrors of war. I remember how, during a family visit to Scotland in 1993, my father and I marvelled at the dimensions of the large cannon on display at Edinburgh Castle. My mother reacted to our enthusiasm with disgust. Having been born during a bombing raid on Münster, Germany, in 1941, she had personally experienced some of the suffering and deprivation that all armed conflicts cause. Like so many innocent victims, she reacts with revulsion any time someone forgets—or, worse yet, attempts to play down—the tragic human consequences of war.

Today, we forget all too easily. We forget the tens of millions killed and maimed and the hundreds of millions whose lives were torn apart. We forget the millions of children who, like my mother, grew up fearful and hungry. And we forget the major diplomatic initiatives undertaken—after the first and second world wars—to prevent further armed conflicts and civilize, as far as possible, the conduct of any future conflicts. The 1925 Geneva Protocol prohibited the "use in war of asphyxiating, poisonous or other gases" as well as "bacteriological methods of warfare." The 1945 United Nations Charter banned aggressive wars and vested responsibility for enforcing the peace in an executive body, the Security Council, made up of fifteen nation-states. The 1948 Genocide Convention bound countries to prevent and punish violent acts committed with the intent of destroying ethnic or religious groups; the four Geneva Conventions of 1949 sought to protect civilians and combatants from unnecessary suffering during times of war. The Allied bomb that struck near the hospital in which my grandmother was giving birth—hastening the delivery and thus, as she later told my mother, fulfilling the role traditionally occupied by storks—would probably have been illegal had it been dropped after the Geneva Conventions had been negotiated and ratified by West Germany and the United States.

It was the development of the atomic bomb in 1945, and especially the thermonuclear hydrogen bomb eight years later, that provided the ultimate incentive for curbing the worst excesses of war and slowing the relentless march of military technology. The charred remains of Hiroshima and Nagasaki, and the horribly damaged bodies of those who survived the blasts, provided stark evidence of what we could expect in the event of a full-blown nuclear conflict. All of a sudden, *Homo sapiens* had acquired the ability to destroy itself.

At least three factors contributed to saving us, all of which were reduced to acronyms by diplomats and strategists. Mutually assured destruction (appropriately known as MAD) provided a perverse and risky deterrent based on the fact that no country could survive the apocalyptic consequences of nuclear war. Its effects were manifest in 1962, when presidents John F. Kennedy and Nikita Khrushchev stepped back from the brink during the Cuban Missile Crisis between the United States and the Soviet Union. Then, in the 1968 Nuclear Non-Proliferation Treaty (NPT), the five countries that already possessed nuclear weapons promised to work towards general disarmament, while sharing nuclear technology for peaceful energy production with those that did not; in return, the latter countries promised never to acquire such weapons. Finally, in 1972, the United States and the Soviet Union negotiated the Anti-Ballistic Missile (ABM) Treaty that, by prohibiting large-scale missile defence shields, ensured that MAD would continue to operate.

That third factor, the ABM Treaty, became subject to a frontal attack in January 1999, in the penultimate year of Bill Clinton's presidency, when a Republican-dominated U.S. Congress adopted an act announcing "the policy of the United States to deploy as soon as is technologically possible an effective National Missile Defense system capable of defending the territory of the United States against limited ballistic missile attack." Referred to by some of its proponents as the "son of Star Wars," missile defence is a scaled-down version of Ronald Reagan's 1983 plan to use land, sea and space-based lasers to shoot down intercontinental ballistic missiles before they could hit the United States. Although the new system uses missiles instead of lasers, at least in its initial phases, the technology that is needed to "stop a bullet with a bullet" is still highly complex, enormously expensive and more than slightly imperfect.

Advocates of missile defence argue that it is needed to guard against "rogue states" such as North Korea and Iran, which are developing long-range missiles and, in North Korea's case at least, nuclear weapons. But other countries, particularly China and Russia, worry that a successful system would undermine the deterrence effect of their own nuclear forces, especially if the system were eventually expanded into a full defensive shield similar to that envisaged by Reagan. By providing some protection against retal-iatory Chinese or Russian strikes, missile defence would make it easier for the United States to contemplate a first strike—or at least more willing to threaten such a strike in order to pressure other countries. George W. Bush's expansive doctrine of "pre-emptive" self-defence has only exacerbated these concerns.

It was precisely this kind of dangerous destabilization that American president Richard Nixon and Soviet general secre-tary Leonid Brezhnev were seeking to prevent when they negoti-ated the ABM Treaty in 1972. The treaty limited the United States and Soviet Union to one anti-ballistic missile system each, cover-ing an area less than 150 kilometres in radius. The Soviet Union built its system around Moscow; a U.S. system was constructed around intercontinental ballistic missile silos in North Dakota, but it was turned off after only one day of operation. Making a mis-sile defence system work, even on a small scale, was proving much more difficult than anticipated. Not that it mattered, because the development of nuclear missile submarines—by providing a plat-form that was essentially immune from the threat of first strikes—was already bolstering both the Soviet and U.S. deterrents. In addition, the ABM Treaty was part of a larger initiative, the Strate-gic Arms Limitation Talks, that led to a series of caps and, eventu-ally, to coordinated reductions in both countries' nuclear arsenals.

The 1990s saw the "peace dividend," a massive reduction in U.S. military spending as the Cold War ended and the threat of nuclear war receded. Then, late in the decade, the Republicans pushed Bill Clinton to amend the ABM Treaty to allow the development of a continent-wide missile defence system. Russian president Vladimir Putin called the proposal "a cure which is worse than the disease," by which he meant mutually assured destruction. The standoff ended when George W. Bush arrived in the White House in Janu-ary 2001. A long-time supporter of missile defence, Bush soon gave Putin the required six months' notice that the United States was withdrawing from the ABM Treaty.

The reaction was prompt and decisive. In February 2004, the Associated Press reported that Russia had designed a "hypersonic" weapon that provided an "asymmetrical answer" to the U.S. missile defence plan. The American action had triggered a new arms race. The strategic stalemate, resulting from mutual full exposure to the threat of nuclear war, was starting to break down.

China is particularly concerned about U.S. missile defence. The People's Republic has a relatively small number of intercontinental ballistic missiles and is therefore susceptible to having its nuclear deterrence nullified by a missile defence system. Its concern has been heightened by the fact that George W. Bush is an ardent supporter of Taiwan, to which China lays claim. Exacerbating things even further, the first U.S. interceptors are based in Alaska, which is the closest part of the United States to China. In response, Beijing has decided to produce more missiles capable of reaching the lower forty-eight American states, so as to ensure an ability to overwhelm the new shield. As the then chief Chinese arms negotiator, Sha Zukang, told the *New York Times* in May 2000: "How can we base our national security on your assurances of goodwill?"

Similar calculations are likely being made in other capitals. Just as China is responding to the United States, India might then respond to China, then Pakistan to India, and so on. This knock-on effect gives vulnerable, previously non-nuclear weapon countries— including Iran and North Korea—more reason to pursue their own missile-borne nuclear deterrents. In short, missile defence, by upsetting the delicate balance between the existing nuclear powers, is helping to create an international climate of fear and suspicion in which a system might one day become justified. What is more, the reciprocal buildups are already generating a perceived need, within the United States, to push missile defence to ever-higher levels of technological sophistication. Indeed, the Bush administration's missile defence plans extend far beyond those of the Clinton administration, to include weapons deployed in and from outer space.

If igniting a new arms race was not bad enough, missile defence—especially on a continental scale—is still unlikely to work. To date, all of the tests have been rigged, including by outfitting the mock incoming warheads with Global Positioning Satellite beacons so that the intercepting missiles can "home in" on them. Some of the supposedly successful tests were in fact misses relabelled as "flybys," which can only be considered successes if the intercepting missiles are designed to be nuclear armed—just like the Bomarc anti-aircraft missiles of the 1960s—so that they can be exploded in proximity to the incoming target. Moreover, there is nothing to suggest that the system could cope with multiple launches or decoys. Technologically simple devices, such as tinfoil chaff, might be able to negate any foreseeable anti-missile system by creating an array of apparently real targets. As Steve Staples explains in *Missile Defence: Round One*: "This problem of missile discrimination was being utterly overlooked by the weapons designers because it was an unsolvable problem."

Even if the technology could be made to work, the effort being put into missile defence is sadly, and perhaps deliberately, misdirected. Why would terrorists and rogue states develop and use intercontinental missiles when it is much easier to sneak across borders and deploy asymmetric force in the form of box cutters, pathogens and primitive radiological ("dirty") bombs? It's no wonder that the Russians and Chinese are nervous, since missile defence is so obviously the wrong answer to the threats being invoked publicly to justify it!

Given the negatives, U.S. missile defence should be the last thing that other countries would wish to join. However, the Bush administration has been keen to induce others to share the expense and just as eager to situate missile interceptors and ancillary radar stations on foreign soil. Foreign participation would also help to bolster the case within the United States, where support has waned. As Staples writes: "Then George W. Bush could show his critics at home and around the world that even Canada the peacekeeper,

Canada the advocate of banning landmines, Canada the champion of nuclear disarmament, embraced his missile-defence system." Persuading Canada to participate became all the more important after our refusal to join in the 2003 Iraq War, as a way of demonstrating to other, potentially unco-operative countries that that decision was just an aberration from an otherwise obedient ally.

For all of these reasons, the February 2005 decision to stay out of missile defence was one of the most important foreign-policy decisions that any Canadian government has ever made. At stake was nothing less than our freedom of action in international affairs, including our ability to play a constructive role in a global system based on co-operation and agreed rules rather than the threat and use of armed force. Yet the decision was hardly an easy one for the Paul Martin government to make, and not just because of U.S. pressure. For decades, Canada's military leaders and an associated "security community" of academics—many of them funded by the Department of National Defence—had been promoting "interoperability" with the U.S. armed forces, and by 2005 this effort had acquired significant momentum.

Interoperability requires compatible command structures, rules of engagement and equipment—the last being especially attractive to generals seeking a larger slice of the budgetary pie. Interoperability is expensive because the U.S. military is technologically very advanced and becoming more so. The increased budgets would give the generals more influence within the federal bureaucracy, as well as the opportunity to work hand in glove with the world's most powerful military.

The non-financial costs of interoperability are also significant. Since interoperability is intended to make it easier for the Canadian Forces to work with the U.S. military, it leads, almost inexorably, to more frequent involvement in U.S.-led training and combat missions. As this happens, the orientation and ethos of the Canadian Forces, as well as the selection of the missions themselves, will increasingly be influenced by U.S. attitudes, interests and decision-making procedures. Before long, Canada's military leadership will be pushing our politicians to backtrack or renege on existing policies and treaties. Just consider how our involvement in the counter-insurgency mission in southern Afghanistan, which came about largely because of pressure from chief of the defence staff General Rick Hillier, has challenged our commitment to international humanitarian law and precluded our involvement in important UN peacekeeping missions elsewhere. In the Arctic, another critical area, interoperability could compromise our independent ability to monitor and protect that vast territory, its remarkable wildlife and its indigenous people.

Missile defence would take interoperability to a whole new level, since Canada would be locked into a continent-wide weapons system that was run by the United States primarily for the United States. Despite contributing political support as well as, quite possibly, money and territory, Canada would have little say in the development, deployment or uses of the system. The day-to-day operation of missile defence is conducted by NORTHCOM, the entirely American "Northern Command." Even the radar stations already located on Canadian soil, previously used for air defence but potentially useful for missile defence (ever since the Martin government amended the North American Aerospace Defence Command agreement to allow NORAD surveillance information to be transmitted instantaneously to NORTHCOM), are owned and operated by the United States. Nobody seriously thinks that Canada would be consulted before interceptors were launched against an incoming missile; indeed, there probably would not be time. When you add in the geopolitical consequences of missile defence, particularly for relations with Russia and China, the rest of the international community would consider that Canada had surrendered most of its foreign-policy independence to the United States. And they'd be right.

Joining missile defence would also have run counter to Canada's long-held position as an advocate and architect of arms control agreements. For decades, Canadian governments insisted that all countries live up to their commitments under the UN Charter, the Nuclear Non-Proliferation Treaty and other related agreements. In particular, Canada has traditionally maintained that those countries that possess nuclear weapons have an ongoing obligation, under the NPT, to work towards the eventual elimination of their nuclear arsenals. Had we joined missile defence, we would have been condoning the Bush administration's preference for military and technological rather than co-operative solutions to the threats posed by weapons of mass destruction and terrorism. And we would have discredited the efforts of our diplomats to secure a multilateral treaty imposing meaningful limits on the use of space for military purposes. As a country with significant commercial interests in outer space, Canada has long advocated keeping that area free of weapons.

In the lead-up to Canada's decision, those politicians, corporate lobbyists, military leaders and their university-based allies in favour of participation sought to conceal or distort these considerations. In *Rushing to Armageddon*, Mel Hurtig recounts how, in April 2004, former Canadian defence minister David Pratt claimed that five of the previous eight tests of the U.S. missile defence system had succeeded. Hurtig convincingly disproves this claim, with forty pages of information, statistics and quotations from reputable U.S. sources such as the Union of Concerned Scientists and the U.S. government's own General Accounting Office. He is similarly thorough in disproving repeated assurances by then prime minister Paul Martin and his defence minister, Bill Graham, that missile defence would not contribute to the weaponization of space. Of all the quotes provided by Hurtig, my favourite comes from the 2004 Strategic Master Plan of the aptly named U.S. Space Command: "Future challenges require that we develop flexible, responsive force projection capabilities to complement our nuclear deterrent force. In short, we must become a full spectrum space combat command." Space Command is headquartered at Peterson Air Force

Base in Colorado Springs, alongside both the joint Canada-U.S. NORAD and the U.S.-only NORTHCOM.

Hurtig goes so far as to accuse Martin and Graham of "intentionally misleading" the Canadian people about missile defence. Indeed, the contrast between their emphatic statements denying the dangers and implications and the pages upon pages of contradicting evidence assembled by Hurtig leads inexorably to the conclusion that "lying" would not be an inappropriate word. Graham admitted as much in September 2004 when—seemingly out of the blue—he stated that the principal reason why Canada should join in missile defence was to maintain good relations with the United States.

Graham and other proponents of Canadian participation felt that Canada's interests must necessarily be aligned to those of the U.S. government of the day, even if that government was and remains opposed to multilateral institutions, systems of justice and forms of international co-operation in which most Canadians firmly believe. The concern of the proponents was overwhelmingly economic: keeping the border open for trade during a period when the United States was increasingly obsessed with national security. As Thomas D'Aquino, the ubiquitous chief executive and president of the Canadian Council of Chief Executives, stated in January 2004: "Our countries need to maintain a strong economic partnership, but also to build a much stronger security and defence partnership to ensure that we do not get caught in any repeat of the disruptions seen in the aftermath of the terrorist attacks of September 11, 2001."

Indeed, one striking characteristic of Canadian proponents of missile defence was how many of them were either members of the corporate elite or financially supported by them. For them, missile defence—indeed, security generally—was almost entirely about the bottom line. They were seemingly unconcerned that joining in the U.S. system would have taken us dramatically away from a course charted by generations of Canadian governments—a foreign policy based on the belief that a predictable rule of law, and not the arbitrary rule of men, is the best way of ensuring both national and global security.

In the end, the missile defence lobby encountered stiff opposition from a much smaller and less well-funded coalition of civil society groups—including the Polaris Institute, Physicians for Global Survival, Canadian Peace Alliance and Montreal-based Échec à la guerre—which mounted a sustained campaign to educate the Canadian public about missile defence. And the more that Canadians learned, the more their opinions shifted against Canadian participation.

In August 2004, the "Canadian Coalition to Oppose Missile Defence" won the first of two major victories. Paul Martin had become prime minister in December 2003, after Jean Chrétien resigned. A more Machiavellian politician would have signed up to missile defence immediately, but Martin, dubbed "Mr. Dithers" by the *Economist*, decided to wait until after he had won his first election as prime minister. He won that on June 28, 2004, but with only a fragile minority government. And so, on August 5, 2004, Martin decided to take only the most cautious of steps—by agreeing to amend the NORAD agreement to allow surveillance information, gathered by the binational aerospace defence command, to be conveyed directly to NORTHCOM. This move ensured that NORAD would not have to be scaled back to its initial function of air-only surveillance and defence as soon as the Americans activated their anti-missile system. However, it incidentally confirmed the fallacy of one of the arguments previously deployed in favour of Canadian participation, namely, that NORAD could only survive if we became fully involved in missile defence.

The second victory came on February 22, 2005, when then foreign minister Pierre Pettigrew told U.S. secretary of state Condoleezza Rice that Canada would not be joining missile defence. Two days later, Paul Martin conveyed the same message to the House of Commons. The prime minister did so with obvious regret, but his hands had been tied by domestic political considerations.

With only a minority government, he could hardly ignore the mounting public opposition to missile defence. Another important factor was that the Young Liberals of British Columbia had submitted a resolution to an upcoming national Liberal Party policy convention unequivocally calling for Canada to remain outside the U.S. system. The Prime Minister's Office put enormous pressure on the Young Liberals to withdraw the resolution, knowing that it would almost certainly be adopted by the relatively progressive majority of delegates who attend such conventions. But the youth members refused to back down. Facing imminent embarrassment in the full glare of the national media spotlight, the prime minister swallowed hard and dispatched Pettigrew to convey the bad news to Rice.

Two weeks later, in Halifax, I participated in a panel discussion on missile defence at the annual conference of the Canadian Institute of International Affairs. It soon became apparent that I was the only member of the panel who approved of Martin's decision. It was also apparent that most of the audience, which was dominated by prosperous-looking men in dark suits, did not share my views either. I had decided not to rub salt in an already sore wound. But then a young woman with dreadlocks, cradling an infant in her arms, asked a perfectly reasonable question about whether the government's announcement meant that it would have to revisit the earlier decision to share NORAD surveillance with NORTHCOM. Her intervention was met with a chorus of derisive snorts and chuckles. Unable to restrain myself, I reached for the microphone: "Excuse me, but would all of you please take a closer look at the woman who just spoke. She's a member of the Halifax Peace Coalition, an organization that played a central role in the campaign against missile defence. Now, since that campaign was successful, it stands to reason that she's one of the most powerful people in this room."

Most Canadians remain opposed to missile defence. For this reason, Stephen Harper wisely avoided the issue after he failed to win a majority government in January 2006. Yet it is likely that we will revisit it if the Conservatives secure a majority any time soon. Harper is a long-time proponent of Canadian participation in missile defence, having made his position clear as early as May 2002. As for Stéphane Dion, the Young Liberals played a key role in his election as party leader. There is therefore reason to hope that he would resist the intense pressure, from the U.S. government as well as the Canadian defence and corporate lobbies, that would be applied to him following any Liberal electoral success.

If and when the issue is forced upon them again, Canadians would do well to remember that the campaign against missile defence began in the United States and the Soviet Union with Richard Nixon and Leonid Brezhnev. This is much more than a Canada-U.S. issue. If stability is to be maintained among the nuclear powers, Dr. Strangelove must be denied legitimacy and political support wherever he is found—including in Ottawa. On missile defence, as on so many other issues, it's time for Canada to look beyond North America. It's time to exercise our influence to prevent the insanity of a new global arms race that will, unless we stop it, soon extend into space.

— 4 —

NUCLEAR NIGHTMARES:

George W. Bush and the NPT

BECAME AWARE of the threat of nuclear holocaust when I was about ten years old. As a child, I spent the summers on my grandparents' farm in southeast Saskatchewan, where I was fascinated by the vast, ever-changing prairie skies. I would lie on my back in a pasture, watching billowing clouds form an almost infinite number of fantastical shapes. It was during this early skywatching that I noticed the contrails of jet aircraft, most flying east–west, but some flying north–south. Curious, I asked my grandfather where the planes were going.

The east–west traffic was easy enough, since Stoughton, Saskatchewan, lies near the flight paths between Toronto and Regina, Calgary and Vancouver. Today, when I fly from Vancouver to Winnipeg and points east, I sometimes see the town's large, orange-coloured grain elevator ten thousand metres below.

The north–south traffic was more difficult to explain. At the southern end, the flights must have been taking off and landing in the United States. Yet there were no large cities directly to the south and, to the north, there was not much more than frozen tundra between Stoughton and the USSR. I remember the look on my grandfather's face when he told me that the contrails were from American B-52 bombers headed to forward-staging locations over Canada's High Arctic, where they would wait for the signal to fly deep into Russia to drop their payloads. "Those are military planes," he said quietly, "carrying atomic bombs." My grandfather taught me many things, but I doubt he had ever expected to be teaching his ten-year-old grandson about the prospect of a nuclear war. I had nightmares for years afterwards.

Some national leaders must have had similar nightmares or been as concerned about their grandchildren's future as my grandfather was about mine. In August 1945, U.S. president Harry S. Truman ordered that nuclear bombs be dropped on Hiroshima and Nagasaki in Japan, incinerating tens of thousands of people—most of them innocent civilians—and condemning hundreds of thousands more to the painful and often fatal effects of radiation exposure. Three months later, a sombre and somewhat regretful Truman said:

> The hope of civilization lies in international arrangements looking, if possible, to the renunciation of the use and development of the atomic bomb, and directing and encouraging the use of atomic energy and all future scientific information toward peaceful and humanitarian ends.

The International Atomic Energy Agency (IAEA) was created in 1957 with a mandate to "accelerate and enlarge the contribution of atomic energy to peace, health and prosperity throughout the world." At the same time, the IAEA was charged with ensuring that "assistance provided by it or at its request or under its supervision or control is not used in such a way as to further any military purpose." Today, the IAEA serves as the world's nuclear inspectorate, regularly visiting nuclear facilities in more than 140 countries to monitor that they are not being used for military purposes.

In 1968, the five "declared nuclear weapon states"—the United States, Soviet Union, Britain, France and China—signed the Nuclear Non-Proliferation Treaty (NPT). So too did most of the countries that had not yet acquired nuclear weapons, including Canada. Under the terms of the NPT, the declared nuclear weapon states promised to share nuclear technology for peaceful energy production with the non-nuclear weapon states, and to work towards "general disarmament." In return, the non-nuclear weapon states, of which more than 180 have now ratified the treaty, forswore the acquisition of such weapons. Under the terms of the NPT, the IAEA is tasked with verifying these commitments.

The deal set out in the NPT is counterintuitive: sharing nuclear technology in return for a promise not to use that technology to build a nuclear bomb. Yet the NPT has been remarkably successful. Over the course of nearly four decades, only four countries have developed nuclear arms, and each of the four—Israel, India, Pakistan and now North Korea—exercised its sovereign right to stay out of, or withdraw from, the treaty. About thirty other countries, including Canada, have chosen not to develop nuclear weapons despite having the technological ability to do so.

Still, the NPT has failed to achieve general disarmament or even significant progress towards it. More than twenty thousand nuclear weapons remain in existence, most of them belonging to the five declared nuclear weapon states. In 1996, the nuclear powers went so far as to argue in the International Court of Justice that international law had nothing to say about whether countries are permitted to use—or to threaten to use—nuclear weapons. It is not surprising that some countries are now questioning the willingness of the nuclear powers to keep their side of the bargain. Several of them are returning to a way of thinking that predates the NPT, namely, that a nuclear deterrent is a desirable and even necessary component of national security. Unfortunately, this trend has only accelerated as a consequence of the policies and actions of President George W. Bush.

Bush's administration has confronted three countries suspected of having nuclear weapon programs: Iraq, North Korea, and Iran. In each instance, the United States has curtailed rather than extended its co-operation with the IAEA, even though the agency is frequently able to gain access to nuclear sites in countries of concern. In 2003, the Bush administration went to war against Iraq despite being told by IAEA director general Mohamed ElBaradei that Saddam Hussein no longer had a nuclear program. The findings of the IAEA inspectors were pushed aside by then U.S. national security adviser Condoleezza Rice and vice president Dick Cheney, both of whom spoke darkly about the looming risk of a "mushroom cloud."

The Bush administration then attempted to shoot the messenger by opposing ElBaradei's reappointment as director general of the IAEA. According to the *Washington Post*, the National Security Agency was even tapping ElBaradei's telephone in an attempt to acquire evidence of bias that it could then have used against him. Any previous U.S. administration would have succeeded in blocking a reappointment to such an important post. That the Bush administration failed to do so is a stark reflection of just how much "soft power" the United States has lost since it invaded Iraq in defiance of international opinion.

The Bush administration has also stymied IAEA efforts to constrain Pakistan, which exploded its first nuclear weapon in 1998 and has provided technical know-how for the North Korean and Iranian nuclear programs. In 2003, A.Q. Khan, who ran Pakistan's bomb-building operation, was exposed as the kingpin of an international black market in nuclear technology. Khan was placed under house arrest but subsequently pardoned by Pakistan's president, General Pervez Musharraf. Officials from the United

States and the IAEA were denied permission to interrogate Khan. According to a report by Seymour Hersh in the *New Yorker*, the Bush administration agreed not to investigate the Khan network in return for an intensified effort on the part of Pakistan to kill or capture Osama bin Laden.

One of the more serious setbacks in the struggle against nuclear proliferation came in June 2002, when President Bush announced that he would "take the battle to the enemy, disrupt his plans and confront the worst threats before they emerge." Preventive military action necessarily involves speculating about the intent and future actions of other actors. Decisions to intervene preventively are consequently susceptible to intelligence failures or even to the deliberate skewing of facts—as occurred before the invasion of Iraq. As a result, the so-called Bush Doctrine dramatically increases the uncertainties for potential target countries and thus the incentive for them to acquire a nuclear deterrent.

Matters have been made worse by a decade of opposition by U.S. Republicans to a number of arms control treaties. In October 1999, the Republican majority in the Senate refused to give the required "advice and consent" to the ratification of the 1996 Comprehensive Test Ban Treaty (CTBT). They did so despite a long history of efforts by leaders of both political parties to develop a treaty of precisely this kind, beginning with President Dwight Eisenhower, who described the failure to conclude an agreement as the "greatest disappointment" of his administration. John F. Kennedy came closest to success with the Limited Test Ban Treaty, which prohibited nuclear tests in the oceans, atmosphere and space but not underground.

The rejection of the CTBT was contrary to public opinion, with polls showing that at that time more than 80 per cent of Americans supported ratification. Key allies—including Britain, France and Germany—had urged the Senate to ratify, but they were similarly rebuffed. And the consequences have been profound, especially in terms of the United States' ability to discourage countries such as

Pakistan and India from testing nuclear bombs. Indeed, both these countries have pointed to the Senate's decision to justify their own refusals to ratify the treaty.

Since gaining office, President Bush has refused to revisit the issue of the CTBT. He has also opposed the negotiation of a verifiable fissile material cut-off treaty, whereby countries would cease the production of weapons grade uranium and plutonium. But neither of these moves compares in its seriousness to his frontal attack on the NPT.

Every five years, the parties to the NPT meet to review developments related to the treaty. At the 2000 review conference, the five declared nuclear weapon states made an "unequivocal commitment" to take thirteen clearly defined steps towards a nuclear-free world. Since achieving power in 2001, the Bush administration has systematically backed away from that commitment. At the political level, it has insisted on maintaining a substantial nuclear arsenal. Covertly, it has been engaged in developing new nuclear weapons. A secret Pentagon report obtained by the *New York Times* in March 2002 revealed plans to construct small nuclear weapons for battlefield use and to destroy deep and heavily fortified bunkers. The same report suggested that testing of nuclear weapons might need to be resumed. The Pentagon has also indicated that it will retain rather than destroy nuclear missiles and warheads removed from active deployment as a result of arms control negotiations with Russia.

At the same time, the Bush administration has pushed for new measures to enforce the obligations of non-nuclear weapon states, including strengthened export controls and improved mechanisms for interdicting weapons shipments on the high seas. In short, the Bush administration seeks to have the United States excused from its obligations under the NPT, while holding the non-nuclear weapon states strictly accountable. Exacerbating the situation yet further, the Bush administration has recently concluded an agreement with India to share U.S. civilian nuclear technology despite the fact that India has refused to join the NPT and has developed a nuclear arsenal.

The excuse for the shift in U.S. policy is, as always, the terrorist attacks of September 11, 2001. Before the 2005 NPT review conference, one unnamed U.S. official was quoted as saying: "We think the international situation with regard to non-proliferation has changed so radically that the review conference should not be looking backward at the past final document." Unfortunately, the change in the U.S. position led to the failure of the entire conference, casting the future of the NPT itself in doubt. In the circumstances, it comes as no surprise that some non-nuclear weapon states are reconsidering their options.

NORTH KOREA: THE MOUSE THAT ROARED

In Leonard Wibberley's novel *The Mouse That Roared* (1955), a tiny, impoverished country declares war on the United States in the hope of being rapidly defeated, occupied and then generously reconstructed. The plan goes awry when the flyweight belligerent inadvertently acquires the world's most powerful weapon and thus the ability to defend itself.

Wibberley's tale was made into a Peter Sellers movie that Kim Jong-il, a film buff, has probably seen. After the 2003 Iraq War, the North Korean dictator speculated that George W. Bush would not have launched an invasion had Saddam Hussein possessed nuclear weapons. In October 2006, North Korea detonated a crude nuclear bomb, sending political shock waves around the world.

The test was a serious blow to the Nuclear Non-Proliferation Treaty. North Korea had withdrawn from the NPT in January 2003. It had also renounced a bilateral treaty, the 1994 "framework agreement" with the United States, whereby, in return for economic aid, it had promised to shut down its sole nuclear reactor and cease the extraction and refinement of plutonium from spent uranium fuel rods into material suitable for nuclear weapons. At the same time, North Korea expelled weapons inspectors from the International

Atomic Energy Agency who had been monitoring its compliance with both treaties.

The North Korean test could well prompt other countries to go nuclear. Japan is the most likely to do so, despite its vehement denials of any such intent. In any event, Tokyo is accelerating work on a joint U.S.-Japanese missile defence system, while South Korea has announced that it will build a similar system on its own. These moves will only make matters worse, by causing Pyongyang—and probably Beijing—to build more bombs and missiles so as to maintain a credible deterrent. The test also raises the stakes with regard to Iran, since, if Pyongyang benefits rather than suffers as a result of acquiring nuclear weapons, Tehran will be encouraged to do likewise.

The North Korean test also poses a challenge to the United Nations. In July 2006, the Security Council ordered North Korea to stop producing ballistic missiles. Three months later, it expressed "deep concern" at the prospect of a North Korean nuclear test, which it said "would jeopardize peace, stability and security in the region and beyond." If the Security Council cannot agree on a unified approach to Pyongyang's clear refusal to abide by its requests, its authority will suffer. That authority could be diminished even further if the lack of a strong and unified response prompts the United States to act forcefully on its own.

At the same time, the situation provides something of an opportunity for the UN, by offering new space for Chinese leadership. China, which is North Korea's primary source of food and oil, has used its status as a permanent member of the Security Council to protect Pyongyang in the past. But its immediate reaction to the North Korean test was to condemn it as a "flagrant and brazen" violation. Although Beijing is justifiably concerned about creating a situation where more of North Korea's 22 million oppressed and impoverished citizens might flee into China, it also, almost desperately, wants to expand its role in international affairs beyond the economic domain.

So far, the Chinese response has been cautious, though not overly so. For nobody—not even the Bush administration—thinks that North Korea will actually use its new weapons. It is a big step from having a nuclear bomb to having one that is small enough to mount on a missile. Moreover, any attempt to attack the United States, or Japan for that matter, would be met with a devastating retaliatory strike. Instead, the main concern is that North Korea might sell nuclear materials or technology to other countries or even terrorist groups. For this reason, China agreed to a Security Council resolution that allows the United States and other countries to board and search vessels, leaving from or headed to North Korea, for nuclear weapons or missile components—provided that any such interdictions are made "in accordance with international law."

Whether the interdiction of foreign vessels on the high seas is allowed under international law has already been a matter of some debate. In 2003, then U.S. undersecretary of state for arms control and international security John Bolton spearheaded the creation of the Proliferation Security Initiative (PSI), a co-operative effort to prevent international trafficking in missiles and weapons of mass destruction that now involves more than sixty countries. Initially, the walrus-moustached U.S. diplomat sought to include recognition of a right of pre-emptive self-defence within the framework of PSI, knowing that such a reference could provide a foothold for unilateral U.S. action against foreign shipping, even in the absence of an immediate threat. But most of the other countries resisted that effort, making it difficult to argue that the new Security Council resolution, by calling for action in accordance with international law, somehow authorizes the interdiction of foreign vessels without the consent of those vessels' flag states.

In addition, the resolution specifically states that it was adopted under Article 41 of the UN Charter. Article 41 is confined to measures short of the use of military force, with the use of force being governed by Article 42. The Security Council could certainly have used Article 42 to authorize the non-consensual boarding of North Korean vessels on the high seas; indeed, there is already a precedent for doing so, dating from 1966 when the council authorized the United Kingdom to interdict oil shipments destined for white-ruled Rhodesia. But China is clearly pushing for more diplomacy instead of any military action against North Korea. In the circumstances, it is imperative that Washington talk directly with Pyongyang. When Bill Clinton was president, he made real progress by allowing his diplomats to engage in bilateral negotiations. Those talks led to the 1994 framework agreement and, in 2000, a summit meeting between Kim Jong-il and South Korea's then president, Kim Dae-jung. Shortly before Clinton left office, American diplomats were so close to achieving an agreement on ballistic missiles that he was seriously considering a trip to Pyongyang.

How did we get into this mess? The simple answer is, by bullying and threatening rather than talking. George W. Bush arrived in the White House determined to reject everything his predecessor had done. When, in early 2001, newly appointed U.S. secretary of state Colin Powell said that he favoured continuing Clinton's approach on North Korea, he was publicly rebuked by the president. Bush, overlooking a fundamental principle of diplomacy—that opponents must be treated as equals—insisted that North Korea's regional neighbours be participants in any negotiations. He labelled North Korea as a member of the "axis of evil," called the diminutive Kim "disgusting" and "a pygmy" and declared that the United States would never tolerate a nuclear-armed North Korea. The latter statement was replete with hypocrisy, given that the United States was flouting its own NPT obligations. As Brazil's representative at a preparatory meeting for the 2005 NPT conference warned: "One cannot worship at the altar of nuclear weapons and raise heresy charges against those who want to join the sect."

A senior U.S. naval officer once told me that the Pentagon's "nightmare scenario" involved North Korea rushing its forces into Seoul—which is only fifty kilometres south of the demilitarized zone between the two Koreas—and then announcing that the soldiers had taken along a nuclear bomb. Such a bomb, if detonated in the heart of that large city, could kill or injure a million or more South Koreans as well as thousands of the American soldiers and expatriates resident there. Undetonated, it would constitute a powerful bargaining chip.

For this reason, the October 2006 test, and the uncertain effectiveness of any pre-emptive military action against North Korea, have forced George W. Bush to retreat to a new position. Any transfer by North Korea of nuclear weapons or material to another country or group will be considered "a grave threat to the United States" for which North Korea will be held "fully accountable." And new talks have been initiated that follow—at long last—the path cut by the Clinton administration a decade before.

The North Korean test represents a serious foreign-policy failure for Bush. From one perspective, there is logic in nuclear proliferation. Backed into a corner, even a mouse may feel the need to roar.

IRAN: WAGGING THE DOG?

George W. Bush has found himself in increasingly desperate straits. His inability to lead was confirmed by Hurricane Katrina. He has lost some of his closest allies: Cheney aide Lewis "Scooter" Libby to perjury, fundraiser "Kenny Boy" Lay to fraud, former secretary of defence Donald Rumsfeld to incompetence. In the November 2006 midterm elections, Bush suffered what he himself described as a "pummelling," with the Republican Party losing control of both the House of Representatives and the Senate. Then the Iraq Study Group, led by former secretary of state James Baker, issued a stinging indictment of Bush's policies in the Middle East and recommended negotiations with both Syria and Iran.

For some of the president's remaining advisers, it might seem time for another war. Margaret Thatcher's defence of the Falkland Islands after Argentina's invasion ensured her re-election as British prime minister in 1983. Fifteen years later, a beleaguered Bill Clinton fired seventy-nine so-called Monica missiles at Sudan and Afghanistan; a film along similar lines, entitled *Wag the Dog*, soon followed. The declaration of a "global war on terrorism" and the invasion of Afghanistan ensured Republican victories in the 2002 midterm elections; two years later, the invasion of Iraq carried Bush to a second presidential term. Evidence of weapons of mass destruction in Iraq, and of links between Saddam and Al-Qaeda, was either spurious or manufactured to provide justification. And the use of military force abroad is one of the few significant things that a weak and unpopular president can do arbitrarily, given the multitude of political and constitutional constraints inherent in the American system of government.

Bush began rattling sabres over Iran shortly after the 2003 Iraq War began, referring to Iran as an "outlaw regime" and explicitly threatening violence. It helped that the Iranian government is hardly composed of angels: in 2003, International Atomic Energy Agency inspectors, following up on leads provided by Iranian dissidents, discovered that Tehran had been trying to enrich uranium for almost two decades. At that point, Washington accused Tehran of having a clandestine weapons program and began pushing for the IAEA, which does not have the power to impose mandatory sanctions, to refer the matter to the UN Security Council. The United States needed the UN in this instance because it could not exert any more economic pressure by itself, having already suspended commercial relations with Iran since the fundamentalist revolution there in 1979.

European governments initially opposed sending the matter to the Security Council, because they feared that Moscow would threaten to veto any stringent resolution and that the resulting deadlock might then be seized upon as implicitly authorizing war, repeating what happened before the invasion of Iraq. Instead, France, Germany and Britain—the "EU Three"—sought to negotiate an agreement whereby Iran would cease enriching uranium in return for membership in the World Trade Organization (WTO), access to new civilian aircraft, and a light water nuclear reactor that, although less useful for producing weapons, would effectively produce electricity. This approach, which was modelled on that taken by the Clinton administration towards North Korea, made considerable progress—until the election of hardliner Mahmoud Ahmadinejad as Iran's new president in June 2005.

Ahmadinejad defiantly reasserted his country's right to enrich uranium, though he did not, it must be said, assert a right to produce a nuclear bomb. It is unclear why Iran, a country with some of the world's largest oil and gas reserves, needs nuclear energy, but it is obvious why it might want a nuclear bomb. Two of Iran's neighbours, Pakistan and Russia, have nuclear weapons; two others, Afghanistan and Iraq, are in effect occupied by U.S. forces, while Israel, less than fifteen hundred kilometres away, is assumed to possess a nuclear arsenal despite a continued policy of ambiguity. In 1981, Israel bombed an Iraqi reactor under construction near Baghdad; last year, it threatened a similar pre-emptive strike on Iranian nuclear facilities.

The threat of an Israeli strike—or, more likely, an American strike in support of Israel—must be taken seriously. In January 2005, Seymour Hersh reported in the *New Yorker* that U.S. commandos were already in Iran pinpointing underground nuclear facilities. Some experts have speculated that the July 2006 bombing of Hezbollah targets in southern Lebanon was in part a test, by Israeli forces on behalf of the United States, of the effectiveness of precision air strikes against deeply buried and heavy fortified targets. In November 2006, Hersh reported that U.S. strikes against Iranian nuclear facilities remained a real possibility, despite the opportunity for a midterm election-boosting "October surprise" having passed.

That Washington is involved on both sides of the affair—stoking Iran's fears while agitating about the transgressions that these fears generate—reflects the depth of U.S. hypocrisy. The CIA estimates that Israel, which has never ratified the Nuclear Non-Proliferation Treaty, possesses more than two hundred nuclear warheads. The same agency can still not produce conclusive evidence that Iran, a party to the treaty, has a nuclear weapon—as opposed to a nuclear energy—program. Yet Iran's leaders are presumed to be seeking weapons and have been vilified on that basis.

Part of the explanation for this dichotomous approach lies in Washington's uncritical support for Israel, especially since George W. Bush became president. Another part of the explanation is revenge. The Iranian revolutionaries revealed the limitations of American power nearly thirty years ago when they were able to hold fifty-two hostages in the U.S. embassy in Tehran for 444 days. A third part of the explanation is fear—that the ongoing chaos in Iraq could work to the advantage of Iran, which, like its neighbour, has a largely Shiite population. But the most important part of the explanation is the usefulness that another demonized enemy provides to a beleaguered American president.

The UN Security Council will not authorize the use of force against Iran. Other countries know that Iran poses no immediate threat and that additional sanctions will take time to bite. They also remember how Washington relied upon a UN resolution to justify the Iraq War just four months after assuring the world that the terms of the resolution provided no "automaticity." Russia has wisely insisted that any new resolutions on Iran specify that they do not authorize military action.

The Bush administration knows this, but it wants to be seen—especially by moderate Republicans, swing voters and a now questioning Congress—to have exhausted multilateral options. If Bush finds that his faltering popularity has become such a liability that it prevents him from advancing any kind of legacy agenda during his final years as president, the U.S. may bomb Iranian nuclear facilities regardless. Efforts are already being made to establish a new "coalition of the willing," not to join in the raids, but to provide the diplomatic cover necessary to weather the ensuing storm. In May 2006, British prime minister Tony Blair fired Jack Straw, his experienced foreign secretary, apparently because he had publicly expressed the opinion that the use of force against Iran was not an option. The Bush administration will also be looking to Canada, which raises the question: where do we, as a country, stand on the critical issue of nuclear proliferation?

CANADA'S ROLE, CANADA'S OPPORTUNITY

The 1963 federal election turned on the issue of whether to allow the deployment of nuclear weapons on Canadian soil. Prime Minister John Diefenbaker had agreed to a U.S. request to locate Bomarc anti-aircraft missiles in Canada, but he refused to allow them to be armed with nuclear warheads. After the U.S. state department publicly criticized this decision, Diefenbaker's Progressive Conservative government collapsed. Lester B. Pearson then fought and won the election partly on the basis that his Liberals would accept the warheads.

Pearson's willingness to accept nuclear warheads had serious consequences. Although Canada had been closely involved in the Manhattan Project that led to the development of the atomic bomb, it chose not to acquire nuclear weapons of its own. When Canada helped found the International Atomic Energy Agency in 1957, the decision to forsake nuclear arms provided the basis for early leadership within that organization.

Although the nuclear warheads for the Bomarcs were never placed under Canadian control, documents obtained by military analyst John Clearwater reveal that Pearson had signed a secret agreement concerning their use. The agreement gave the commander-in-chief of the North American Air Defence Command ("Air" became "Aerospace" in 1981 as NORAD's mission extended into space) the authority to release the warheads to the Canadian military if and when he deemed this necessary—without any need to consult the Canadian government. As a result, Canada could have been transformed into a nuclear weapon state almost instantly, solely as the result of a decision by a U.S. general.

Accepting the warheads may have bolstered the U.S. system of nuclear deterrence and thus the effectiveness of the strategy of mutually assured destruction. But it was a step backwards in Canada's efforts to persuade other countries not to use nuclear technology for military ends. Pierre Trudeau understood just how important it was for Canada to serve as a role model in the nuclear domain. One of the first things he did after becoming prime minister in 1968 was to ask the United States to remove the warheads from Canada. Even then, it took a decade and a half for the request to be fulfilled. When my grandfather told me what the B-52s overhead were carrying, he did not mention that our own country was a participant in the nuclear arms race. Perhaps he did not know; in the late 1970s, relatively few Canadians did.

Today, few Canadians realize just how exposed we still are to the dangers of nuclear conflict. Just as industrial pollutants and pesticide residues drift across oceans and contaminate our air and watersheds, radioactive fallout from a nuclear conflict anywhere would almost certainly reach our shores. One has only to think of the fallout from the 1986 accident at Chernobyl in Ukraine; it spread across central Europe, Scandinavia and the United Kingdom, to the point where sheep raised on some British farms still cannot be sold until they have been tested for safe levels of the radioactive isotope cesium-137. For this reason alone, the Canadian government should be doing all that it can to reduce the nuclear threat.

Canada is well positioned to engage in constructive diplomacy concerning the North Korean nuclear weapons program. We are, after all, a Pacific Rim country with an advanced economy and significant ties to both China and the United States. The Canadian government should be pushing for a UN maritime peacekeeping operation to search all vessels travelling to or from North Korea, one that is explicitly authorized by the Security Council and does not involve ships from the United States. We should commit several of our own naval vessels to such a mission. In the meantime, however, we should resist any U.S. pressure to participate in searches of North Korean vessels without further, much clearer authorization from the UN. For such searches would undermine that organization, engender hostility in Beijing and risk dragging Canada into another unnecessary and costly U.S.-led war.

As for Iran, our relations with that country have been in decline since 1980, when Canadian ambassador Ken Taylor helped six Americans who had escaped Iranian hostage-takers at the U.S. embassy. Relations worsened in July 2003 when Canadian photographer Zahra Kazemi was raped and killed in Iranian custody. The Canadian government responded by sponsoring a UN resolution that expressed "serious concern" about human rights in Iran; that resolution has been re-adopted on an annual basis ever since. Since May 2005, Canadian diplomats have been allowed by the Canadian government to deal with their Iranian counterparts only on matters concerning Canadian citizens, human rights and nuclear proliferation. We do not even have an ambassador in Tehran; therefore, any diplomatic contact is left to more junior envoys, whose lack of status deprives them of influence.

Cutting diplomatic ties is almost always counterproductive. Since Tehran does not recognize attempts to renounce Iranian citizenship, tens of thousands of Canadians are by default also Iranian nationals. When they travel to Iran to visit family or friends, they are at considerable risk. Having an ambassador in the country would enable Canada to intervene more promptly and at a higher level when something goes wrong. In April 2006, Canadian academic Ramin Jahanbegloo was arrested in Tehran. He was later released, but only after repeated requests from the Canadian embassy.

Diplomatic ties also create opportunities to help the citizens of other countries. Ken Taylor provided one example; Raoul Wallenberg another: in 1944, the Swedish envoy saved tens of thousands of Hungarian Jews from the Nazis. This could not have happened if Sweden had decided to pull its diplomats out of Budapest.

Our diplomatic presence in Tehran is particularly important because the United States, having severed all diplomatic and commercial relations in 1979, has very little leverage there. European countries and the UN are doing what they can, but there is no guarantee that they will succeed. Should they fail, the world might need a well-respected middle power to step into the gap. That is why we should appoint an ambassador to Iran immediately, and let him do his job—while we do all that we can to dissuade the U.S. and Israeli governments from taking military action.

Canada has a particularly important role to play in rescuing the Nuclear Non-Proliferation Treaty. As Pierre Trudeau explained in 1978, Canada was "not only the first country in the world with the capability to produce nuclear weapons that chose not to do so, we are also the first nuclear-armed country to have chosen to divest itself of nuclear weapons." Very few other countries—the most notable exception being Japan—can speak with as much authority and credibility as Canada on nuclear matters. Our authority is only enhanced by the fact that we have become a leading exporter of peaceful nuclear materials and technologies, in the form of medical isotopes as well as uranium and reactors for electric-power generation.

In the past, Canada did not hesitate to articulate a progressive position. In January 2002, Canada's policy at the time was set out on the Department of Foreign Affairs Web site as follows:

> The objective of successive Canadian Governments has been and remains the complete elimination of nuclear weapons. Canada will continue to resist any movement to validate nuclear weapons as acceptable currency in international politics or any attempt—de jure or de facto—to legitimize any new nuclear-weapon state. Canada's approach to nuclear disarmament is based on the view that the most viable and practicable way forward is by a continuous step-by-step process to reduce and eliminate nuclear weapons through steadily advocating national, bilateral and multilateral steps.

The policy reflected some long-standing differences between Canadian and U.S. approaches to nuclear weapons, particularly with regard to the obligation—on the part of the declared nuclear weapon states—to work towards general disarmament.

However, a new policy was recently posted on the same Web site:

> Canada's longstanding policy objective is the non-proliferation, reduction and elimination of nuclear weapons and other weapons of mass destruction. Canada is pursuing this objective steadily, persistently and energetically, consistent with our membership in NATO and NORAD, and in a manner sensitive to the broader international security context.

The new policy would be fine if it stopped after the word "energetically." However, the subsequent qualifications—"consistent with our membership in NATO and NORAD, and in a manner sensitive to the broader international security context"—strip the policy of meaning and indicate that Canada is surrendering its traditional role as a leader in this domain. The Canadian government has bought into the exact same argument that is advanced by every country that already possesses or seeks to possess nuclear weapons, namely, that the needs of security trump the obligation to disarm.

To be fair, Canada has long been conflicted on the matter of nuclear weapons. In addition to hosting U.S. warheads for twenty-one years, we have long been a member of NATO's nuclear planning group which, in apparent violation of the UN Charter, maintains the option of engaging in a nuclear first-strike against any aggressor country. Membership in the group—which is not a requirement of NATO membership—places us in the awkward position of supporting disarmament with our words but weakening it through some of our actions.

It does not help that most of the nuclear non-proliferation experts in the Canadian bureaucracy have gained their expertise in Washington, D.C., and Los Alamos, New Mexico. To some degree, their immersion in the U.S. security community skews their analysis and recommendations. Take, for example, the head of Canada's delegation to the 2003 "nuclear suppliers group" meeting in

South Korea, who at a preparatory meeting in Ottawa argued that Canada should move its negotiating position closer to that of the United States—in order to help repair relations after our refusal to join the Iraq War!

Canada's position entering the 2005 NPT review conference was similarly conflicted. The Canadian delegation proposed a nebulous concept for improving "civil society participation" as well as reporting and review mechanisms under the NPT, in what was described as a "bridging strategy" between the United States and developing countries. Many observers, however, saw the strategy as little more than an effort to retreat from the fray.

Canada does have progressive options. We could join the "new agenda coalition," a group that already includes Brazil, Egypt, Ireland, Mexico, New Zealand, South Africa and Sweden. Together, these countries seek to decrease the political legitimacy of nuclear weapons and persuade the nuclear powers to move decisively towards disarmament. With Canadian support, they might be able to rescue the NPT at the next review conference in 2010.

Canada could also declare itself a "nuclear-weapons-free zone," a possibility encouraged under Article 7 of the NPT and already seized upon by many countries. Nearly half the Earth's surface and one-third of humanity already fall within officially declared nuclear-weapons-free zones. The City of Vancouver took the plunge in 1983, with no apparent deleterious effect. Whenever I drive into my adopted city, I feel encouraged by the sight of a sign that informs motorists they are entering a nuclear-weapons-free zone. Although Vancouver City Council does not have any formal powers in foreign affairs, it is the thought that counts. It expresses a willingness to imagine a better world—and to do what one can to make it happen.

If Canada were to declare itself a nuclear-weapons-free zone, it would be forbidden to produce, test, store, acquire or deploy nuclear weapons or to have nuclear weapons deployed on its behalf by other countries. As it happens, we currently do none of these things, so we are, in practical terms, already nuclear weapons–free. What a wonderful, cost-free opportunity! Just by being frank about our nuclear-free status, we could enhance our credibility and exercise leadership on the world stage.

When it comes to nuclear proliferation, we should do the same thing that Paul Martin eventually did on missile defence. We should stop the dithering and mealy-mouthed excuses and set a powerful example for the rest of humanity.

– 5 –

CANADA
AND GLOBAL
GOVERNANCE:

One for One, or All for All?

IN 1992, I travelled by bus across the Sinai Peninsula between Tel Aviv and Cairo. Burned-out
tanks littered the desert, a stark reminder of
the death and destruction of war. Most of the machines and their
crews were casualties of the 1967 Six Day War, though some went
back to an earlier conflict in 1956, when Egyptian president Gamal
Abdel Nasser nationalized the Suez Canal, prompting an invasion by Israel, Britain and France. The Soviet Union threatened to
intervene on Egypt's behalf, raising the spectre of a direct conflict
between the USSR and at least two NATO countries. The United
States strongly disapproved of the risk being taken by its allies
and threatened to punish them economically. Eventually it was
a soft-spoken Canadian foreign minister, Lester B. Pearson, who
brokered a solution to the crisis, for which he won the Nobel Peace
Prize in 1957.

Students of Canadian history are well versed in our signal accomplishments in the field of international affairs—accomplishments that span a relatively brief period, since Canada only achieved foreign-policy independence from Britain in 1931. Canada played a major role in the Second World War, joining the Allied effort two years before Pearl Harbor. Our soldiers, sailors and airmen fought on the beaches of Normandy, on the waters of the North Atlantic and in European skies. More than 45,000 Canadians were killed in combat, out of a population of only 11 million. At home, the Herculean efforts of our farmers and factory workers, many of them women, produced much of the food and materiel that fuelled the Allied effort. After the war, Canada participated in the conferences at Dumbarton Oaks and San Francisco that founded the United Nations. Had we not been a relatively new entrant into international affairs, we might have demanded—and would likely have received—a permanent seat on the United Nations Security Council.

Canada, which at the end of WWII possessed the world's third-largest navy, played a central role in the newly formed North Atlantic Treaty Organization. Our principal mission was a continuation of our wartime role, protecting the North Atlantic sea lanes against foreign submarines that were now Soviet rather than German. Today, the unified Canadian Forces' three active Iroquois-class destroyers and their ancient Sea King helicopters are mere reminders of our once formidable fleet. During the same postwar period, the Royal Canadian Air Force and the Canadian Army formed part of NATO's presence in West Germany, with the RCAF also contributing to the new North American Air (later Aerospace) Defence Command (NORAD). By helping to keep the Soviet Union at bay, we may have prevented a nuclear cataclysm.

At the same time, Canada established itself as a leader on the softer side of international relations. In 1948, McGill University law professor John Humphrey, French diplomat René Cassin and American first lady Eleanor Roosevelt drafted the Universal

Declaration of Human Rights. The declaration, which detailed a wide range of civil, political, economic, social and cultural rights, set in motion the human rights revolution of the twentieth century. It led to the recognition of human rights as part of a universally applicable body of customary international law, the adoption of an array of treaties and the creation of numerous—and often surprisingly effective—commissions, committees, councils and special rapporteurs. It also led to the inclusion of systematic human rights abuses within the UN Security Council's conception of "threats to international peace and security"; the development of a vibrant international "civil society" made up of grassroots activists and increasingly sophisticated non-governmental organizations (NGOS), and a widespread recognition that nation-states had lost the authority to treat their citizens as they wished without comment or constraint.

These two faces of Canadian foreign policy—the harder, military side and the softer, humanitarian side—soon proved an influential combination. Pearson's diplomatic success during the Suez Crisis depended on the deployment of a sizable UN force, including many Canadians. It brought Canada recognition as a leader in the suppression and resolution of conflicts, not through brute force but through the use of well-trained and well-equipped soldier-diplomats. Instead of supporting one or the other of the belligerent parties, these "peacekeepers" would insert themselves between them, with the goal of discouraging further death or suffering.

During the past decade, a few commentators have suggested that Canadian foreign policy is returning to the dizzying heights of the post–Second World War period. Certainly, some of our diplomats and a few of our politicians have performed exceptionally well in certain domains. At the same time, Canada's recent foreign-policy accomplishments suffer from a lack of broad-based, ongoing support by successive federal governments. The Ottawa Landmines Convention provides a sobering example of how our ability to do great work abroad is often hindered—or subsequently undermined—at home.

OTTAWA LANDMINES CONVENTION: WALKING WITHOUT FEAR

During the past thirty years, more than one million people, most of them civilians, have been killed by anti-personnel landmines: small devices placed in the ground and designed to explode when stepped upon. Millions more have been seriously injured. World-wide, hundreds of thousands of landmine amputees suffer ongoing pain, social stigma and economic hardship. Yet literally hundreds of millions of these indiscriminate devices remain in the ground—years, even decades after they were laid—in countries as far-flung as Cambodia, Mozambique, Lebanon, Nicaragua and Afghanistan.

In 1992, grassroots activists and NGOs, led by Vermont-based Jody Williams and including the International Committee of the Red Cross and the Vietnam Veterans of America, came together to create the International Campaign to Ban Landmines. The coali-tion, which quickly grew to include more than a thousand groups, campaigned for a multilateral treaty that would prohibit the use and possession of anti-personnel landmines. Such a treaty would, quite literally, enable many millions of innocent people to "walk without fear" (to quote from the title of a book co-edited by my UBC colleague Max Cameron).

Since treaties are negotiated and ratified by nation-states rather than NGOs, a governmental "champion" was needed to carry the anti-landmines initiative into the sphere of interstate diplo-macy. Lloyd Axworthy, then Canada's minister of foreign affairs, served as that champion, making a landmines convention one of Canada's principal international objectives. Axworthy sought to return Canadian foreign policy to its "Pearsonian" roots by fus-ing the hard diplomacy of military power to the softer diplomacy of human rights, multilateral institutions and international law. The result was the concept of "human security," which Axworthy described as follows in *Navigating a New World*, written shortly after he left politics:

We proposed a way of seeing the world and tackling global issues that derived from serving individual human needs, not just those of the nation-state or powerful economic interests. This is not through some form of all-powerful, centralized world government. Rather, it is a form of global governance that operates under global rules, works through global institutions and will require a form of global democratic politics to make decisions. It seeks a way to transcend particular interests for a common good.

With Axworthy's support, the initiative to ban anti-personnel landmines rapidly gained momentum. Other countries were soon persuaded to join, thanks in part to the media attention generated by the initiative—which increased dramatically when Diana, Princess of Wales, joined the campaign just months before her death in August 1997. Public awareness of the horrific consequences of landmines increased dramatically, as did the number of grass-roots activists and NGOs lobbying national governments. Before long, the snowballing support created an opportune moment for international law making. In December 1997, the Canadian government hosted a negotiating conference involving delegates from 150 national governments and even more NGOs. After three days of meetings, the deal was done, in the grand old railway station across from the Château Laurier hotel. The Ottawa Landmines Convention, formally known as the 1997 Convention on the Prohibition of the Use, Stockpiling, Production and Transfer of Anti-Personnel Mines and on Their Destruction, has since been ratified by 151 countries—with Canada being the first to do so.

The success of the Ottawa Convention can be best measured by the way in which those countries that did not choose to ratify are, nevertheless, reducing their use of anti-personnel landmines. Only a handful of countries continue to use these obscene devices. Prominent among them is the United States, and its continued use of landmines, especially in Afghanistan, has caused ethical problems for Canada and some of the other countries participating in American-led operations there.

Read in a straightforward manner, the Ottawa Convention categorically prohibits any possession, use or reliance on anti-personnel landmines. Such a reading is consistent with the convention's spirit—what international lawyers refer to as a treaty's "object and purpose"—which aims at the complete elimination of this particular weapon. However, such a reading could be inconvenient when Canadian soldiers are operating alongside U.S. forces that are using anti-personnel landmines or when Canadian soldiers wish to locate their camps, bases or other facilities in close proximity to existing minefields.

Some civil servants in Ottawa evidently anticipated this problem, and they found a way around it. When the Canadian government notified the UN secretary general that it had ratified the Ottawa Convention, it attached a qualification in the form of what is called an "understanding." The understanding explains that Canada interprets the prohibition on use and reliance as not extending to "indirect reliance" on landmines laid by others, provided that the country responsible for having laid the mines had not yet ratified the Ottawa Convention. Significantly, the same understanding was submitted by Britain, another country whose soldiers regularly serve alongside U.S. forces. It seems that there was a coordinated effort to prevent the Ottawa Convention from hindering military co-operation between the United States and its closest allies.

The text of the "understanding" can be found on the Department of Foreign Affairs Web site, but I did not think to look for it until after I was told, by two separate military sources—one Canadian, one American—that Canadian soldiers in Afghanistan had benefited from landmines laid by U.S. soldiers on their behalf. This was precisely the sort of situation where the understanding would take effect and, arguably, this meant that the Canadian soldiers had not violated international law. At the same time, relying indirectly on anti-personnel landmines is contrary to the spirit of the Ottawa Convention. It undermines one of this country's most significant foreign-policy achievements and has real consequences for our moral authority—an important element of "soft power" in international affairs.

Troubled by what I had learned, I resolved to ask Lloyd Axworthy for an explanation. My opportunity came soon enough, during a visit to Vancouver in April 2003. The response was surprising: "What are you talking about?" When I explained about the understanding and the corresponding qualifications set out in the implementing legislation, Axworthy expressed his disapproval of what the civil servants had done to *his* convention in language that would have made a prairie farmer proud.

Canadians like to "talk the talk" of a progressive, human rights–oriented foreign policy. And from time to time we do "walk the walk," thanks to the vision and commitment of individuals such as Lester B. Pearson and Lloyd Axworthy. But then, all too often, we fail to carry through. The reasons for this are manifold, but they include decades of financial and personnel cutbacks that have left our foreign-policy apparatus overstretched, overwhelmed and increasingly dependent on information, analysis and ideas obtained from other countries. When remarkable figures such as Pearson and Axworthy move on, the cold hand of bureaucratic inertia squeezes the life out of much of what they have accomplished. All too often, all that is left is a limp and convoluted deference to the policies and prerogatives of the United States.

INTERNATIONAL CRIMINAL COURT: THE END OF IMPUNITY

In 1998 and 1999, I spent the better part of a year helping a coalition of human rights groups push for the extradition of Augusto Pinochet from Britain to Spain to face charges concerning torture committed in Chile during his years as president. We established an important precedent: that former heads of state do not benefit from immunity with regard to the most egregious of crimes. But we also learned that domestic courts are hardly the best forum for prosecutions of this kind. The British government, led by

Tony Blair, was distinctly unenthusiastic about the proceedings and eventually ordered the former dictator released on medical grounds, just as his extradition was about to take place. We now know that the doctors chosen by the British government to assess Pinochet's health were not acting on the basis of medical objectivity. On arriving back in Chile, the alleged torturer walked across the tarmac, his arms raised triumphantly above his head. He made many public appearances during the next seven years, until his death in December 2006.

The idea of a permanent international criminal court had been around since the end of the Second World War, when the Nuremberg and Tokyo tribunals were created to prosecute leading members of the German and Japanese regimes. These tribunals were international in the sense that they were created jointly by the Allied powers but, despite U.S. president Franklin D. Roosevelt's insistence on rigorous standards of due process, they still gave the impression of victor's justice. In 1949, the United Nations International Law Commission began work on a draft statute for a permanent international criminal court. Five years later, the initiative was abandoned as the rivalry between the United States and Soviet Union intensified, paralyzing much of the UN.

In the early 1990s, the end of the Cold War raised hopes for what U.S. president George H.W. Bush referred to as the "new world order," by which he meant a system of international relations based on multilateral co-operation and international law. The mass murder of hundreds of thousands of innocent civilians in Bosnia-Herzegovina and Rwanda prompted new calls for a system of international justice to deal with such cases, which the UN Security Council answered by creating two specific and temporary tribunals: the International Criminal Tribunal for the Former Yugoslavia, based in The Hague, and the International Criminal Tribunal for Rwanda, based in Arusha, Tanzania. However, it took years of preparation for judges to be appointed, rules and procedures to be drawn up, buildings to be renovated or constructed and then—and only then—for investigations to be conducted and indictments issued. Since justice delayed can be justice denied, the delays associated with setting up the two "ad hoc" tribunals gave new force to the arguments in favour of a permanent international criminal court.

As it did with the Ottawa Landmines Convention, "civil society" played a central role in creating the public awareness and political pressure to turn arguments into action. All told, more than a thousand NGOs joined together in a so-called Coalition for the International Criminal Court. But again, the grassroots activists and NGOs needed a governmental champion to carry their initiative into the realm of interstate diplomatic relations. And again, Lloyd Axworthy answered the call.

British foreign secretary Robin Cook was a key ally. The diminutive Scotsman possessed a razor-sharp mind and a deep commitment to social justice. Appointed by Tony Blair after New Labour's first electoral victory in May 1997, Cook immediately announced that their government would follow an "ethical foreign policy." The new approach was human security by a different name, and it fit the proposal for a permanent international criminal court like a glove. Along with his Canadian counterpart, Cook was convinced that an effective, objective and universal system of criminal justice would make a major contribution to the cause of peace and human rights. Within a year, the two men achieved their first goal: a negotiating conference, this time held at the palatial headquarters of the UN Food and Agriculture Organization in Rome.

Canada was exceptionally well represented at what became known as the Rome Conference, thanks in part to an unexpected vacancy in the chairmanship of the gathering. At the last moment, the designated chair, a Dutchman, withdrew for health reasons. Philippe Kirsch, the head of the Canadian negotiating team, was immediately called upon to take his place. Kirsch was already well known for his negotiating and drafting skills, but in the eight weeks of the conference he surpassed even the highest expectations. The new "Rome Statute of the International Criminal Court" provided the NGO coalition with most of what it had been seeking, while still being acceptable to almost all governments. Even the five permanent members of the Security Council either supported the statute or acquiesced in its adoption, even if a few of them— notably China and Russia—had no intention of ever ratifying the instrument. No matter: to date, the Rome Statute has been ratified by 104 countries. The International Criminal Court has a purpose-built headquarters in The Hague, a full complement of prosecutors and judges and an accomplished, widely respected Canadian president, in the form of Philippe Kirsch.

Kirsch's appointment as the chair of the Rome Conference created the need for a new head of the Canadian negotiating team. The position was filled by Kirsch's deputy, John Holmes, who later served as Canada's ambassador to both Jordan and Iraq. Under Holmes's guidance, the Canadians exerted considerable influence on the negotiations, heading a group of so-called "like-minded states" that defeated an attempt, led by the United States, to limit the jurisdiction of the International Criminal Court to those instances where the Security Council had specifically requested it to act. As for Lloyd Axworthy, he made a point not just of being in Rome at the conclusion of the conference but also of arranging for the champagne with which he and the negotiating team toasted Canada's success.

In January 2001, George W. Bush arrived in the White House fiercely opposed to the International Criminal Court. Bush and his advisers believe that the court threatens U.S. interests, and not just because it represents a triumph for multilateralism and international law. In addition to having jurisdiction over the citizens of any country that has ratified the Rome Statute, the International Criminal Court has jurisdiction over anyone—regardless of their nationality—who is accused of having committed a war crime or crime against humanity *on the territory* of any ratifying country. As a result, the United States, which has soldiers deployed in more than 140 countries, is more exposed to the International Criminal Court than most other countries—even if it itself never ratifies the statute.

The Bush administration began pushing for the UN Security Council to override the Rome Statute and permanently suspend the jurisdiction of the International Criminal Court with regard to the citizens of non-ratifying countries. It seemed likely that the effort would succeed, since there are only fifteen countries on the Security Council, and most of them were either already sceptical of the court or small enough to be highly susceptible to U.S. pressure. That is, until Canada intervened. Paul Heinbecker, our then ambassador to the United Nations, insisted on being allowed to speak to the Security Council on the matter. The request was granted, and Heinbecker laid out the case for respecting the intent of those who had drafted and adopted the statute in Rome. He argued that it would be improper for the council to amend treaties that had been negotiated in good faith by a large number of countries. He argued that the court's jurisdiction was well founded in international law, since it was already widely accepted that domestic courts had universal jurisdiction over war crimes and crimes against humanity. And he appealed to the members of the council to recognize that the International Criminal Court was part of a larger, decades-long effort to humanize international affairs.

As a result of Canada's efforts, the Security Council made a small and seemingly meaningless concession. Instead of suspending the jurisdiction of the International Criminal Court over the citizens of non-ratifying countries on an indefinite basis, it did so for one year only, explicitly envisaging that the suspension would be renewed annually. Most observers assumed that Canada had lost, and they seemed to be right when, one year later, the suspension was renewed with almost no debate. But then, in April 2004, the photographs of the atrocities committed at Abu Ghraib Prison were published. Shocked by what they had seen, the other members of the Security Council began to turn against the United States on the issue of the International Criminal Court's jurisdiction. As the year-long suspension drew to a close, American diplomats at the United Nations frantically consulted the other delegations and then, remarkably, chose not to seek another renewal. Canada, acting on behalf of international justice, had taken on the superpower and won.

Countries that ratify the Rome Statute of the International Criminal Court take on certain obligations. Prominent among these is the obligation to investigate and prosecute, under their domestic criminal laws, any individual located on their territory who is accused of any crime prohibited by the statute. This is because the International Criminal Court operates on the basis of a principle called "complementarity," whereby most prosecutions are supposed to take place in domestic courts. The International Criminal Court steps in only when it deems that the relevant domestic court is unable or unwilling to fulfill that role, or when the UN Security Council refers a situation directly to it.

In 2000, the Canadian Parliament adopted legislation implementing the Rome Statute into Canadian law. The Crimes Against Humanity and War Crimes Act provides Canadian domestic courts with jurisdiction over a wide range of international crimes, regardless of the nationality of the alleged perpetrator or the location where he or she allegedly committed the crime. The act also goes further than the Rome Statute by providing jurisdiction retroactively over crimes committed before the coming into existence of the International Criminal Court. It goes even further by not limiting its jurisdiction to alleged crimes committed by the nationals of or on the territory of countries that have ratified the Rome Statute. As a result, anyone who is present in Canada and alleged to have committed genocide, torture or another particularly egregious crime anywhere, at any time, can be prosecuted here.

But the Canadian government has been reluctant to use the Crimes Against Humanity and War Crimes Act, as the case of Léon Mugesera shows. In 1992, the Rwandan politician made a widely broadcast speech in which he urged ethnic Hutus to stamp out the *inyenzi*—the Hutu word for cockroaches, used pejoratively to designate Tutsis. Within two years, more than 800,000 Tutsis had been massacred and Mugesera had moved to Quebec City. The Canadian government responded by seeking to deport Mugesera back to Rwanda. The case went all the way to the Canadian Supreme Court, which held, in December 2005, that there was sufficient evidence of incitement to genocide to permit the deportation. At this point, the government found itself in a bind. For in 2001, the same court had ruled that two men accused of a triple murder in Seattle could be deported only if U.S. authorities promised that they would not be executed. Since Mugesera is wanted for genocide by the now-Tutsi-dominated government of Rwanda, he would almost certainly be executed if sent there. And so the Canadian government asked for an assurance from Rwanda that the death penalty would not be applied.

Curiously, while the Canadian government was willing to argue that Mugesera had incited genocide when seeking to deport him, it resisted the option of prosecuting him in Canada under the Crimes Against Humanity and War Crimes Act, even though any such prosecution would have trumped the deportation proceedings. It is only now, after Rwanda has refused to provide the requested assurance, that our government is coming round to doing what it should have done in the first place: prosecuting Mugesera here in Canada, thus fulfilling our obligations under international criminal law. That it has taken so long to come to this decision reflects a desire, in Ottawa, to avoid the trouble and risk inherent in a high-profile prosecution concerning crimes committed half a world away. As an unnamed Department of Justice employee told the *Globe and Mail*'s Stephanie Nolen in April 2001, the government preferred the easier route of deportation in dealing with Mugesera and others who face such charges.

Unfortunately, detrimental consequences could flow from this privileging of expediency over principle. Other governments may decide to follow our lead by not prosecuting alleged war criminals found on their territory, thus undermining the principle of complementarity and, ultimately, the International Criminal Court itself. Individuals who have committed war crimes may come to regard Canada as a safe haven and move here—either legally or illegally—to escape the possibility of prosecution or revenge attacks elsewhere. Those who contemplate committing war crimes in the future might well conclude that there is no such thing as an effective, objective and universal system of criminal justice and that they will never be held accountable for their acts.

For all these reasons, it is time for Canada to get serious about using the Crimes Against Humanity and War Crimes Act, and not just in the Mugesera case. It is time to show the world that Canada stands behind the vision and commitment of Lloyd Axworthy, Philippe Kirsch, John Holmes and Paul Heinbecker, and that we really do intend to lead when it comes to international human rights and global justice.

PROTECTING CULTURAL DIVERSITY

One of Canada's most decisive and least well known international law-making successes came in October 2005. That month, in Paris, a convention on cultural diversity was adopted that is designed to help defend cultural industries against globalizing forces emanating from within the World Trade Organization.

In 1997, the WTO ruled that Canadian content requirements for magazine advertising were illegal, raising the prospect that quotas and subsidies protecting Canadian culture would be stripped away. In response, Canada's film, television, music, theatre and publishing industries submitted a report to Pierre Pettigrew, then international trade minister, recommending that we negotiate a treaty giving countries the right to take protectionist measures in the cultural domain.

Sheila Copps, then Canadian heritage minister, had already organized an international network of culture ministers and funded the formation of a parallel non-governmental association; the proposed convention was the perfect cause for her to champion. Canada's cultural industries, meanwhile, created a Coalition for Cultural Diversity and encouraged the formation of similar groups elsewhere; there are now thirty-six such national coalitions worldwide.

Industry representatives and government officials began working on a draft convention that could provide a framework for international negotiations. The draft was completed in September 2002, the same month the United States announced—at First Lady Laura Bush's behest—that it would rejoin the United Nations Educational, Scientific and Cultural Organization, after two decades on the sidelines. With UNESCO about to gain greater relevance, it was the obvious negotiating forum.

Pettigrew and Copps's officials mounted a diplomatic offensive at UNESCO headquarters in Paris and forged alliances with countries such as France, China and Brazil. Liza Frulla, who succeeded Copps at Canadian Heritage in July 2004, became an enthusiastic proponent of the draft convention. Pettigrew, meanwhile, was shifted into a new portfolio as minister of foreign affairs.

By the time experts from UNESCO countries met for final discussions in June 2005, Canada's efforts had ensured a recommendation that the draft convention be adopted at the organization's annual conference in October of that year. In due course, that is what happened. Thirty ratifications were all that was then needed to transform the convention into binding international law; that threshold was achieved in December 2006.

The Cultural Diversity Convention had been criticized for not providing a binding dispute-settlement mechanism and for thus being subordinate to the WTO. But the convention's drafters never sought a binding mechanism, because the WTO agreement in question (the General Agreement on Trade in Services) operates on a "bottom up" rather than a "top down" basis. Instead of automatically requiring non-discriminatory treatment for all services regardless of their country of origin, national governments indicate which specific services they are prepared to open up to competition, provided reciprocal concessions are received from other states. This offer-and-acceptance process results in a web of bilateral deals that liberalize select services between discrete pairs of countries, under the WTO's general umbrella.

Successive Canadian governments had said that they would never subject trade in cultural services to non-discriminatory treatment. But this blanket stand would have become more difficult to maintain over time, because the "bottom up" approach is based on the premise that countries will gradually work towards ever greater harmonization and liberalization. The Cultural Diversity Convention does not try to challenge the WTO directly, but rather to buttress the position that culture differs from other economic sectors. This approach avoids the legal problems that can arise when a new treaty includes rules that conflict with WTO obligations.

Until 2005, U.S. officials had assumed that the lack of a binding dispute-settlement mechanism would render the convention toothless. When they realized that the convention's intent was political rather than legal, they fought hard to delay or at least water it down. The United States argued that UNESCO had no mandate to adopt a convention that was primarily about trade; that trade barriers are not a valid way to promote cultural liberty because "such measures reduce choices"; and that the convention could have a negative impact on further WTO negotiations. Left unsaid was the fact that U.S.-based companies such as Disney and Time Warner already account for cultural exports of more than US$80 billion a year and would stand to benefit most from free trade in cultural services.

In June 2005, at a WTO meeting on trade in services, the United States expressed "great concern" over efforts to create a general exclusion for audiovisual services, which is where the bulk of future profits lie. But the U.S. effort to block the convention started too late; the momentum established by Canada could not be overcome.

The United States could have lobbied hard for then prime minister Paul Martin to intervene. But the convention had attracted considerable support in Quebec, where protecting cultural diversity is almost an obsession. A change in position would have provided the Bloc Québécois with a campaign issue. Even in English Canada, concessions on trade in cultural services would have seemed odd, given Ottawa's defence—up to that point, at least—of the softwood lumber industry.

For all these reasons, Canada's ministers, bureaucrats and cultural industries were able to succeed. International law making requires vision and a sustained willingness to play as a team. On those occasions when we decide to play hard, it is a game at which we excel.

RESPONSIBILITY TO PROTECT

Under international law, force may be used only in the face of an armed attack or if the UN Security Council has authorized military action or, arguably, if two-thirds of the UN General Assembly has voted in favour. In 1999, Canada and other NATO countries broke the law when they intervened—properly, on moral grounds—to protect the Muslim population of Kosovo from Slobodan Milosevic and his Serbian paramilitaries. The intervention took place without UN Security Council or General Assembly authorization and over the strong objections of Russia, China and many developing countries.

Then UN secretary general Kofi Annan found himself in a difficult position. His initial reaction to the Kosovo War was to say: "Emerging slowly, but I believe surely, is an international norm against the violent repression of minorities that will and must take precedence over concerns of state sovereignty." Later in 1999, however, Annan acknowledged that this norm had not yet achieved legal status and, moreover, that its development could have undesirable consequences for the international order. He said: "What is clear is that enforcement action without Security Council authorization threatens the very core of the international security system founded on the charter of the UN. Only the charter provides a universally accepted legal basis for the use of force."

Like the Ghanaian-born former secretary general, all those who seek a more peaceful world immediately encounter a dilemma. The constraints imposed by the existing rules on the use of force may—by preventing at least some armed conflicts—have already saved many lives, and this benefit could be compromised by any attempt to create a new right of humanitarian intervention that does not depend on UN authorization. In other words, modifying international law to allow for a right of unauthorized humanitarian intervention might actually result in more wars—more death and destruction—particularly if the new right were abused by powerful states. Yet surely countries should act when mass atrocities are unquestionably occurring and the UN is paralyzed or proves impotent?

In 1999, Lloyd Axworthy established an independent body, the International Commission on Intervention and State Sovereignty, to address precisely this dilemma. He charged the commissioners, who included former Australian foreign minister Gareth Evans, former Philippine president Fidel Ramos, former U.S. senator Lee Hamilton and Canadian then author, now politician Michael Ignatieff with finding "some new common ground." But a careful reading of the resulting report, "The Responsibility to Protect," shows they failed to agree on the central issue. Some passages of the report favour a right of humanitarian intervention in the absence of UN authorization:

> Based on our reading of state practice, Security Council precedent, established norms, emerging guiding principles, and evolving customary international law, the Commission believes that the Charter's strong bias against military intervention is not to be regarded as absolute when decisive action is required on human protection grounds.

But in their chapter "The Question of Authority," the commissioners come to a final conclusion that cuts against this analysis and is distinctly unhelpful to proponents of unauthorized humanitarian intervention:

> As a matter of political reality, it would be impossible to find consensus... around any set of proposals for military intervention which acknowledge the validity of any intervention not authorized by the Security Council or General Assembly.

Since international law is made and changed by the global community of nation-states, consensus—or at least very widespread agreement—is a necessary condition for making or changing rules on the use of military force. And whether we like it or not, many governments are concerned that powerful states might abuse any new right to intervene. Following the 1999 Kosovo intervention, the now 133 members of the Group of 77 coalition of non-industrialized states twice adopted declarations in which they unequivocally affirmed the illegality of humanitarian interventions not specifically authorized by the UN Security Council.

The concerns were only heightened after March 2004, when British prime minister Tony Blair retroactively applied to Iraq the concept of the responsibility to protect, stating: "We surely have a responsibility to act when a nation's people are subjected to a regime such as Saddam's." Suddenly, a highly contentious war—justified at the time on the basis of a series of ambiguous Security Council resolutions—was being rationalized, one year after the fact, with a concept that had already been rejected by many of the world's governments.

At this point, the Canadian government had a choice: embark on a long and difficult campaign to shift international opinion towards a right to unauthorized humanitarian intervention, at least in certain clearly defined conditions, or work within the existing legal constraints.

Lloyd Axworthy would have chosen the more challenging course, but he left politics before the International Commission on Intervention and State Sovereignty released its report in 2001. In his absence, Prime Minister Paul Martin selected the second, less ambitious option. In a speech to the UN General Assembly in September 2004, he advanced a watered-down, parsimonious version of the responsibility to protect that focussed on generating political will to intervene among the fifteen members of the Security Council, using their existing powers under Chapter VII of the UN Charter. Martin refrained from suggesting that interventions could occur without the expressed authorization of the UN Security Council, saying that that body "should establish new thresholds for when the international community judges that civilian populations face extreme threats." Indeed, he stressed that "the responsibility to protect is not a licence for intervention; it is an international guarantor of political accountability."

In one fell swoop, Martin conceded the point that had motivated the development of the responsibility to protect in the first place: that some mechanism should exist for interventions to prevent mass suffering where the UN is unable or unwilling to act. In the search for international consensus—and a diplomatic accomplishment that he could brag about back home—the prime minister stripped the meaningful content out of the responsibility to protect, leaving the existing legal constraints on humanitarian intervention firmly in place.

Unilaterally conceding your most important point is hardly the optimal way to commence negotiations. Worse yet, the other side will invariably seek further concessions. These have come in the form of limitations on the kinds of humanitarian crises to which the responsibility to protect is supposed to apply. In September 2005, the UN General Assembly adopted a declaration that limits the responsibility to protect to "genocide, war crimes, ethnic cleansing and crimes against humanity," even though there is nothing in the UN Charter to suggest that the Security Council's powers should be constrained in this way. In the past, the council has authorized humanitarian interventions for other purposes, including preventing mass starvation in Somalia and restoring democracy in Haiti after a military coup. Perversely, limiting the responsibility to protect to a pre-established list of atrocities creates the risk that fewer humanitarian interventions will now take place.

The paragraphs concerning the responsibility to protect in the UN General Assembly's declaration were endorsed by the Security Council in April 2006. But nobody expects the criteria to be treated as anything more than non-binding guidelines. The council is a political body that bases its decisions on diplomatic, political and economic concerns, and its decisions trump any criteria—including all but the most fundamental rules of international law. In future humanitarian crises, the greatest challenge will remain that of generating the political will to act. In 1994, the situation in Rwanda would have met anyone's threshold for action, but nothing was done to prevent a genocide that every member of the council knew was taking place. By deciding to promote the responsibility to protect only within the existing legal constraints, Paul Martin did little more than provide already reluctant states with more excuses for inaction. How will Canadians feel about this diplomatic initiative if, faced with the next mass starvation, the Security Council declares that famines do not fall within the criteria of the responsibility to protect?

Even when the Security Council authorizes a humanitarian intervention, there is no guarantee that countries such as Canada will act. Since 2003, millions of people in Darfur have been displaced, raped or killed by the Janjaweed, a mounted militia that acts in tandem with the Sudanese military. In August 2006, the Security Council finally used its powers under Chapter VII of the UN Charter to authorize the deployment of a UN peacekeeping force with a robust mandate to prevent further atrocities. But instead of rushing to contribute to—or even lead—the mission, the Canadian government has held back, claiming that its commitments in Afghanistan preclude another mission elsewhere. As a result, hundreds of thousands of innocent Sudanese are still being terrorized by their own government while the rest of the world stands by.

As far as the responsibility to protect is concerned, it is nice to see made-in-Canada terminology in a UN declaration. But before celebrating another Canadian foreign-policy success, we should ask ourselves: how much protecting have we actually done?

OVERSEAS DEVELOPMENT ASSISTANCE

Not so long ago, the responsibility to protect encompassed far more than military action. In 2001, the International Commission on Intervention and State Sovereignty, having concluded that consensus on a new right to unauthorized humanitarian intervention was impossible to achieve, stressed that a main element of the responsibility to protect was a "responsibility to prevent"—by addressing the root causes of internal conflicts and other human-generated threats to civilian populations.

The commission's report identified numerous dimensions of prevention, including support for democratic institutions, press freedom and the rule of law; the provision of development assistance and improved terms of trade; and the promotion of arms control, disarmament and nuclear non-proliferation. And the commission was absolutely right. Much more attention should be given to these sorts of non-military measures, even if they entail significantly larger transfers of wealth from developed to developing countries. If developed countries were to redirect just a portion of their current military budgets to overseas development assistance (ODA), the number of armed conflicts and humanitarian crises would almost certainly decrease.

In 2005, the United States spent US$478 billion on its military. The fifteen highest-spending countries, including the United States, spent a staggering total of US$839 billion. In comparison, the total amount spent on overseas development assistance by all of the world's countries during the same year was US$106 billion. Even then, much of that assistance was tied to the purchase of goods and services from the donor state or involved the forgiveness of long-standing foreign loans of only nominal value. Canada's record is better than that of some of the largest military spenders, but it is still less than admirable. Our current military budget of $16 billion dwarfs our foreign-aid budget of $4 billion, and the military budget is growing faster.

Each day, around the world, more than fifty thousand people die for poverty-related reasons and another 800 million people go to sleep hungry. More than 2.7 billion people—almost half the world's population—live on less than two dollars per day.

In 1968, shortly after stepping down as prime minister, Lester B. Pearson chaired a World Bank commission on international development. The Pearson Commission concluded that, with sufficient assistance, developing countries could achieve developed-country status. Indeed, thanks to overseas development assistance, some developing countries were already achieving higher rates of growth than many developed countries had reached at comparable stages of their own history. The commission strongly recommended that, by 1975, developed countries contribute 0.7 per cent of their gross domestic product (GDP) to overseas development assistance. The report was quickly embraced by the World Bank, the Organization for Economic Co-operation and Development and the UN General Assembly. The 0.7 per cent target has remained the leitmotif of development economists and international organizations ever since. But we are still a long way from attaining that goal.

By the target date of 1975, Canada's commitment to overseas development assistance had risen to 0.53 per cent. But then it began to slide. During his final term in office, Pierre Trudeau sought to revive the so-called North–South dialogue—an effort to promote equity between developed and developing countries—but chose not to increase Canada's financial contribution significantly. Perhaps for this reason, he failed to persuade other countries to give more.

During Jean Chrétien's tenure as prime minister, the deficit-cutting regime of Finance Minister Paul Martin caused Canada's overseas development assistance to fall from 0.42 in 1994 to a dismal 0.25 per cent in 2000. That same year, the UN General Assembly adopted the Millennium Development Goals, the eighth goal of which was to "develop a global partnership for development," including through "more generous official development assistance for countries committed to poverty reduction." When Paul Martin addressed the UN General Assembly in September 2004, he might have wondered why most of the seats were empty. Part of the explanation was obvious: our miserly contributions to overseas development assistance have undermined our international influence, especially in the developing world.

This is a crucial point. Overseas development assistance is not charity. It is the price we pay for "soft power," the ability to persuade rather than coerce. Soft power is the principal currency of diplomacy—especially between middle-power and less powerful states.

Overseas development assistance also engages our national interest in another way. Poverty and underdevelopment contribute to a wide range of global problems that are infinitely more difficult and expensive to deal with after they have emerged and grown. Whether with respect to terrorism, forced migration or contagious diseases such as avian flu, antibiotic-resistant tuberculosis or HIV/AIDS, overseas development assistance is almost always money well spent: a penny for prevention is, truly, often worth a pound of cure.

As the International Commission on Intervention and State Sovereignty explained with regard to the intervention that prompted its own creation and thus the very concept of a responsibility to protect: "In Kosovo, almost any kind of preventive activity... would have had to be cheaper than the US$46 billion the international community is estimated to have committed at the time of writing in fighting the war and following up with peace-keeping and reconstruction." The commission's report was written during the summer and autumn of 2001. The UN Interim Administration Mission in Kosovo is still saddled with authority over the territory, requiring the support of sixteen thousand NATO-backed peacekeepers and substantial ongoing financial assistance from developed countries.

Worse yet are the opportunity costs borne by populations in other needy countries and territories, which, as a result of the redirection of peacekeeping resources and overseas development assistance to Kosovo, have for eight years been deprived of much-needed support. The subsequent interventions in Afghanistan and Iraq have only exacerbated the problem of a relatively small pool of money being siphoned from one crisis to another in response to the shifting attentions of Western governments. Today, Afghanistan is the largest recipient of Canadian overseas development assistance: more than $100 million per year. But as the University of Ottawa's Amir Attaran has discovered, the Canadian International Development Agency either cannot or will not divulge how most of that money is spent. What matters most, it seems, is that our money is being directed to the country currently dominating the headlines.

The best that one can say about Canada's recent record on overseas development assistance is: we have been consistent. As of June 2005, Canada was contributing 0.26 per cent of its GDP, or less than $4 billion annually. Worse yet, when asked that summer, just before the G8 summit at Gleneagles, Scotland, whether he would join other leaders in committing to a firm timetable to take Canada up to 0.7 per cent by 2015, then prime minister Paul Martin said: "I am not prepared to make a commitment that I'm not unalterably convinced that we will hit within the time period." Instead, Martin committed only to raising Canada's contribution by 8 per cent a year, a rate of increase that should take us to 0.35 per cent of GDP by 2010 but will not enable us to reach 0.7 per cent of GDP by 2015. Doing that would require doubling the annual increase to approximately 16 per cent. In 2006, Canada's ODA reached 0.34 per cent of GDP, but only because of an extraordinary debt cancellation for Iraq.

To their credit, and our shame, a number of countries have been much stronger on this issue. Pushed by a growing public awareness (caused in part by the Make Poverty History campaign), some wealthy countries have upped their commitment to overseas development assistance substantially. Eleven have pledged to achieve or maintain levels of ODA at 0.7 per cent by 2015. Five more, all of them members of the European Union, have committed to achieving a more near-term target of 0.51 per cent by 2010.

Bono, who endorsed Paul Martin when the latter became Liberal leader and prime minister in 2003, responded in the bluntest of terms: "No, I'm not satisfied and I'm gonna kick his butt." The U2 star added, poignantly, that "Canada has lost its chance to lead." And the opportunity for Canadian leadership matters, including in terms of the lives we could save. The Canadian economy is large enough that every 0.1 per cent of GDP (our total GDP is about $1.4 trillion) directed into overseas development assistance would literally save several million lives. Just as important, a firm commitment by Canada would help shame other, even larger economic players such as Japan and the United States into becoming less stingy. An increase of just 0.1 per cent by those two countries would amount to an additional $16 billion in overseas development assistance each year—more than ten times the amount dispersed annually by the charitable Bill and Melinda Gates Foundation.

The fact of the matter is, Canada *can* afford to raise its overseas development assistance to 0.7 per cent of GDP. Real incomes in this country have, on average, increased by about 20 per cent over the past two decades. Canada has the most robust economy of any G8 country, and it has posted large budget surpluses for the past decade. We also have far more than our fair share of some of the world's most valuable resources.

Arguably, one of the reasons why Canadian politicians have refused to lead on this issue is because of subtle pressure from the United States. The U.S. government contributes only 0.1 per cent of GDP to overseas development assistance and would be at risk of being embarrassed if its northern neighbour began contributing seven times more. Curiously, however, most Americans believe that their country is much more generous, and they respond with either disbelief or dismay when told the truth. For Americans—like Canadians—are actually far more generous than their politicians seem to think. On the subject of overseas development assistance, it's time for all of us, on both sides of the Canada-U.S. border, to reach out to the poor and downtrodden—for everyone's sake.

CANADA CAN DO BETTER!

Whether on landmines, international criminal justice or overseas development assistance, one thing is clear: even in those areas where Canadians think this country has done well in international affairs, we could do much better. Across the board, Canadian leadership is episodic, often overblown and all too frequently absent.

Take the following recent example. At an arms control conference in Geneva in November 2006, government officials from the United States and Britain defeated a proposal to begin negotiations on a treaty banning cluster bombs. Although cluster bombs are widely used, they are inherently indiscriminate, since many of the hundreds of small "bomblets" scattered by each cluster bomb do not initially explode but instead lie in wait until disturbed by an unsuspecting passerby—usually a civilian, often a child. Although the American and British delegations argued that any discussion of cluster bombs belonged within the framework of the 1980 UN Convention on Conventional Weapons, this move was clearly intended to stymie any attempt at a meaningful ban. Indeed, the same two countries had used the exact same tactic when opposing a ban on anti-personnel landmines a decade earlier.

At that time, Canada showed real leadership in breaking out of the inconclusive negotiating framework established under the Convention on Conventional Weapons. It established a new, more focussed and accelerated negotiating process that quickly led to the 1997 Ottawa Landmines Convention, which in turn saved many thousands of lives.

Today, there is nobody in the Canadian government with the courage and moral conviction of Lloyd Axworthy or Lester B. Pearson. It was left to the Norwegian foreign minister, Jonas Gahr Støre, to announce: "We must now establish concrete measures that will put an end to the untold human suffering caused by cluster munitions. Norway will organize an international conference in Oslo to start a process towards an international ban on cluster munitions that have unacceptable humanitarian consequences." Good for Norway. But again, where were we? And what will be our contribution going forward, in Oslo and beyond?

— 6 —

CLIMATE CHANGE:

Our Greatest Challenge

"WHERE HAS ALL the ice gone?" asked Joe Immaroitok. "It never used to be like this."

It was October 24, 2006, and he was staring at Foxe Basin. A shallow expanse of ocean the size of Lake Superior, the basin usually freezes over by early October, enabling the Inuit to travel across to Baffin Island to hunt caribou. Now, the hamlet council in Igloolik, Nunavut, was considering chartering a plane to take the hunters across the unfrozen sea.

Just a few hours before I spoke with Immaroitok, I had sailed through Fury and Hecla Strait aboard the *Amundsen*, Canada's research icebreaker. All we saw were a few chunks of thick, aquamarine "multiyear" ice—formed when ice survives one summer or more and new ice accretes onto it—which had floated down from higher latitudes and were easily avoided. The previous day, we had passed through Bellot Strait, the first ship ever to do so in October.

Although we were seven hundred kilometres north of the Arctic Circle, there was absolutely no ice.

The two straits are part of the Northwest Passage, the so-called Arctic Grail. From Martin Frobisher in 1576 to John Franklin in 1845, generations of European explorers searched for a navigable route through the Arctic islands to Asia. Many of them, including Franklin and his men, died in the effort. Their greatest challenge was sea ice, which has almost always filled the straits, even in summer. When combined with strong currents and relatively narrow channels, the ice rendered these waterways impenetrable to all but the most patient of explorers or, more recently, powerful icebreakers. William Parry spent the summers of 1821 and 1822 waiting for the ice to clear from Fury and Hecla Strait. But though the strait is named after his ships, he never made it through. Francis Leopold M'Clintock, dispatched by Lady Franklin to search for her husband on King William Island, tried six times to penetrate Bellot Strait during the summer of 1858 before continuing his journey by dogsled. When Roald Amundsen completed the first full transit of the Northwest Passage in 1906, it took him three years, including two winters lodged in the ice.

In 2004, the Arctic Climate Impact Assessment—a collaborative effort by more than three hundred Arctic scientists, climatologists and Inuit elders—reported that the average extent of sea ice cover in summer had declined by 15 to 20 per cent over the previous thirty years. More than two million square kilometres of ice had been lost, an area more than twice the size of British Columbia. The remaining ice was 10 to 15 per cent thinner overall and 40 per cent thinner in the middle of the Arctic Ocean. And these trends were expected to accelerate, so that by the end of the twenty-first century, there might be no sea ice at all in the summer.

Recent satellite measurements analysed by the U.S. National Snow and Ice Data Center are even more alarming. The area covered during the winter by sea ice was at an all-time low in March 2006, down 300,000 square kilometres from the previous year. At this rate, the entire Arctic could be without sea ice as soon as the summer of 2030.

The scientists who were with me on the *Amundsen* are acutely aware of climate change. Jody Deming from the University of Washington in Seattle is studying how phytoplankton in cold Arctic waters take carbon dioxide out of the atmosphere by converting it into the organic content of their bodies. When they die, this captured carbon sinks into the ocean depths, where it remains for hundreds of years. Deming worries that a warming of the water might disrupt this process, as it does at more temperate latitudes, by increasing the activity level of marine bacteria which, when they feed on the plankton, release some of the carbon dioxide before it reaches the ocean floor.

Gary Stern from the Canadian Department of Fisheries and Oceans is studying mercury levels, which have been rising far more steeply in beluga whales than can be explained solely on the basis of the contaminant being carried on the wind from industrial sources farther south. One possible explanation is that, as the Arctic permafrost melts, naturally occurring mercury leaches out of the soil and into the marine environment, where it is carried up the food chain.

Climate change is having more apparent effects on other Arctic mammals. In Queen Maud Gulf, we encountered the only new "first-year" ice of our voyage—as well as our only polar bear. The bear was thin, and as he walked his hind feet kept breaking through the ice. But he was likely going to make it through the winter, since he would soon be able to catch ring seals. Farther south, where the ice-free season is even longer, other polar bears may be less lucky. In Hudson Bay, the birth rate of the bears is plummeting as lengthening summers impose famine-like conditions on a species that has evolved specifically to hunt on ice for seals.

Off Cape Felix, near where Franklin died, our ship stopped alongside a multiyear ice floe the size of a hockey rink to enable scientists to extract an ice core, a cylindrical cross-section cut out with a hand-powered auger. An Arctic fox, snow white and no bigger than a cat, scampered behind a small ridge. In previous years, the fox would not have been stranded, apparently without food, since first-year ice would already have formed across the entire surface of the ocean. Fortunately for the fox, the Canadian Coast Guard takes its search and rescue mandate seriously; as we sailed away, a sailor tossed some baloney onto the ice.

CLIMATE CHANGE: WAKE-UP TIME

If you have not yet accepted the reality of human-caused climate change, please be assured, the moment is coming. CBC newsanchor Peter Mansbridge had his moment on July 31, 2006, when, from the deck of CCGS *Louis S. St-Laurent*, he told the country: "Well, it doesn't take long to realize, if you had any doubt, that global warming is a thing of the present." Jeffrey Simpson's moment came sometime earlier in 2006, leading to a series of *Globe and Mail* columns, including one entitled "The Prime Minister is blowing a lot of hot air" and another quoting approvingly from British Conservative Party leader David Cameron: "The first great challenge we face is the urgent need to protect our planet... The threat of climate change is real and the costs of failing to act are huge."

My own moment of acceptance came in September 2004 when I read the Arctic Climate Impact Assessment and immediately began writing an article about it for the *London Review of Books*. That it had taken me so long to accept the obvious was a matter of some embarrassment. Compelling evidence of human-made climate change had existed for decades, and some prominent people had already been expressing alarm. In 1990, British prime minister Margaret Thatcher told the United Nations that the threat of climate change was "real enough for us to make changes and sacrifices, so that we do not live at the expense of future generations." In 1991, Ivan Head, Pierre Trudeau's foreign-policy adviser, wrote that: "It is unlikely that any other single environmental issue contains a potential hazard to human well-being as great as climate change."

I have since realized that climate change is a bit like death: most people just try not to think about it, perhaps because it overwhelms our sense of significance or seems impossible to control. Seen in this light, some climate change deniers, rather than being misinformed, could simply be trying to explain away their subliminal fears.

The basics of climate change are easy to understand. In the two centuries since industrialization—a geological millisecond—the concentration of carbon dioxide in the Earth's atmosphere has increased by 35 per cent; a third of that has come during the last four decades. Carbon dioxide and other greenhouse gases, such as methane, trap solar heat that would otherwise radiate back into space. As the levels of greenhouse gases rise, the lower atmosphere warms up and the climate changes. The global average temperature has already increased by about 0.6 degrees Celsius over the past two centuries, and the ten hottest years on record have occurred within the past twelve years. And since greenhouse gases remain in the atmosphere for decades, they have an ongoing, cumulative effect. In 2001, the United Nations Intergovernmental Panel on Climate Change—a multinational group of 2,500 scientists—predicted an additional increase during the twenty-first century of between 1.4 and 5.8 degrees Celsius. In 2007, they repeated the exercise, this time predicting an increase of between 1.1 and 6.4 degrees Celsius.

Beyond the basics, climate change involves some extremely complex phenomena. Today, scientists are especially concerned about "feedback loops," the first of which involves the open water and bare ground exposed by melting ice and snow. These darker surfaces reflect 75 per cent less heat away from Earth's surface and thus contribute to further warming, which melts more ice and snow, which reflects less heat, and so on. Already, in the Arctic, the average annual temperature has increased by almost twice as much as it has globally. The winter of 2005–6 was the warmest on record, with temperatures averaging between 4 and 6 degrees Celsius higher than usual. In February 2006, Peter Irniq, the former commissioner of Nunavut, began a lecture in Vancouver with the following words: "Something very strange is happening in Iqaluit today. It is raining."

The effects of climate change are not confined to the North. In British Columbia, some salmon stocks are plummeting as summer water levels in their spawning streams drop, and water temperatures rise, due to diminished snowpacks and glaciers. The Prairie provinces are also affected: as David Schindler of the University of Alberta has explained, summer flows of the Peace, Slave and Athabasca rivers are down by 35 to 40 per cent, and the summer flow in the South Saskatchewan River basin has declined 80 per cent since 1910.

Our forests are also at risk, due to an explosive increase in the extent and severity of mountain pine beetle infestations. As Terry Glavin succinctly explained in the *Georgia Straight* in August 2005:

> If you want to get your head around the scale of British Colum-
> bia's mountain-pine-beetle crisis, try this: the number of trees
> it has killed in the dry forests of the Interior in recent years
> is more timber than you'll find in all the trees growing in the
> United Kingdom. That's its scale, so far.
>
> Here's its pace: in 1999, the terrain that succumbed to a
> full-blown "red attack"—the term used to describe the red and
> dying trees in the full fury of the beetles' advance—amounted
> to 164,000 hectares. In 2000, the red-attack zone took another
> 184,000 hectares. In 2001, it grew by 785,000 hectares. In 2002,
> another 1.96 million hectares. In 2003, another 4.2 million
> hectares. During the year 2004, the beetles added to their car-
> nage another seven million hectares, an area of land roughly
> the size of the Republic of Ireland.

The mountain pine beetle, a native species, cannot survive winter temperatures below minus 35 degrees Celsius. As a result, the beetle population was, until a decade or so ago, kept in check by winter cold snaps. But climate change has led to warmer winters and thus more beetles, which are now spreading northward and eastward into the boreal forest. Now Canada's largest ecosystem—stretching from the Yukon to the Northwest Territories, Alberta, Saskatchewan, Manitoba, Ontario, Quebec and even Labrador—is at risk.

A second climate change feedback loop involves fresh water from melting Arctic and Greenland ice flowing south into the North Atlantic and potentially altering the Gulf Stream, the warm ocean current that sweeps across from the Caribbean and moderates temperatures in northern Europe. In December 2005, scientists reported that the Gulf Stream has recently slowed by 30 per cent. If this continues, winter temperatures in Ireland, Britain and Scandinavia could be dramatically reduced, and the worldwide system of ocean currents known as the Global Thermohaline Circulation thrown out of kilter. It is because of the possibility of temporary cooling in some regions that the term "climate change" is preferred to "global warming." It is also why polemicist Rex Murphy was wrong when, in August 2004, he argued that cold weather on the Canadian prairies the month before somehow disproved the existence of climate change.

One hopes Murphy is paying attention to the weather where he lives, in Toronto. In 2005, Canada's largest city experienced forty-eight smog days. I have visited most of the world's largest cities, but the air has made me physically sick in only two places: Santiago, Chile, during a temperature inversion that trapped the air between the adjacent mountain ranges, and Toronto during a smog alert in October—yes, October—2005. Coal-fired power plants and vehicles are partly to blame, but it is the combination of pollutants with hot sunny days that creates the worst of the smog. In 2005, there were twenty-six heat alerts in Toronto. And this is only a harbinger of things to come, with the Toronto Public Health agency predicting that heat-related deaths could double by 2050 and triple by 2080. And then there was the winter of 2006–7, which brought the warmest December on record, with an average temperature of 1.9 degrees Celsius, a staggering 4.8 degrees Celsius above the historic norm.

Extreme weather events are increasing in frequency and severity. In just one hour on August 19, 2005, one neighbourhood in Toronto received 17.5 centimetres of rain. The deluge caused extensive damage to basements, sewage systems and roadways and resulted in more than $400 million in insurance claims, making it one of the most expensive weather disasters in the history of Ontario. In British Columbia, more than two million people were under a boil-your-water alert in November 2006, after record rainfalls washed large amounts of sediment into the water reservoirs on Vancouver's North Shore. A series of windstorms then tore through the city's iconic Stanley Park, toppling trees that had stood for five centuries.

In 2005, for the first time ever, the number of tropical storms and hurricanes in the North Atlantic exceeded the number of letters in the Roman alphabet. After Hurricane Katrina in August of that year, Ceres, a U.S.-wide network of investment funds and environmental organizations, commissioned a report that documented a fifteen-fold increase over the previous three decades in insured losses from catastrophic weather events. The report predicted that climate change would cause significantly higher losses in the years ahead—in homes lost to hurricanes, crops lost to drought and floods and interruptions to business caused by electrical outages resulting from lightning strikes—leading to higher insurance premiums, reduced limits and more restrictions on coverage.

A third climate change feedback loop involves the melting of Arctic permafrost and the subsequent release of large quantities of methane and carbon dioxide as the organic material in the soil decomposes. Methane, which is released by the anaerobic decomposition that predominates in cold, wet soils, is twenty-three times more effective than carbon dioxide at trapping heat in the atmosphere. As methane and carbon dioxide from the permafrost enter the atmosphere, they cause further temperature rises, which in turn cause more melting and more methane and carbon dioxide release. This third feedback loop may already be having a discernible impact on the atmosphere: measurements at Hawaii's Mauna Loa Observatory show that atmospheric carbon dioxide concentrations increased by 2.08 parts per million in 2002 and 2.54 ppm in 2003, considerably higher than the 1.50 ppm average of recent decades.

Massive quantities of methane are also trapped on the frozen bed of the Arctic Ocean in the form of solid gas hydrates. As the temperature of the seabed rises, these hydrates might decompose, releasing additional methane into the atmosphere. Although the Arctic Climate Impact Assessment describes this as "a less certain outcome," it warns that "if such releases did occur... the climate impacts could be very large." Roughly one-third of the world's Arctic region is located in Canada, meaning that an equivalent proportion of the methane released from melting permafrost and gas hydrates would originate from our territory and continental shelf. At the moment, and despite Canada's extremely high per capita greenhouse gas emissions, our population of just 32 million means that emissions in Canada constitute but a fraction of those in the United States or China. But if this third feedback loop begins to operate, our relative contribution could escalate quickly. In this sense, Canada's Arctic permafrost and seabed could constitute a climate change bomb.

Rising sea levels are also a serious concern. Melting of sea ice does not affect the water level any more than an ice cube melting in a glass. But there are about three million cubic kilometres of land-based ice in the Arctic, and in most places it is also melting. The Arctic Climate Impact Assessment foresees a rise of 3 degrees Celsius in Greenland's temperature over the course of this century and the eventual disappearance of the Greenland ice sheet. In August 2004, the Geological Survey of Greenland and Denmark reported that, in the southernmost part of the island, the ice is already thinning at a rate of ten metres per year. The ice cap is now losing ice at the staggering rate of 225 cubic kilometres per year. In August 2006, I crossed Greenland on a flight from London to Vancouver. Rivers and lakes of water were visible on the surface of the ice, and the turbulence—probably caused by the intense evaporation ten thousand metres below—was unsettling.

If the Greenland ice sheet melts completely, sea levels worldwide will rise by about seven metres. Concurrent melting of the Antarctic ice cap would add greatly to that. But, until recently it seemed that such severe changes were far in the future, with most predictions placing the sea-level rise during the twenty-first century at around fifty centimetres, with much of that resulting not from melted ice but from the expansion of water as the oceans warm. Still, fifty centimetres would inundate several island nations and large areas of the world's best farmland, displace hundreds of millions of people and impose potentially unbearable costs on low-lying cities such as Amsterdam, Calcutta, London, Manila and New Orleans as they tried to prevent inundation. During high tides in November 2004, 80 per cent of Venice was underwater.

Here in Canada, one hundred square kilometres of the Fraser River delta already lie within one metre of sea level. In the spring, when the snowmelt is rushing down the river, many of the nearly 200,000 residents of Richmond, B.C., live below sea level. Making matters worse, the delta is slowly subsiding due to compaction and the absence—because of the existing dikes—of any replenishment of sediment from the river. In February 2005, Ken Cameron, the former manager of policy and planning for the Greater Vancouver Regional District, told me that catastrophic flooding was already a serious threat during high tides and strong inshore winds, circumstances that could easily be exacerbated by an earthquake or spring meltwater. Confirmation of the warning came just one year later when the seawall at Tsawwassen was breached, necessitating the evacuation of some two hundred homes.

But here is the kicker: some of the most recent peer-reviewed science anticipates much faster rates of sea-level rise. In March

2006, an article in *Science* predicted that sea level will increase in an exponential rather than linear fashion as a result of climate change feedback loops, leading to a rise of between four and six metres by 2100. A major real estate market correction is inevitable, involving tens of billions of dollars, and hundreds of thousands of Canadians will have to find new homes.

Even my office at the University of British Columbia is threatened. Until 1982, the edge of the sea cliff at the western tip of Point Grey peninsula had been retreating by up to sixty centimetres per year. Then, huge amounts of coarse gravel were dumped along the shoreline to stop the clay soil from eroding. But as the sea level rises, the erosion will recommence. Building a seawall along Wreck Beach below the bluff would postpone the event but only for a few decades.

Climate change could also be bad for our health. For example, increasing levels of greenhouse gases could be delaying the recovery of atmospheric ozone levels. The ozone layer had been badly damaged by the escape into the atmosphere of chlorofluorocarbons (CFCs) used in refrigerators, fire extinguishers and some industrial processes. The 1987 Montreal Protocol, an international treaty to protect the ozone layer by phasing out substances that deplete it, and a consequent switch to alternative substances and technologies caused CFC emissions to drop dramatically. So far, so good, until climate change entered the equation. Greenhouse gases, by trapping heat in the lower atmosphere, actually cool the upper atmosphere; thus they contribute to the formation of stratospheric clouds that support ozone-destroying chemical reactions. For this reason, the Arctic Climate Impact Assessment projects elevated ultraviolet levels at northern latitudes for decades to come, which helps to explain the increasing prevalence of skin cancer and cataracts.

Globally, it is difficult to overstate the gravity of the situation. In June 2005, the Millennium Ecosystem Assessment, a US$22 million study funded by the World Bank, concluded that environmental degradation linked to climate change is threatening the health and livelihoods of two billion people. In October 2006, a report commissioned by British prime minister Tony Blair and written by Nicholas Stern, a former chief economist of the World Bank, predicted that climate change could impose costs equivalent to 20 per cent of global gross domestic product by 2050. This would constitute the greatest market failure in history.

Then there is the ethical dimension of climate change. Beyond the impact on natural ecosystems, the economy and our own lives, surely we have a moral obligation to our fellow human beings? What about the citizens of developing countries, who bear little responsibility for climate change but are, perversely, the least able to adapt to it? What about future generations, including our children and grandchildren? Is anyone prepared to argue that we do not have an obligation to safeguard the planet for them?

The Arctic Climate Impact Assessment concludes with the following message:

> Strong near-term action to reduce emissions is required in order to alter the future path of human-induced warming. Action is also needed to begin to adapt to the warming that is already occurring and will continue. The findings of this first... Assessment provide a scientific basis on which decision makers can consider, craft and implement appropriate actions to respond to this important and far-reaching challenge.

The scientists who wrote this must have been deeply disappointed when the eight countries that make up the Arctic Council—the same countries that had commissioned the report—issued a three-page response that merely "noted" its findings and "acknowledged" that it would "help inform governments as they implement and consider future policies on global climate change." Sadly, the eight countries included Canada, which deferred to a U.S.-led campaign to downplay the scientists' warnings and avoid any implication of a responsibility to act.

THE POLITICS OF CLIMATE CHANGE

Stephen Harper had been in office for almost a year before public opinion forced him to admit the reality of climate change: "I think the preponderance of the evidence is clear, that it's a real long-term challenge, but... it can't be fixed overnight. This country is headed to be 50 per cent above its Kyoto target in 2012." On climate change, the prime minister was content—as were his predecessors Jean Chrétien and Paul Martin—to hide behind the misdirected policies of the U.S. government.

In April 2001, U.S. vice president Dick Cheney said of the Bush administration's energy plan (which the soon-to-implode Enron helped to write): "Conservation may be a sign of personal virtue, but it is not a sufficient basis for a sound, comprehensive energy policy." The assertion showed a lack of objective analysis, since switching the U.S. car and truck fleet to currently available hybrid technology would eliminate the need for Middle Eastern oil. For this reason, and because the United States accounts for 24 per cent of global carbon dioxide emissions, the Bush administration's refusal to deal with climate change constitutes not just bad policy, but also a major abdication of responsibility.

Several factors are likely responsible. First, Cheney and his boss are so deeply embedded in the oil, gas and coal industries that even the most rigorous scientific analyses could not shake their commitment to fossil fuels. Second, there is a tendency for right-wing Americans to see human relations in competitive, individualistic, game-theory terms. From this perspective, climate change presents a collective-action problem ("the tragedy of the commons," as ecologist Garrett Hardin termed it) that simply cannot be resolved. With hundreds of governments, thousands of stateless transnational corporations and billions of consumers relentlessly pursuing growth inside fossil fuel–based economies, the necessarily co-operative exercise of stabilizing the atmosphere seems so complex—so replete with opportunities for "free riding"—that it is destined never to begin.

A third, more sinister explanation for the Bush administration's approach concerns the centrality of military strategy in contemporary U.S. policymaking. Cheney and his colleagues may have calculated that climate change will enhance rather than detract from their country's long-term security and economic position. The United States, with its flexible economy, temperate location, low population density and presumed access to Canadian energy resources, agriculture and fresh water, would suffer less than other major countries as a result of climate change. "With diverse growing climates, wealth, technology and abundant resources," a report prepared for the Pentagon in 2004 concluded, "the United States could likely survive shortened growing cycles and harsh weather conditions without catastrophic losses... even in this continuous state of emergency the U.S. will be positioned well compared to others."

In comparison, China and India would struggle to cope with decreasing agricultural production, energy shortfalls, severe storms and mass population displacements, while the European Union is ill prepared for the colder continental climate that would follow the collapse of the Gulf Stream, not to mention the waves of environmental refugees from North Africa, Central Asia and the Middle East that would overwhelm its borders. If the weakness of one's opponents is as important as one's own strength, carbon dioxide emissions could be conceived—by conspiracy theorists, at least—as an insidious weapon in a ruthless struggle for power.

In 2004, senator and presidential challenger John Kerry twice raised the issue of climate change in his first election debate with President Bush, despite the likely absence of any payoff with undecided voters. Had he prevailed, he would have found allies on Capitol Hill. Republican senator John McCain, for instance, has said of the Arctic Climate Impact Assessment that it "clearly demonstrates how the Arctic region is acting as the canary in the coal mine." In 2004, McCain and Democrat fellow senator Joseph Lieberman sponsored a bipartisan bill calling for cuts in greenhouse gas emissions. But

Bush's electoral victory and the increased influence of the Republican right meant there was no prospect of the bill being adopted, let alone signed. More recently, Democrat victories in the November 2006 midterms have certainly changed the equation, though much depends on how frequently the president resorts to his veto.

In contrast to the United States, some European countries have shown leadership on this issue. In September 2004, Tony Blair identified the current rate of climate change as "simply unsustainable in the long term. And by long term I do not mean centuries ahead. I mean within the lifetime of my children certainly; and possibly within my own." Prime Minister Blair promised to make climate change the central thrust of his chairmanship of the G8 in 2005, and he raised the possibility of a government-encouraged but market-led retooling of British industry that would make the United Kingdom the leading instigator and beneficiary of alternative energy technologies. "We need," he said, "to develop the new green industrial revolution that develops the new technologies that can confront and overcome the challenge of climate change" and "combine reducing emissions with economic growth."

Blair's approach is one that appeals to many experts. But it has inherent problems. First, alternative energy sources can provide only a partial solution. They cannot on their own achieve the almost immediate 60 per cent worldwide reduction in emissions that is required to stabilize greenhouse gas levels. It will take decades to bring alternative sources fully on line—in developing countries it will probably take even longer—and we simply do not have the time. As the Arctic Climate Impact Assessment points out, the climate will continue to change significantly even if all emissions stopped tomorrow, as the atmospheric system responds to the level of greenhouse gases already present and the feedback loops kick in. Much more dramatic reductions in the consumption of fossil fuels are needed if catastrophe is to be avoided. This truth is inconvenient, as Al Gore has poignantly explained, but at least there remains an opportunity to engage with and solve the problem. We need to seize that opportunity, rather than wasting precious time with procrastinating half measures.

A starting point would be to introduce steeply graduated transportation taxes, as the French government did in 2004, to get people out of their gas-guzzling vehicles and into trains, buses and hybrid cars. Higher taxes on air travel are also necessary. The encouragement of low-cost flights is one of the greatest environmental failings of Western governments: jetting from Vancouver to Honolulu and back for a discount vacation introduces more greenhouse gas into the atmosphere than an entire year of driving—and yet, because aviation fuel is tax exempt, the contribution to climate change is effectively being subsidized.

Second, relying on a market-based approach to climate change is like betting your house on a promising racehorse. There is no room for such risk taking when the existence of millions of species—and the welfare of future generations—is in play. Yes, we need to strongly encourage alternative energy. But we also need to tame energy-extravagant consumerism. Preventing runaway climate change may well require drastic alterations in how we live. Taxes, regulations and subsidies designed to reduce unnecessary travel, promote local holidays and the use of local products, improve public transport, retrofit homes and businesses with more efficient heating, insulation and lighting, and provide a far-reaching program of environmental education and practice in workplaces and schools are the kinds of policies that cannot responsibly be ignored or postponed. They are a necessary complement to the quest for alternative energy sources.

Then there are the large industrial emitters, including the tarsand extraction plants at Fort McMurray, Alberta. Taxes and royalty rates must be raised to levels sufficient to ensure that these companies are not undercutting cleaner sources of energy. In November 2006, the Pembina Institute estimated that oil companies operating in the tar sands receive $1.38 billion in federal tax breaks each year. In addition, the Alberta government charges them royalty rates that are significantly lower than those charged for conventional oil and gas, the extraction of which causes less harm to the atmosphere.

At the same time, the federal government needs to introduce stringent caps on industrial emissions, along with a market-based carbon credit–trading regime, similar to those already being implemented in Europe and California. Cap-and-trade systems provide companies with a financial incentive to reduce and prevent emissions, including through the development of new extraction and refining technologies, since they can then sell any unused emission credits. The use of government regulations to create markets is, of course, nothing new: just consider how property law and land registries enable people to buy, sell and speculate in real estate.

CANADA'S DISMAL RECORD

Canada is on the front line of climate change as an Arctic country, as one of the highest per capita emitters of greenhouses gases and as the main resource base for an energy-challenged superpower. For all these reasons, you might expect that our federal government would be particularly concerned and eager to act. But when it comes to this critically important issue, Canada is a hypocritical laggard.

Since 1990, our carbon dioxide emissions have increased by 24 per cent, despite the fact that Jean Chrétien's government committed us to a 6 per cent reduction when it ratified the 1997 Kyoto Protocol (which falls within the 1992 UN Framework Convention on Climate Change). Successive Liberal and Conservative governments have refused to impose stringent fuel-efficiency requirements on new automobiles, waive the GST on hybrid cars, tax aviation fuel, or ban incandescent light bulbs (as the Australian government has recently done). In the negotiations leading up to the Kyoto Protocol, Canada stood staunchly beside the United States, sharing its preference for less stringent emission targets, greater reliance on market mechanisms and the inclusion of nebulous "carbon sinks" in any multilateral agreement. When the United States finally pulled out of the Kyoto process, Canada stayed in—and secured terms that were actually worse for the environment that those that had been proposed by the Americans.

This apparent schizophrenia results from the Canadian government's desire to export more and more of our non-renewable fossil fuels to the United States. Although the extraction of these resources, especially from the tar sands, generates huge amounts of emissions that count against carbon-production quotas, there is no disputing that oil and gas exports boost the economy, at least in the short term. Canada already exports more than $30 billion worth of energy annually to the United States. When George W. Bush encountered opposition to his plans for drilling in the Arctic National Wildlife Refuge, Jean Chrétien promptly offered alternatives in Canada. Ralph Klein, the then premier of Alberta, hustled off to Washington to tell Dick Cheney that his province "had energy to burn" and was "open for business."

In November 2004, representatives from the California State Assembly travelled to Ottawa to ask that Canada adopt measures in line with California's Pavley Bill, legislation that tightens the emission standards for cars and light trucks by 30 per cent. Nine other American states, including New Jersey and New York, were planning to adopt similar regulations; if Canada had joined the effort, a third of the North American automobile market would have been subject to the higher standards. The Martin government responded to the Californian legislators in a manner that was polite but noncommittal.

Canadian legislators were treated with less respect. When then environment minister Stéphane Dion was asked about the matter in the House of Commons, he dismissed the question with a disdainful wave of his hand. Instead of seizing the opportunity to create meaningful environmental change across an entire continent, Dion sat down with the Canadian automobile industry and negotiated weak voluntary targets—which, because they were not legislated, fell by the wayside as soon as the Liberals lost power. Once again, short-term politics and economic growth trumped long-term planning.

The Martin government went so far as to try to renegotiate Canada's Kyoto commitment so that it could receive emissions credits for the export to the United States of large volumes of natural gas, which when burned produces less carbon dioxide than oil. It failed to make significant investments in alternative energy technologies, notwithstanding a burgeoning federal surplus. Indeed, the performance of the Chrétien and Martin governments on climate change was so bad that, in November 2005, the CEOs of some of Canada's leading corporations—including Alcan, Bombardier, Falconbridge, Home Depot Canada, Power Corporation and Shell Canada—called for immediate measures to avoid the "severe consequences for human health and security and the environment" posed by climate change.

Sadly, Stephen Harper's Conservatives have to date been even more irresponsible than their Liberal predecessors. Within two months of taking office, they stopped funding groups that had been promoting the One-Tonne Challenge, a program that encouraged individual Canadians to reduce their carbon dioxide emissions by one tonne annually. The commercials featuring comedian Rick Mercer were corny and perhaps ineffective, but there is no denying that some sort of government-funded effort is needed to persuade individual Canadians to reduce greenhouse gas emissions. At the same time, the Conservatives eliminated subsidies for the installation of high-efficiency furnaces and improved insulation in Canadian homes. Only then did Environment Minister Rona Ambrose tell the House of Commons, "It is impossible, impossible for Canada to reach its Kyoto targets."

Six environmental groups—the Climate Action Network, David Suzuki Foundation, Pembina Institute, Greenpeace Canada, Toxics Watch Society and World Wildlife Fund Canada—immediately called for Ambrose to resign as chair of the upcoming meeting of the parties to the UN Framework Convention on Climate Change. She chose not to do so, making the briefest possible appearance at the gathering in Bonn, Germany. The audacity and hypocrisy of that appearance, coming as it did on the heels of her admission that Canada intended to violate its international legal obligations, damaged this country's reputation as a fair and honest player on the world stage.

Let there be no doubt: the violation is intentional. One month before Ambrose's appearance in Bonn, the *Globe and Mail* obtained leaked cabinet papers indicating that the Harper government would impose an 80 per cent cut on Environment Canada programs designed to curb climate change, along with a 40 per cent reduction in the climate change funding provided to other departments. The documents also indicated that the tax breaks for public transit passes, promised by the Conservatives during the 2005–6 election campaign, would have no significant effect on emissions. Finally, the documents showed that the Conservatives planned to renege on a $260 million pledge that the Martin government had made to UN climate change programs.

In June 2006, the Conservatives shut down the government's main Web site on climate change. They expunged mention of the Kyoto Protocol from other government Web sites as well as from speeches delivered by ministers. Instead of admitting the scale of the climate change threat and making any effort to deal with it, the Harper government chose to focus on those environmental issues that were having a more immediately visible impact on Canadians, including smog and the dumping of untreated sewage along Canada's coasts. These issues are important, but they pale in comparison to the medium- and long-term threat posed by climate change. One can reasonably suspect that attention was devoted to them primarily for short-term political benefit.

Then, in August 2006, the *Ottawa Citizen* reported that the Conservatives were developing an environmental plan that would push for greater co-operation with the United States "on key aspects of air pollution and climate change policy." The plan ignores the reality that the Bush administration has an abysmal environmental track record, not only on climate change but also on air pollution; it has loosened the regulatory requirements for coal-fired power plants in spite of the objections of many U.S. states. The *Citizen* quoted Pierre Alvarez, the president of the Canadian Association of Petroleum Producers, who called the proposed change "something that we have been asking for at both the federal and provincial level for years now." The Conservatives, it was reported, were also considering transferring the responsibility for enforcing environmental regulations to the provinces—a strange suggestion given the national, indeed global character of many environmental problems.

Stephen Harper's calculations concerning climate change were quickly proved to be flawed. By the end of 2006, the environment and, above all, climate change had become the primary concern of Canadian voters. A series of damaging storms in British Columbia and a near-tropical December in Ontario were the final straws. In January 2007, the prime minister responded with a series of cosmetic changes, including a cabinet shuffle that installed John Baird as the new minister of the environment. Unfortunately, Baird's only previous engagement with the environment seems to have been his role as the head of the Treasury Board in shutting down the City of Ottawa's plan for a fuel-efficient light rail transit system. Baird and Harper then reintroduced some of the Liberal half-measures that their government had cut the previous year, repackaging and re-labelling them so that they appeared novel. The fact that it was all electorally-oriented window dressing was confirmed within days of Baird's appointment, when Harper fatalistically declared that Canada would breach its Kyoto commitments by 50 per cent in 2012. This in the face of incontrovertible evidence of a global crisis, from a prime minister who had been in power for a year and prides himself on being smart and decisive!

TIME FOR A CHANGE

It is time for a change. It is time to harness the emotional connection that many Canadians have with nature, our sense of responsibility for human beings elsewhere and our deep concern for future generations. It is time to take strong and decisive action on climate change, with or without the co-operation of other countries. Through unilateral efforts, Germany has reduced its carbon dioxide emissions to 18.5 per cent below 1990 levels, mostly through conservation measures. Denmark has become a leader in alternative energy technologies and produces 20 per cent of its electricity from wind power. It also has a thriving industry producing wind turbines for export, an activity that has created twenty thousand new jobs. Canadian politicians could do a great deal more than they have been—and they should be voted out of office if they do not.

For starters, the Canadian government should publicly acknowledge what the vast majority of scientists already know: climate change is the principal predictable challenge facing humanity in the twenty-first century, and there is no time to waste. Leadership involves informing citizens of the full scope of economic, health and ecological threats, rather than taking advantage of public apathy and media negligence to delay tough decisions until after the next election.

The Canadian government should then take strong and immediate measures to reduce greenhouse gas emissions. Making these reductions matters in itself, and it also creates momentum for other countries. It goes without saying that these measures must be strong enough to make serious progress towards meeting our Kyoto Protocol commitments. Contrary to what Stephen Harper believes, this is technologically possible, it can be done without impairing the overall Canadian economy, and there is no need to buy emission credits from other countries. Reducing our emissions dramatically would also help prepare the Canadian economy for the eventual and inevitable global shortage of oil and natural gas. As Nicholas Stern pointed out in his October 2006 report, spending large sums on reducing climate change now will, in fact, generate much larger financial dividends in the future, at a return rate of about twenty to one.

In theory, the necessary action could come from any of Canada's political parties. Environmental protection is something that Canadians of all political colours care about: just think about the tens of thousands of rural Canadians who donate money to Ducks Unlimited for wetlands preservation. Or think about Arnold Schwarzenegger, the Republican governor of California, who has imposed stringent caps on industrial and automobile emissions and invested billions of dollars in alternative energy technologies. The Canadian government should match Schwarzenegger's climate change policies and challenge the provinces to do likewise. It might even want to draw an explicit connection to "the Terminator"—in order to make the fight against climate change more compelling to those Canadians who do not yet consider themselves environmentalists. The point is two-fold: climate change is not a left/right issue; it is a right/wrong issue. And confronting and defeating climate change will require conviction and perseverance.

Finally, individual Canadians do not need to wait for tardy politicians. When we moved back to Canada, my wife and I committed to reducing our carbon footprints. We bought a Toyota Prius, a gas-electric hybrid that burns only five litres of gas per hundred kilometres and is especially efficient in stop-and-go city driving. I began cycling to work and taking the bus downtown. We purchased Energy Star appliances, installed a clothes-drying rack in our backyard, high-efficiency light bulbs throughout the house, a high-efficiency furnace with a programmable thermostat, and we installed much more effective insulation. We are also buying offsets for the carbon dioxide that we still produce, including when we fly, so that our remaining emissions are balanced by emission reductions elsewhere—for example, through a program that is replacing millions of ordinary light bulbs in South Africa with high-efficiency ones. We are now considering solar panels and a mini-windmill for our roof, with the goal of heating all the water and generating much of the electricity we need. But even without these last two steps, we have already accomplished more than what Stephen Harper and other sceptics say Canada cannot achieve. We have reduced our emissions by significantly more than the Kyoto Protocol requires of all Canadians. And to top it off, we will actually save money in the long term. Of course, not all Canadians can afford to do all that Katharine and I have done, but everyone can— and should—do what they can to help.

Climate change is real and will have truly devastating consequences unless we act quickly and decisively. Canada is one of the wealthiest countries on Earth. Canadians know, deep in their hearts, that our prosperity should not be borne on the backs of more vulnerable people elsewhere, nor stolen from future generations. We have the resources and technologies necessary to create an ecologically sustainable economy. With foresight and political will, we can help to overcome the threat of climate change and, by doing so, exercise leadership on the world stage. Real leadership, of the kind the Bush administration and recent Canadian governments have so badly failed to provide.

As I write, the European Commission has just announced a plan that will see greenhouse gas emissions reduced to 20 per cent below 1990 levels by 2020. And the Europeans have issued a formal challenge to the United States, Australia and Canada. If we sign on to the 20 per cent reduction, they will increase their commitment by an additional 10 per cent. We should of course accept the challenge, and then do what it takes to meet it. For what better manifestation of an "intent for a nation" could one imagine than joining the charge against the greatest global threat of our time?

– 7 –

A TRUE NORTH
STRONG AND FREE

IN 1969, Humble Oil (now Exxon) sent an ice-strengthened supertanker, ss *Manhattan*, on a test voyage through the Northwest Passage. The U.S. Coast Guard dispatched two icebreakers to accompany the vessel and made a point of not seeking permission from Canada. The Canadian government granted unsolicited permission anyway, sent one of its own icebreakers to tag along, and then argued that Canada's sovereignty had not been undermined—because we had provided permission and our assistance had been accepted. A more convincing defence of Canadian sovereignty came from an unexpected source, according to John Amagoalik, the chief negotiator of the 1993 Nunavut Land Claims Agreement: As the *Manhattan* ploughed through the ice near Arctic Bay, on the north shore of Baffin Island, two Inuit hunters drove their dogsleds into its path. The vessel was halted until the hunters—having made their point—moved aside.

Most Canadians know nothing of Amagoalik's story, for we suffer from a most peculiar handicap. We can see east, west and, of course, south. Yet for some strange reason many of us do not see north. Indeed, for most Canadians, our home and native land might as well be the long, thin country of Chile, turned sideways. Seventy-five per cent of us live within 160 kilometres of the U.S. border. A staggering 99.7 per cent live south of 60 degrees latitude, the line separating the western provinces from the Yukon Territory, Northwest Territories and Nunavut. This leaves just 104,000 people occupying 40 per cent of the second-largest country on Earth, and well over a third of them are concentrated in the cities of Whitehorse (population 23,000) and Yellowknife (20,000).

For most of the rest of us, in terms of our lives, our travels, our personal geographic referents, our vast Arctic spaces simply do not exist. They constitute a collective, national blind spot. And as any driver knows, blind spots present danger. In some instances, they can also present opportunity.

WHO CONTROLS THE NORTHWEST PASSAGE?

Canada's High Arctic is a vast archipelago made up of about nineteen thousand islands and countless rocks and reefs. Baffin Island alone is nearly as large as Manitoba, and two of the other islands, Ellesmere and Victoria, are about twice the size of Newfoundland. Until very recently, the straits and channels between the islands were choked with thick, hard, multi-year sea ice, fusing the archipelago into a triangular mass that was three thousand kilometres wide at its base and stretched to within nine hundred kilometres of the geographic North Pole.

Today, with the ice melting as a result of climate change, the straits and channels are opening to the point where an experienced sailor could take a tanker through during late summer or early autumn. Governments are gradually waking up to this new reality. In 2001, a report prepared for the U.S. Navy predicted that, "within 5-10 years, the Northwest Passage will be open to non-ice-strengthened vessels for at least one month each summer." A briefing book given to Canadian defence minister Gordon O'Connor in February 2006 stated: "If the current rate of ice thinning continues, the Northwest Passage could be open to more regular navigation by 2015."

Shipping companies are watching closely. A navigable Northwest Passage offers a route between Asia and the Atlantic seaboard that is seven thousand kilometres shorter than the current route through the Panama Canal, saving time, fuel and transit fees. In the short term, uncertainties concerning the weather, availability of search and rescue services plus the erratic movement of the remaining multiyear ice will—along with consequently higher insurance premiums—dissuade reputable companies. But less reputable outfits might take the risk. There are more than a few rusting-out tankers and tramp steamers sailing the world's oceans with Liberian flags and disgruntled creditors.

International shipping in the Arctic entails serious environmental risks for one of the greatest, relatively unspoiled ecosystems left on Earth. An oil spill would cause catastrophic damage. The emptying of ballast tanks, a likely practice on the part of large ships entering these shallow waters, could introduce destructive new species such as fish parasites or toxic algae. These risks are of great concern to the Inuit. When I asked Maria Kripanik, the deputy mayor of Igloolik, about the possibility of increased shipping through the Northwest Passage, her first thought was for "our animals." The waters of the archipelago, she explained, are home to whales, seals and walrus, which the Inuit depend on as a local source of healthy food.

There are also security concerns. Ships carrying illicit cargoes could be attracted by the relative absence of a police or military presence. Smugglers, illegal migrants, even terrorist groups could regard an ice-free Arctic as a back door to North America. Indeed, transnational criminal activity was the focus of an Arctic Capabilities Study conducted by the Canadian Directorate of Defence in 2000. Since then, concerns about global terrorism and illicit trafficking in weapons of mass destruction and missile components have only increased.

Most people would be surprised by how many attempts at illegal immigration already occur in our North. In October 2006, two Turkish sailors jumped ship at Churchill, Manitoba, and bought train tickets to Winnipeg. The previous month, a Romanian man sailed a six-metre fibreglass motorboat from Greenland to Grise Fjord on Ellesmere Island. In 1999, a Chinese research icebreaker showed up unannounced in Tuktoyaktuk, with nearly one hundred scientists and crew members wanting to come ashore. There is a regular charter flight from Frankfurt to Whitehorse that requires the occasional deportation back to Germany, from the Yukon.

Cruise ships are already frequent visitors to Canada's Arctic waters. The *Kapitan Khlebnikov*, a Russian-flagged converted icebreaker, offers luxury trips through the Northwest Passage for us$13,000. The Canadian Coast Guard's 2005 Arctic Traffic Summary lists another six cruise ships and eight pleasure craft as visitors to the Canadian Arctic that year.

The greatest incentive for future shipping, however, will be the increasing scarcity and value of oil and gas. The U.S. Geological Survey estimates that 25 per cent of the world's undiscovered fossil fuels are located under the Arctic Ocean. Big oil is already planning against the day when exploitable deposits are discovered: Shell has recently commissioned an analysis of the legal status of the passage, which is the subject of a long-standing international dispute.

Ownership of the islands along the Northwest Passage is not at issue. They were assigned to Canada by Britain in 1880, and the resulting title has never been contested—with one exception. Hans Island, a tiny (1.3 square kilometres), barren, otherwise inconsequential islet between Ellesmere Island and Greenland, is claimed by both Canada and Denmark. In recent years, the dispute over the islet has been seized upon by journalists keen to sell newspapers and by politicians looking to strengthen their nationalist credentials in a risk-free way. In July 2005, then defence minister Bill Graham even flew to Hans Island by helicopter, despite the fact that a group of Canadian soldiers had visited the island to assert our sovereignty just one week earlier.

As for the straits and channels between the islands, the nearly impenetrable ice meant that the issue of ownership and control was, for decades, never even discussed. Only the development of powerful icebreakers—and more recently climate change—has brought the issue to the fore.

Canada claims that the Northwest Passage constitutes Canadian internal waters. In 1985, the Canadian government drew "straight baselines" around the Arctic islands. Under international law, straight baselines may be used to link the outer headlands of an archipelago or fragmented coastline. Provided the lines are of a reasonable length, the straits and channels within them are then subject to the full force of the coastal state's domestic laws. Canada argues that the baselines are consolidated by historic usage, including the occupation of the sea ice by the Inuit. In Kugluktuk, at the western end of the passage, I met Alice Ayalik, who is a living manifestation of this aspect of Canada's claim. The 69-year-old artisan spent most of the first thirteen years of her life on the frozen surface of Coronation Gulf, where her family lived in igloos, fished through the ice and hunted seals. The Inuit, a largely maritime people, are Canadian citizens.

The United States insists that the Northwest Passage is an "international strait," a waterway that connects two expanses of high seas and is used for international navigation. The coastal state retains title to the waters, but foreign vessels have a right of "transit passage," much like walkers on a footpath through a British country estate.

Straight baselines cannot be used to close off an existing international strait. As a result, the crux of the dispute between Canada and the United States concerns the requirement that the strait be used for international navigation. In the past century, only two vessels have passed through the Northwest Passage overtly without asking Canada's permission: the *Manhattan* in 1969 and the *Polar Sea*, a U.S. Coast Guard icebreaker, in 1985. Some submarine voyages have almost certainly taken place, but their covert nature deprives them of any ability to contribute to a right under international law.

Ottawa argues that two transits do not create an international strait. Washington points to a judgement of the International Court of Justice, in a case concerning the Corfu Channel between the Greek island of Corfu and Albania, which suggests that the volume of traffic is irrelevant. The U.S. position has received some support from the European Commission, which in 1985 joined the State Department in protesting against Canada's drawing of straight baselines around the Arctic islands.

The Canadian government should be very concerned about the prospect of additional unauthorized transits, for they would seriously undermine its claim. Yet it is poorly equipped to prevent them from happening. The bulk of Canada's military presence in the North is provided by the Canadian Rangers, fourteen hundred part-time volunteers, many of them Inuit, who live in fifty-nine hamlets stretching from Baffin Island to the Alaskan frontier. The rangers know the land and ice, but they are neither trained nor equipped to intercept ocean-going vessels.

The Canadian Coast Guard's small fleet of icebreakers is incapable of operating in the Northwest Passage in winter, and it is redeployed to the Gulf of St. Lawrence each autumn. The ships are also growing old: the largest, the *Louis S. St-Laurent*, was built in 1969; the *Amundsen* is just a decade younger. Yet if Canada is to control the Northwest Passage, it will need ships that can operate there for twelve months a year.

Before being elected prime minister in January 2006, Stephen Harper promised "three new armed naval heavy icebreakers." But after being elected, he hesitated. The icebreakers were not mentioned in his first budget, nor did they feature in a $17.1 billion defence procurement package announced in June 2006. Perhaps Harper had realized that the new vessels weren't ideal for navy use and should instead be supplied to the coast guard, which uses its icebreakers to clear paths for other ships, provide search and rescue services, support research scientists and help in the enforcement of fisheries, environmental, customs and criminal laws. With the addition of light armament and a few police or military personnel, they could also fulfill an enhanced security role.

Harper's indecisiveness has been unfortunate—because American interests have recently changed, and they may well be more willing to accept Canadian sovereignty. During the Cold War, the United States was focussed on maintaining open access for its navy and especially its submarines. Under the law of the sea, submarines may pass through an international strait without surfacing or otherwise alerting the adjacent coastal state or states, something not permitted in internal waters. From Washington's perspective, the Canadian claim threatened to create an inconvenient precedent for straits and channels elsewhere.

Today, Washington is more concerned about terrorists sneaking into North America or rogue states using the oceans to transport weapons of mass destruction. And these challenges would best be addressed through a domestic legal system's criminal, customs and immigration laws, rather than the much looser constraints of international law. As it happens, the Canadian system is the only domestic legal system that could plausibly be applied in the Northwest Passage. It simply does not benefit the United States—or most other countries—to have foreign vessels shielded from reasonable regulations and scrutiny by maintaining that the passage is an international strait.

Access to the waterway is not really at issue, since Canada would never deny entry to one of its allies, or indeed to a reputable shipping company. As Pierre Trudeau declared in 1969, "to close off those waters and to deny passage to all foreign vessels in the name of Canadian sovereignty . . . would be as senseless as placing barriers across the entrances of Halifax and Vancouver harbours." Washington's concern about an inconvenient precedent is also misplaced, since the sea ice—and the resulting near-absence of international navigation to date—has created a situation where the Northwest Passage is distinct from the other waterways it claims are international straits.

In March 2005, then U.S. ambassador to Canada Paul Cellucci revealed that he had asked the U.S. State Department to take a "serious look at our long-standing policy" on the Northwest Passage. This has created an opportunity to resolve the dispute. The Canadian government should seize the initiative, first by investing in the equipment necessary to police the passage on a year-round basis, then by offering to provide open access for all U.S. government vessels and reputable international shipping companies—in return for the United States recognizing Canada's claim. But we must move quickly. Having seen an almost totally ice-free passage in late October 2006—when I sailed through on the *Amundsen*—it is clear to me that we have no time to waste.

SECURING THE RUNWAYS

The failure to defend Canadian interests in the Arctic extends beyond the land, sea and ice. Northern skies have become busy of late, and we are woefully underprepared for any emergencies that might arise from that.

The development of global positioning technology and ultralong-range aircraft such as the Airbus 340-500 and Boeing 777-LR have led to a dramatic increase in air traffic over the High Arctic. In 2006, nearly 150,000 commercial flights took "transpolar" or "high latitude" routes, flying from the east coast of North America to Southeast Asia or from the west coast to Europe and the Persian Gulf. Air Canada flies transpolar from Toronto to Beijing, Hong Kong, Seoul and Tokyo. Some of its other flights traverse the Arctic without going "over the top." I am a frequent passenger on the Vancouver-to-London flight, which passes over the middle of Baffin Island some 2,500 kilometres north of Montreal. Indeed, on any given day, as many people fly over Canada's three northern territories as live there on the ground.

Arctic routes reduce distance and are less likely to encounter strong headwinds, thus reducing flight time and fuel consumption. They are relatively safe, thanks to the new, technologically advanced equipment deployed. But even the newest and best-maintained aircraft can have mechanical problems, and passengers occasionally become dangerously ill. Canadian and U.S. regulators require airlines flying Arctic routes to specify a series of alternative airports, which must have a runway with sufficient length and strength to allow for a safe landing by the plane in question. In most circumstances, 2,100 metres of asphalt are required for an Airbus 340 or Boeing 777. As a point of comparison, the shortest runway at Toronto's Pearson International Airport is 2,700 metres long, and even this proved insufficient for an Air France Airbus 340 landing during a thunderstorm in August 2005.

The longest runway in Canada's North is at Whitehorse, with 2,877 metres. On September 11, 2001, two Korean Air 747s destined for the United States were safely diverted there. Iqaluit, with 2,606 metres, hosted the new, 555-passenger Airbus 380 for cold-weather testing in February 2006. Iqaluit sees about one unplanned landing each month, usually because of medical emergencies. Yellowknife has 2,286 meters of runway, barely over the minimum. Moreover, its instrument-landing system, required during poor visibility, works in one direction only—a direction that leads, just beyond the runway, to a drop-off into a lake. In March 2004, a United Airlines Boeing 777 with mechanical problems diverted to Yellowknife. The plane landed safely, but the airport was deemed too small to fly in a replacement engine. The engine was flown to Edmonton and then trucked the last 1,500 kilometres.

There are no other Canadian airports above 60 degrees north latitude where a long-range passenger jet could land safely. Inuvik and Rankin Inlet both have 1,829 metres of asphalt. The Government of Nunavut has recently spent $3 million to improve the instrument-landing system and apron at Rankin Inlet and an additional $18 million to pave the 1,515-metres-long gravel strip at Cambridge Bay. Resolute Bay, centrally located 1,500 kilometres northward of Yellowknife and Iqaluit, has 1,981 metres of gravel. One thousand kilometres farther northward, the runway at Alert is also gravel, and it is only 1,666 metres long. Faced with this inadequate infrastructure, regulators are allowing airlines flying Arctic routes to designate alternative airports that fall short of the usual requirements.

Arctic airports are expensive to maintain. Freeze-thaw cycles cause runways to crack and heave, a problem that is being exacerbated as climate change causes the underlying permafrost to melt. And although northern ground crews are adept at removing snow and ice from runways, they are hampered by limits in equipment and personnel. Most northern airports lack instrument-landing systems, and rescue and firefighting services are generally provided by volunteer fire departments—if they're available at all. Nor do most northern airports offer twenty-four-hour service, which poses a problem for an overnight flight from Beijing to New York that urgently needs to land.

The federal government collects "overflight" fees for the use of Canadian airspace. That money used to go to Transport Canada, a federal department, which spent some of it on airports, runways and rescue and firefighting services. Today, the revenue generated by overflight fees goes to Nav Canada, the private corporation that has been responsible for air traffic control in Canadian airspace since 1996. Northern airports, meanwhile, have been "devolved" to the governments of the three territories, which have been forced to shoulder most of the financial burden without the previous revenue stream. To make matters worse, these changes occurred at the same time that the federal government was concluding an air liberalization agreement with Russia to enable more transpolar routes, thus increasing the need for improved infrastructure on the ground. A similar agreement has recently been concluded with China.

In these circumstances, it behooves the federal government to provide the three northern territories with sufficient funds to lengthen and pave their runways, install or improve instrument landing, upgrade snow-clearing, firefighting and rescue services and to staff airports at night. In addition, the Department of National Defence should lengthen and pave the runway at Alert right away. Some of the expenditure could then be recouped, over time, through a small increase in overflight fees.

Internationally, frustration with the present situation has led to suggestions that airlines pay service charges directly to their designated alternative airports. Given the importance of strengthening Canada's governmental presence in the North for sovereignty assertion purposes, such an approach is far from ideal. Territorial governments can do the job, provided that some of the money generated by the traffic through the Arctic is directed their way from a federal source.

There is also the issue of crash landings away from airports. Although such events are very rare, frigid temperatures during the long Arctic winter demand that rescuers reach the site within hours. At the moment, they are hard pressed to do so. In 1991, after a Canadian Forces Hercules crashed twenty kilometres from Alert, the pilot froze to death during the two days it took help to arrive.

A small number of Arctic-trained paratroopers could make a difference, although to be effective in a crash scenario some of them would need to be based in the North. Stephen Harper promised new paratroopers for the Arctic in 2005, but he made no mention of them after becoming prime minister. At the same time, Joint Task Force North, the Canadian Forces' northern headquarters in Yellowknife, was promised new fixed-wing search and rescue aircraft specifically designed for parachuting, but no search and rescue personnel ("SAR techs") to do the actual jumps. Federal bureaucrats claim that the small number of incidents that might require search and rescue in the Arctic does not justify the expense of basing specialized personnel there. But unlikely events do occur and can have serious consequences. Imagine the outcry if an international airliner crash-landed on Canadian territory and the three hundred or more passengers and crew froze to death while waiting the two or three days it took for help to arrive.

Last but not least, there is an issue concerning the adequacy of communications facilities. In February 2006, I received an e-mail from a former Canadian Forces pilot who now flies for Cathay Pacific, including making transpolar flights between Hong Kong and New York. As he explained:

> As I'm sure you can imagine there's not much to do on a 15:45-hour over-the-pole flight. Notably, VHF, and eventually HF, comms end in Canada in the vicinity of Resolute Bay. It was the same 16 years ago when I flew the Herc, so one can see where NavCanada is not spending its money. So it's complete comms silence until one gets into Russian Airspace. Arctic Radio (CZUL/CZEG/CZWG) doesn't even have CPDLC data link comms. Meanwhile Russian ATC has all the latest toys with immediate data link comms (whilst still well within Canadian airspace) and shortly thereafter VHF with Magadan. I know the Canadian Gov't is concerned about its arctic sovereignty and its lack of presence but it's troubling to note the complete lack of "infrastructure" up there. Canada had better assert itself before someone else does.

Far more people fly over Canada's Arctic than have ever set foot there. We need to ensure that they can do so safely.

ARCTIC RESEARCH: EXPLORING CANADA'S NEXT FRONTIER

Globally, Arctic research has become a very big deal, with Britain, China, Denmark, Finland, France, Germany, Japan, Norway, Russia, Sweden and the United States all being major players. Canada has been in the game for decades too: one of my first childhood memories is of my father, a federal government scientist, returning from a research expedition to Bathurst Island with a new, very bushy beard. More recently, funding for Arctic research in Canada dipped to developing-country levels until Allan Rock, as minister of industry, committed $41 million of new funding in 2003.

The result was ArcticNet, a consortium of over one hundred researchers from twenty-seven Canadian universities and five federal departments that is designed to support cutting-edge science on the effects of climate change in Canada's North. Its central asset is the *Amundsen*. Previously named the *Sir John Franklin*, the twenty-eight-year-old Class 3 icebreaker has been refitted as a research vessel. In addition to laboratories and computer rooms, the *Amundsen* has a "moon-pool" that provides researchers with ice-free access to the ocean through the bottom of the ship—while providing reciprocal access to the ship for the occasional seal! The *Amundsen* has also been fitted with retractable "dynamic positioning" thrusters on the sides of its hull, enabling it to remain stationary in moving water or ice while samples are collected from the ocean floor or seabed. The modifications make it a near-perfect platform for Arctic scientists, particularly those specializing in sea ice, marine ecosystems and underwater geology.

Like Canada's other icebreakers, the *Amundsen* is not powerful enough to move throughout the Arctic in winter. It usually returns to its home port of Quebec City and is used to break ice for commercial traffic in the Gulf of St. Lawrence. However, in 2003–4 the *Amundsen* was deliberately frozen into the ice of the Beaufort Sea. There it sat through the long, dark Arctic winter, providing a warm, safe, high-tech research station for forty-six scientists at a time, flown in on ski planes for six-week rotations.

Another research initiative is the International Polar Year, which is actually taking place over two years—from March 2007 to March 2009—and concerns both the Arctic and the Antarctic. Previous international polar years were observed in 1882–83, 1932–33 and 1957–58. Involving up to fifty thousand scientists from sixty countries, this internationally coordinated campaign is cosponsored by the International Council for Science and the World Meteorological Organization. In September 2005, the federal government announced it would budget $150 million over six years to support Canadian research relating to the International Polar Year, with the money being targeted at research into climate change and health issues particular to northern communities.

There is no disputing that $150 million is a significant amount of money. Yet it represents only about 5 per cent of what is being spent on the International Polar Year worldwide. Given that Canada is the world's eighth-largest economy and that one quarter of the Arctic falls within its borders, this is somewhat miserly. The money was also announced too late for many Canadian projects to secure matching international funds. That said, it still represents a significant improvement over previous decades, and Canadian Arctic researchers, some of whom are already world leaders, are putting it to good use.

CANADA'S MOON MISSION

Canada is a big country, but it could soon become even larger. Along our northern coast, Canadian scientists are working to increase the size of Canada by hundreds of thousands of square kilometres. And if that does not sound audacious enough, they have been doing so in co-operation with the Danes—the very same people who have been challenging Canadian sovereignty over Hans Island.

In early 2005, a joint Canadian-Danish expedition mapped the floor of the Arctic Ocean several hundred kilometres north of that contested islet. Hundreds of seismic sensors and depth charges were lowered through the ice at intervals along the Lomonosov Ridge, an undersea mountain range that runs northward from Ellesmere Island and Greenland, towards the North Pole. When the explosives were detonated, shock waves bounced off the ocean floor and off layers of sediments and bedrock up to forty kilometres below the ocean floor, providing detailed geographical and geological information.

The data are being collected not just for science's sake. Coastal states have sovereign rights over their adjoining continental shelves. These rights extend to the resources of the seabed and underlying strata, including all minerals, oil, gas and gas hydrates. Until recently, such rights did not extend more than two hundred nautical miles from shore. But under the 1982 United Nations Convention on the Law of the Sea, countries may—depending on the depth and shape of the seabed and the thickness of underlying sedimentary layers—claim a shelf that reaches much farther. Any such claim must be submitted, with supporting scientific data, to the Commission on the Limits of the Continental Shelf, a body of scientists elected by parties to the UN convention. The commission's recommendations are not legally binding. Its role is to alert countries to exaggerated claims, as well as to help legitimize reasonable claims. It is left to those countries whose claims overlap to negotiate mutually satisfactory agreements among themselves or to take their disputes to an international court or tribunal.

Once a country ratifies the convention, it has ten years in which to make its submission. Russia ratified the UN convention in 1997 and submitted its claim to an extended continental shelf just four years later. The claim encroached on areas that Canada, Denmark and the United States hope to claim for themselves, and all three countries filed protests. The commission responded by recommending that Russia submit a revised claim, as well as more supporting data. Russia has since engaged in a major seismic mapping exercise: in the summer of 2005, it sent one of its research vessels all the way to the North Pole.

Canada ratified the UN convention in 2003; therefore, its submission must be complete by 2013. Conceivably, Canada could assert sovereign rights over an underwater expanse larger than Alberta—with comparable natural resources. As mentioned before, the U.S. Geological Survey estimates that 25 per cent of the world's undiscovered oil and gas reserves lie under the Arctic Ocean. As prices rise, new technologies are developed and climate change makes northern regions increasingly accessible, that ocean could become humanity's last major source of fossil fuels. Alternatively, from an environmental perspective, Canadian sovereignty could be used to help keep the fossil fuels locked in place, where they could not contribute to further climate change.

For Canada, the expedition to the Lomonosov Ridge is just a beginning. Of the $70 million for seabed mapping allocated by the 2004 federal budget, more than half was designated for the northwest flank of the Arctic archipelago, that vast, frozen expanse of ocean stretching from west of Ellesmere Island to the Beaufort Sea. Logistically, mapping that area is as challenging as mounting an expedition to the moon. Two heavy icebreakers working together could take four or more summers to complete the job. Canada has only one such vessel, the aging *Louis S. St-Laurent*, which means that another would have to be chartered or bought. Alternatively, the *Amundsen*, whose dynamic-positioning thrusters could be an asset in such work, might be diverted from its other research activities. Exacerbating the situation, icebreakers consume vast quantities of fuel, the price of which has risen sharply since 2004. As a result, the money allocated by Paul Martin's government will probably not suffice.

The United States could be of considerable assistance. During the Cold War, the U.S. Navy mapped much of the sea-floor topography of the Arctic Ocean, using nuclear submarines operating under the ice. Recently, it declassified the data obtained from areas more than two hundred nautical miles offshore. Yet it will not, officially at least, even admit to having data from within two hundred nautical miles of other countries, since collecting that data would have been illegal without the coastal state's consent. More recently, Ottawa invited Washington to send its mapping submarines into Canadian waters, but the specialized vessels were decommissioned before that could be done. In these circumstances, consideration should be given to providing retroactive consent to any clandestine mapping that occurred.

Our ambassador in Washington could engage in some supportive diplomacy. The United States has not yet ratified the UN

Convention on the Law of the Sea, though the Bush administration has initiated the process by asking the Senate for its "advice and consent." At the same time, it would not be in the United States' interest to have Canada's claim endorsed by the commission before the U.S. makes its own position—and the scientific basis for that position—clear. Ideally, the two countries would concurrently file mutually supportive claims. But before they could do so, Ottawa and Washington would have to resolve a lingering maritime boundary dispute in the Beaufort Sea, offshore from the border between the Yukon and Alaska, since the line within two hundred nautical miles provides the starting point for the line farther out. That dispute, over just sixty-five square kilometres of seabed, pales in significance when compared with the sovereign rights available to both countries farther offshore.

Even if Washington co-operates, much remains to be done. Submarines are not particularly useful for mapping the geology of the seabed, and data on sediments is an essential component of any claim to an extended continental shelf. The seismic mapping along the northwest flank of the archipelago must begin soon, and with the full support of the Canadian government. Any hesitation could result in Canada missing the 2013 deadline, thus losing out on the essential legitimacy that would flow from an endorsement of its claims by the UN commission.

The stakes are high. A complete, scientifically sound, punctual submission could result in Canada having widely recognized sovereign rights over a large and potentially very important expanse of seabed. Once again, the Arctic is Canada's new frontier.

LOOK UP, WAY UP: ARCTIC POLICY AS FOREIGN POLICY

For many people, looking at the Canadian Arctic from a foreign-policy perspective seems counterintuitive. Surely the main issues up north concern the treatment of indigenous Canadians, federal-territorial relations or the exploitation of resources on Canadian soil? But let's think about these and other issues for a moment.

Canada's longest international boundary is located in the Arctic, mostly in the form of the continental coastline and the straight baselines connecting the outer headlands of the archipelago. Although much of our northern boundary is between Canadian territory and the internationalized zone known as the "high seas," Canada does have territorial disputes in the Arctic with three other countries: the United States over the boundary in the Beaufort Sea; Denmark over Hans Island and the boundary in the Lincoln Sea north of Ellesmere Island and Greenland, and (in all likelihood) Russia over overlapping continental shelf claims in the Arctic Ocean. And, of course, it has a dispute with the United States over the legal status of the Northwest Passage.

Acute environmental degradation is occurring in the Arctic as the result of pollution produced many thousands of kilometres away. Some steps to address these challenges have been taken through multilateral treaties, including the Stockholm Convention on Persistent Organic Pollutants and, less successfully, the Kyoto Protocol. Canada's relationship with its indigenous peoples is directly implicated in most of these international issues.

The support of the Inuit is an important element of Canada's claim to the Northwest Passage. The advocacy efforts of the Inuit Circumpolar Conference played a key role in securing a meaningful treaty on persistent organic pollutants. The Inuit have also mounted a significant international effort to address climate change, the leading global issue of the twenty-first century, by filing a complaint against the U.S. government with the Inter-American Commission on Human Rights. Seen from this foreign-policy perspective, it becomes all the more inexplicable that successive Canadian governments have neglected the indigenous people of the Arctic, including, most recently, by failing to implement key provisions of the 1993 Nunavut Land Claims Agreement.

In March 2005, I attended a workshop on the Northwest Passage in Iqaluit. John Amagoalik was there. So was Sheila Watt-Cloutier, then president of the Inuit Circumpolar Conference. Some of the other participants were among the first graduates of the Akitsiraq Law School, a satellite program of the University of Victoria. I have never encountered as much brain power around a single table as I did that day, not even in an Oxford dining hall.

Meeting Amagoalik was a particular pleasure. Relocated from northern Quebec to Resolute Bay in 1953, Amagoalik and his family were the victims of a heavy-handed Canadian government move to assert sovereignty over the High Arctic. He was then taken from his family and sent to residential schools in Churchill and Iqaluit. A subsequent political career earned him the title of "father of Nunavut," the Inuit homeland and, since 1999, Canada's third territory. As president of the Inuit Tapirisat of Canada, chair of the Nunavut Constitutional Forum, political adviser to the Tungavik Federation of Nunavut and then chief commissioner of the Nunavut Implementation Commission, Amagoalik negotiated on behalf of his people with a series of Canadian prime ministers. And he did so directly, on the basis of equality of status as a national leader. This was underlined for me when, during a conference dinner in Ottawa in June 2006, I asked Amagoalik if he remembered Ivan Head, Pierre Trudeau's chief adviser on foreign policy and Arctic issues. "No," he replied, without the slightest hint of hubris, "I only dealt with the principals."

Yet many of the people Amagoalik represented are suffering from grossly inadequate housing and astonishingly high rates of unemployment, illiteracy, preventable disease and suicide. One month after our dinner, Amagoalik sent an e-mail to inform me that, two days after returning to Iqaluit, he had been "medevaced" back to Ottawa with an advanced case of tuberculosis. How many Canadians know that TB, historically one of the world's most deadly diseases, is endemic in our North today, in this, one of the richest and most medically advanced countries on Earth? Four months later, when visiting Kugluktuk in the western Arctic, I noticed that many of the Inuit—who are normally very friendly—were greeting me without smiles. Meeting the town's Anglican priest in the local museum-cum-Internet café, I asked what was wrong. "We buried a young man yesterday," he said, "the third suicide in four months."

To his credit, Lloyd Axworthy took some positive steps on Arctic issues when he was minister of foreign affairs. In 1996, Axworthy led the creation of the Arctic Council, a mechanism that draws together the eight countries and the indigenous people of the circumpolar North, to address common environmental, social and economic concerns. Among other accomplishments, the Arctic Council set in motion the 2004 Arctic Climate Impact Assessment, one of the world's most significant efforts to understand and raise awareness about climate change.

There are other examples of how looking at the North from a foreign-policy perspective can create opportunities. Georgiy Mamedov, the Russian ambassador to Canada, is strongly promoting the idea of an "Arctic bridge," an international shipping route linking Murmansk in Russia to Churchill in Manitoba and then, by rail, to the heartland of the United States. His efforts have been well received, not least by the U.S. railway company OmniTRAX which, in 1997, bought the Port of Churchill for the fire-sale price of ten dollars, as well as the rail line from Churchill to Winnipeg. As climate change extends the shipping season, OmniTRAX—and some residents of northern Manitoba—should profit handsomely in the decades ahead.

The full co-operation of all three territorial governments is required. Just as Ottawa needs to help those governments expand and improve northern airports, a strong case can also be made for building a deepwater port at Iqaluit, as has been requested by the Government of Nunavut. A second deepwater port could usefully be constructed at Tuktoyaktuk, at the mouth of the Mackenzie River. And one way to improve the capacity of the territorial governments to address the challenges of a changing Arctic would be to change their fiscal relationship with Ottawa. At the moment, there is a certain incongruity between Prince Edward Island (5,660 square kilometres) being a province with control over its natural resources and the Northwest Territories (1,346,106 square kilometres) being a territory that does not have the right to receive any of the royalties received by Ottawa on its oil, gas and diamonds.

Canada, by fate and geography, is destined to be an Arctic country. Climate change and the global demand for natural resources are only accelerating the process, while introducing international elements—such as an ice-free Northwest Passage and a continental shelf dispute with Russia—that previous generations could not have imagined. Whether we like it or not, Arctic policy has become foreign policy. At the same time, the success of much of that foreign policy will depend on our ability to co-operate with the people who have long called the Arctic their home. In the North, the Inuit and other indigenous peoples are our sentinels, soldiers and diplomats. It is time for southern Canadians to look up, way up, and provide serious support for their efforts to build a true North strong and free.

— 8 —

CANADA-U.S. MILITARY RELATIONS:

Who to Serve?

CANADA EXISTS in a constant state of tension between the gravitational pull of the world's pre-eminent superpower and an enduring, self-affirming drive to be different from our southern neighbour on matters as profound as the social contract, relationships with minorities and the role of war in the pursuit of justice, democracy and peace. This tension plays out in many different ways, but it is nowhere more evident than in the institutions and policies concerning military co-operation.

BINATIONAL PLANNING GROUP:
CONTINENTAL INTEGRATION BY STEALTH

They seemed innocuous enough at first: two midlevel Canadian Forces officers and a mild-mannered, bespectacled American consultant explaining the work of their forty-eight-member Binational

Planning Group (BPG) to audiences across Canada. Their professed goal was to improve co-operation between the Canadian and U.S. militaries, the better to defend both countries. Yet a close reading of BPG's final report, released in March 2006, revealed that their actual intent—or at least the intent of the politicians and generals who set their mandate—was far from benign. They sought nothing less than the complete integration of Canada's military, security and foreign policy into the decision-making and operating systems of the United States.

As part of a comprehensive post-9/11 effort to secure North America against terrorist attacks, Ottawa and Washington began developing a "combined defence plan" that would have placed the Canadian Forces under the umbrella of the United States' new Northern Command (NORTHCOM). Opponents of the plan attracted enough public attention to cause the Jean Chrétien government to hesitate. In 2002, the plan was quietly shunted out of view and into the newly created BPG. Based at the headquarters of NORTHCOM and the North American Aerospace Defence Command (NORAD) in Colorado Springs, the BPG was intended to devise counterpoints to the critics' concerns while postponing formal decision making until a more politically opportune moment.

Two Canadian elections later, the authors of the BPG report could hardly believe their luck. Stephen Harper had obtained only a minority government in January 2006, but there was little doubt that he desired closer ties with Washington. When in Opposition, the Conservative Party leader had advocated Canadian participation in both the 2003 Iraq War and missile defence.

The BPG recommendations were far-reaching. They aimed at "enhanced coordination and co-operation among our foreign policy, defence and security organizations" at "the level (although not necessarily the form) of co-operation that now exists in NORAD."

In NORAD, the defence of Canadian and U.S. airspace is assigned to a single command that, while supposedly based on an equality of the two countries, is always headed by a senior U.S. officer. As a result, the BPG was, in fact, advocating co-operation at the level of a single, U.S.-dominated command for all of Canada's territory and our surrounding seas. Under this plan, the entire Canadian Forces, unless deployed overseas in operations not led by the United States, could find themselves under U.S. "operational control," with Americans making all key day-to-day decisions. Not to worry, the BPG assured us calmly; "command" would remain in Canadian hands. And that was true, insofar as Canadians would retain responsibility for administrative tasks such as hiring, promotion and pensions.

The BPG also recommended closer co-operation in security and foreign policy: "Canada and the U.S. must continue to act as partners; indeed . . . the partnership must be expanded, to shape the future of North American defence and security, using all of the instruments of diplomatic, economic, informational and military power." Those concerned about the rendition and torture of Maher Arar, the monitoring of telephone calls and e-mails without judicial oversight, the development of missile defence and the related push for the weaponization of space will be especially disturbed by the BPG report's heavy emphasis on "seamless binational information sharing" and "interoperability" in order to achieve "full network-centric operations (NCO) / network-centric warfare (NCW) capabilities."

It was within the context of information sharing that the BPG recommended the immediate extension of NORAD into the maritime domain. The Harper government quickly followed this recommendation, bringing a revised NORAD agreement, complete with a provision on maritime surveillance sharing, before the House of Commons for a non-binding vote. It won the vote handily, with support from the Liberals and Bloc Québécois, and against the objections of the NDP. In normal circumstances, the instantaneous sharing of information on ships approaching North America makes sense. In an age of sea-launched missiles, approaching vessels could pose security threats on timelines that are too short for conventional communication protocols. But the BPG changed the circumstances by indicating that maritime surveillance sharing was intended as a forerunner for much closer co-operation: it called the upcoming renewal of the NORAD agreement "an important step toward enhancing the defence and security of our continent. To continue this momentum a 'Comprehensive Defence and Security Agreement' is the logical next step. . ."

The BPG presented several alternatives for the new agreement. The first was an expanded NORAD responsible for "all-domain warning"—in the air, at sea, on land and in cyberspace—but with its response capability limited to the air. This new, surveillance-focussed NORAD would exist in parallel with the Northern Command and the recently established, Canadian-run Canada Command. Curiously, the BPG saw only one advantage with this approach: "Since NORAD has great appeal among the Canadian public, strengthening NORAD would likely be viewed favourably in Canada." Indeed, a remarkable aspect of the BPG report is how many of its recommendations concerned how best to persuade Canadians to accept further military integration.

A second alternative for the new agreement involved a NORAD command that would provide both "all-domain warning and response to asymmetric threats and attacks." Under this approach, NORTHCOM and Canada Command would continue to exist separately, with "the capability to respond unilaterally to threats against their respective countries." However, in reality, the single command would prevail in most defence matters on the North American continent, including armed responses at sea and on land. It would also, inevitably, be dominated by the United States—a fact the BPG admitted would generate "concerns over sovereignty and maintaining freedom of action."

Another, even more ambitious alternative involved "a truly integrated approach to continental defence and security through a deliberate melding of defence and security functions." This would be achieved by "establishing a single organization responsible for all-domain, binational warning and execution in the realms of defence and security."

This alternative, full integration, was presented as the ultimate goal of improved co-operation, since "any of the previous concepts presented could be used as a stepping stone in the interim." The BPG report thus revealed that the expansion of NORAD to include maritime surveillance was intended to create momentum towards complete military, security and foreign-policy integration. It is part of a deliberately fostered trend that includes Canada's involvement in the U.S.-led counter-insurgency in southern Afghanistan, the instantaneous sharing of NORAD aerospace surveillance for U.S. missile defence, and the Harper government's support for the Bush administration's policies on nuclear proliferation, the Middle East and climate change.

We are being targeted for continental integration by stealth. Indeed, the BPG report warned of a "small but vocal minority" concerned about Canadian sovereignty and recommended the use of an "incremental" approach. Canada, once proudly independent, is in danger of allowing itself to be suffocated in America's militaristic embrace.

MILITARY SPENDING: A QUESTION OF PRIORITIES

Debates about military spending usually focus on the size of defence budgets, both in regard to the total amount and as a percentage of gross domestic product (GDP) when compared with other countries. These debates matter, since military spending draws money away from other areas such as overseas development assistance. But an equally important issue concerns how defence budgets are spent. Many Canadians would support sizable defence budgets that focussed on peacekeeping and sovereignty assertion, but they are less keen on large budgets that focus on being able to participate seamlessly in U.S.-led wars. Unfortunately, in recent decades Canadian defence budgets have tended to follow the latter approach.

Canada currently spends about $16 billion on its military each year, which works out to about 7 per cent of the federal budget or 1.3 per cent of GDP. This level of spending is slightly lower than that of other middle-power, non-nuclear NATO countries. In 2004, Germany spent 1.4 per cent of GDP, the Netherlands 1.7 per cent, Italy 1.8 per cent and Norway 1.9 per cent. Our overall spending may seem reasonable, even parsimonious when one considers that Canada is the world's second-largest country and has the longest coastline. But the key question remains, what is the money best used for?

When the Cold War ended, many countries took advantage of the improved geopolitical situation to reduce military spending. Even the United States cut back. Here in Canada, the defence budget was reduced by one-quarter between 1993 and 2000, to $9 billion per year. But this reduction went beyond a simple "peace dividend," since the federal government was in the midst of a deep-reaching deficit reduction campaign. Necessary purchases were postponed, such as new helicopters to replace the navy's aging Sea Kings. An element of "free riding" was also involved, with Canada's proximity to the militarily predominant United States being seen as ensuring protection regardless of the state of the Canadian Forces. Little thought was given to the possible effects of the cutbacks on Canada's ability to police its coastal and Arctic waters or its ability—independently from the United States—to engage in peacekeeping and humanitarian missions.

The combination of air, land and sea forces necessary to project force abroad cannot be achieved for $9 billion a year. And so, Canadian defence policy became focussed on an even closer partnership with our powerful ally, whereby a modicum of war-fighting capability could be maintained through "interoperability." Under this approach, equipment was obtained and soldiers were trained with a view to plugging them into the much larger U.S. war-fighting machine, without having to field all of the components of a stand-alone military.

However, interoperability is expensive, and the costs go up as the U.S. military grows ever more technologically advanced. Canadian generals, the defence industry and their university-based supporters soon turned this situation to their advantage. They did so by transforming an approach that was designed to preserve an overseas military capacity in the face of declining budgets into an argument for stabilizing and then increasing those budgets. Canada's twelve Halifax-class frigates have been kept fully interoperable with U.S. Navy vessels, but at considerable financial cost; further upgrades, mostly involving expensive computer equipment, will soon be required if interoperability is to be maintained. The same is true of our CF-18 fighter-bombers, eighty of which are having their electronics substantially upgraded. According to some reports, even our second-hand Victoria-class submarines were purchased, in part, to provide Canada with a new means of participating in U.S.-led training exercises: the submarines' diesel-electric engines are extremely quiet, making them a challenge for U.S. anti-submarine forces to detect and locate.

Tight budgets and the rising cost of interoperability also led defence planners to reduce the number of permanent civilian employees and, increasingly, to contract out work that was previously done by Canadian Forces personnel. These contracts extend to deployment support and even to training. Today, when Canadian soldiers are deployed abroad, civilian contractors are often sent with them to provide food and sanitation services, maintain and repair equipment and manage ammunition supplies. The companies that secure these contracts generally use non-unionized and often foreign workers. Some of the companies are not Canadian; others are subsidiaries of large U.S. firms.

Despite these various developments, Canada's military retains a capacity for modern peacekeeping. Some of our older soldiers have considerable experience in UN operations, though we are losing more and more of this experience—and training capacity—to retirements each year. We also possess some relatively new, highly suitable equipment, including more than six hundred light armoured vehicles (LAV IIIs) and two hundred Coyote reconnaissance vehicles. On the naval side, with ships playing an increasingly important role in peacekeeping, our frigates and their soon-to-be-acquired Cyclone helicopters are top of the line.

We are also acquiring more first-rate equipment suitable for peacekeeping. In June 2006, the Harper government allocated $4.7 billion for 16 medium- to heavy-lift helicopters, $1.2 billion for 2,300 medium-sized logistics trucks, $2.9 billion for three joint-support ships and $8.3 billion for four "strategic-lift" and 17 "tactical-lift" transport aircraft. Properly deployed, all of this equipment would strengthen significantly the Canadian contribution to humanitarian and peacekeeping missions. To give just one example, immediately after the 2004 Boxing Day tsunami that devastated regions bordering the Indian Ocean and killed more than 200,000 people, UN emergency relief coordinator Jan Egeland stated that the top priority on his wish list was long-range strategic-lift aircraft. But again, it is a question of how we make use of our capabilities, since the same helicopters, trucks, ships and aircraft would greatly augment the Canadian contribution to U.S.-led wars. Indeed, some of the current purchases have been accelerated in order to support the mission in Afghanistan. The $8.3 billion in fixed-wing aircraft contracts is untendered, making the planes much more expensive than they would otherwise be. Moreover, the decision to avoid a regular tender process has ensured that the planes will be purchased from American rather than European firms.

Overall, the push for interoperability continues unabated. In its 2005 Defence Policy Statement, the Paul Martin government reaffirmed a commitment "to improve... interoperability with allied forces, particularly the United States, through smart investments in evolving technology and doctrinal concepts, training opportunities, and exchange and liaison programs." In December 2006, the Harper government also signed on to the third phase of the development program for the F-35 strike fighter. According to the Department of National Defence, our participation in the program "will strengthen relationships and interoperability with our Allies."

That may be so, but the United States is willing to share only so much. Before I returned to Canada in 2004, I visited Langley Air Force Base in Virginia, where I was accorded a thirty-minute meeting with the four-star general in charge of Air Combat Command. Sitting on the general's desk were models of the latest high-tech warplanes being produced for the U.S. military: the single-engine F-35 and its sister aircraft, the twin-engine F-22. The general had test-flown prototypes of both planes, and he chatted happily about them, displaying an obvious preference for the faster, more manoeuvrable and longer-range F-22. I mentioned that the Canadian government would likely be in the market for new planes, since the CF-18s were beginning to age.

"Yes," the general said, pointing to the F-35. "They're going to buy some of these."

"What about those?" I asked, pointing to the other model. "What if Canada wanted some F-22s?"

The general fixed his fighter-pilot eyes on mine and replied, "I don't think those are for sale."

Still, the U.S. government is more than willing to share the cost of developing the F-35, which is estimated at an astonishing US$276 billion. And foreign sales of the F-35 will offset the even higher cost of developing the F-22, which is based largely on the same technology. The Canadian government insists that Canadian aerospace companies will benefit from being allowed to bid on billions of dollars worth of production and maintenance contracts. However, none of those contracts are guaranteed; nor can we be certain that we are getting the best equipment for Canada's needs. What is certain is that the Canadian taxpayer will, once again, end up supporting the U.S. defence industry.

INTEROPERABILITY OR INDEPENDENCE?

Whereas the pursuit of interoperability is directed primarily at maximizing Canada's ability to fight wars alongside the United

States, high-tech interoperability is less important for humanitarian missions, peacekeeping operations, policing our coasts and asserting sovereignty in the Arctic—even if some of these missions were to involve U.S. forces. Indeed, the expense associated with interoperable war-fighting capability diverts funding from other capacities, and thus other possible missions, which helps explain why the Canadian Forces are currently doing little peacekeeping or sovereignty assertion. This became evident in January 2007, when it was revealed that some of Canada's naval vessels were being kept in port instead of being sent out on regular fisheries and coastal security patrols, because of the high cost of supporting the mission in Afghanistan.

The reductions in peacekeeping and sovereignty assertion also affect Canada's standing and influence abroad. Historically, Canada has punched above its weight, not because of a powerful military but because of a willingness to act for the global good, and not just our own. A continued reduction in peacekeeping could also have consequences in terms of Canadians' sense of national identity. In a poll conducted by Angus Reid for *Maclean's* magazine in October 2006, 87 per cent of Canadians agreed that the role played by our soldiers in peacekeeping was "essential."

But despite this majority opinion, the turn away from peacekeeping—and towards U.S. war fighting—will soon become irreversible if we don't change tack. Suppose that Canada wished to send its soldiers on a peacekeeping mission that the Americans opposed. It is one thing to say that Canada could opt out of its commitments to the United States in order to free up resources for a separate action; it's an altogether different thing to take such action once integrated structures are in place and forces and equipment have been permanently assigned. An early manifestation of this occurred in 2006, when Chief of the Defence Staff Rick Hillier ruled out participation in peacekeeping missions in both Lebanon and Darfur on the basis that the Canadian Forces were fully committed in Afghanistan. General Hillier's position broke a promise he had made in March

2005, when he told Prime Minister Paul Martin that the deployment of 2000 troops to Kandahar would not preclude a parallel deployment to a UN mission elsewhere. The existence of the promise was confirmed in documents obtained in May 2006 by the NDP through an access-to-information request and by Martin himself in October 2006, when he said to the *Globe and Mail*: "Rick Hillier told me he would. That was what we agreed on."

Nor is closer military co-operation likely to enhance Canada's influence with the United States, despite what most proponents of integration argue. As Joel Sokolsky of the Royal Military College of Canada has explained in the context of co-operation between the Canadian and U.S. navies:

[C]onvincing allies to dispatch ships to join the USN, and encouraging them to be as interoperable as their budgets allow, is yet another manifestation of the American pursuit of global dominance... [E]ven when allies contribute forces and there is agreement on specific tasks, there is no concomitant expectation that smaller contributors, such as Canada, will therefore share in the higher strategic and political decisions associated with the operation. Interoperability may allow the Canadian navy to make a useful contribution at sea, but it is not likely to permit Ottawa greater voice or leverage in Washington.

If Canada is to remain independent, our soldiers, sailors and pilots must—for the most part—remain under Canadian "operational control." They must be provided with equipment that is chosen for the kinds of missions that serve Canadian interests, whether protecting this country at home or serving the United Nations abroad.

RADARSAT-2: A CANADIAN-FUNDED U.S. MILITARY SATELLITE?

In November 2003, I attended a dinner at Duke University in honour of the Canadian political philosopher James Tully and the Portuguese sociologist Bonaventura de Sousa Santos. Tully and Sousa

Santos are wonderful conversationalists, but the discussion that I remember most involved a young Hispanic academic who was very interested in the fact that there was a Center for Canadian Studies at Duke. I explained that the centre supported work on topics as varied as French Canadian literature, the history of western Canadian settlement, the economics of federal-provincial relations and the political science of voter preferences. He then asked about my own work.

"I'm interested in sovereignty," I explained, "and whether a relatively small country like Canada can retain political independence while interacting closely with a country as large and powerful as the United States."

"Good luck," the young man smiled bitterly, "I come from Puerto Rico where we lost our political independence a long time ago. But we're still not allowed to vote; we just pay taxes and do what we're told."

I remembered that conversation a year later when, after moving to Vancouver, I discovered that the United States was about to acquire a new military satellite courtesy of Canadian taxpayers.

In 1998, the Chrétien government announced plans for a new Earth observation satellite, Radarsat-2, to be owned and operated by a private company, MacDonald Dettwiler of Richmond, British Columbia. Radarsat-2 was intended to replace Radarsat-1, Canada's first microwave radar satellite, which was launched in 1995 and has served as an important tool in map making, natural resource management and ice navigation ever since. When I sailed through the Northwest Passage on the *Amundsen* in October 2006, the captain used Radarsat-1 imagery to plot our course. Radarsat-1 is owned and operated by the Canadian Space Agency; in 2004, data and images produced by it were sold to six hundred customers worldwide, generating $26 million in revenue for the federal government.

The Chrétien government supported the move from the public ownership of Radarsat-1 to private ownership of Radarsat-2 by prepurchasing $242 million of satellite-generated data from Mac-Donald Dettwiler. In return, the company agreed to invest $80 million of its own funds. This constituted a very good deal for the company, with CEO Daniel Friedmann predicting that Radarsat-2 would, over its seven-year projected lifespan, generate $1 billion in revenue. At the same time, it was expected that the benefits to Canada would be significant. The federal government would obtain a large amount of high-quality imagery as well as "priority access" to Radarsat-2 in emergency situations such as natural disasters. Several thousand well-paid jobs might also be maintained or created.

Radarsat-2 was supposed to have been launched by NASA in 2001, in return for a specified amount of free data. But that plan was axed after Washington expressed concern about the satellite's ability to capture features as small as three metres in size—even at night and through clouds—and the possibility that hostile countries or groups might be able to purchase fine-resolution images of U.S. facilities and forces. As the U.S. government imposed obstacle after obstacle, the launch date began to slip, first from 2001 to 2003, then to 2005 and finally to March 2007, when Radarsat-2 was due to be sent into orbit—on a Russian-made Soyuz rocket.

The delays in turn led to escalating costs: in 2000, the Canadian government paid MacDonald Dettwiler an additional $167 million, and the company added $12 million of its own money. Ottawa made a further payment of $6 million in 2001, bringing its overall contribution to $415 million, or 82 per cent of the $507 million total cost to date. But as the costs went up, the value of Canada's investment went down: after six years of sitting on the ground, Radarsat-2 is no longer at the technological cutting edge and is therefore less globally competitive.

The Canadian government sought to address the U.S. concerns about security by negotiating a bilateral treaty, which was signed by then Canadian foreign minister Lloyd Axworthy and U.S. secretary of state Madeline Albright in 2000. The treaty imposes restraints on the use of Radarsat-2, but the details of those restraints were deemed "commercially confidential" and confined to an unpublished annex. When the House of Commons considered the matter in 2005, members of Parliament were not allowed to see the annex. As Conservative MP Ted Menzies told the *Winnipeg Free Press*, all that government officials would say is that Canada retains "shutter control," which refers to the power to control images downloaded from the satellite.

"Does the minister have the power to trump this annex in the treaty?" Menzies asked. "They claim the minister has shutter control, but they won't tell us if the annex trumps the minister."

One can speculate as to the contents of the annex. Washington undoubtedly obtained the right to prevent others from obtaining Radarsat-2 images of U.S. military facilities and real or potential theatres of operation, such as Afghanistan, Iraq, Iran and North Korea. The U.S. government has a strategic interest in ensuring that high-resolution images of its military and government installations, or of U.S. forces in the field, are not available on the open market; similarly, U.S. law prohibits commercial satellite imagery of territory within nations such as Israel. It is also possible that the United States secured the power, pursuant to Canada's right of priority access, to conscript Radarsat-2 in support of its intelligence and military operations. When I put this last speculation to Lloyd Axworthy in March 2005, it elicited a wry smile.

We do know that cutbacks to the United States' own remote-sensing programs have forced it to seek data elsewhere. Today, the U.S. National Geospatial-Intelligence Agency is one of the world's largest purchasers of commercially produced, fine-resolution satellite imagery. It is therefore possible that a satellite owned by a Canadian company and paid for by Canadian taxpayers may soon become the United States' newest military satellite, available on demand to facilitate and fight wars and perhaps even pre-emptive strikes. MacDonald Dettwiler certainly anticipates that this might happen: it has signed a contract with the U.S. Air Force to test the usefulness of Radarsat-2 in combat situations.

All this raises serious issues of international law. Since Radarsat-2 will be licensed and purportedly controlled by Ottawa, the use of its data in any military intervention could make us a party to that action—and equally culpable for any violation of the UN Charter that occurs.

The potential use of Canadian satellites by other countries for military purposes raises other concerns. When Steve Staples of the Rideau Institute testified before the House of Commons Standing Committee on Foreign Affairs in 2005, he took along two brochures that had been produced by MacDonald Dettwiler and the Canadian Space Agency to promote the uses of Radarsat-1 and Radarsat-2. As he explained:

> The first one . . . would be fairly reflective of what Canadians would expect RADARSAT satellites to be doing. It promotes offshore and continental oil exploration, crop monitoring, ice mapping, and disaster monitoring. I call these the "green" uses of the RADARSAT-1 and RADARSAT-2 satellites, and this is what Canadians think the Canadian Space Agency is doing.
>
> However, there is another application, and there's another brochure to go along with it that MacDonald Dettwiler has produced to tout the uses of RADARSAT-1 and 2; it's from their defence systems. It points out that MacDonald Dettwiler sees space-based technology for surveillance and command control systems, and here they say "We represent a new breed of defence contractor—using commercial space and information management technology to solve the surveillance and command control problems of defence customers." So I fear that what we are seeing with our overall space agency is that these green uses of our satellite technology are being taken over by these more black uses—military use—of our systems, and I think this is of great concern to Canadians.

Staples went on to point out that "Canada closely controls the export of military goods and technologies to countries that pose a threat to Canada, are involved in imminent threat of hostilities, are under UN sanctions, or whose governments have a persistent record of serious human rights violations." Why, he asked, should remote-sensing data be treated any differently? He suggested, provocatively but correctly, that any export controls on remote-sensing data should extend to the United States:

> While most of the time our foreign policies are in sync with the United States, as we know with Iraq, that is not always the case. There has been suggestion that remote sensing data produced by RADARSAT-1 may have been exported to the U.S. in support of their operations in the war in Iraq. Clearly, if you go to the RADARSAT international website, as I did last night, there are a number of photographs of Iraq taken by RADARSAT-1 that are being promoted for use.

The issue of remote-sensing satellites is rarely mentioned in discussions about Canadian foreign policy. We tend, when thinking about foreign affairs, to do so within long-established parameters. But as technology moves on, new issues arise. Today, Canadian taxpayers are paying for a satellite that could be used to help fight other countries' wars. In some instances, those wars might be illegal or otherwise inconsistent with Canada's principles and long-term interests. We need to regain control over our satellites in order to protect our commitments to the United Nations, to international law and to our own status and reputation as a sovereign nation-state.

OUR OWN WORST ENEMIES?

During the height of the campaign to keep Canada out of the U.S. missile defence program, the Department of Foreign Affairs invited me to participate in a public debate with Jack Granatstein, a retired Canadian military historian. But before the plans could be finalized, they were abruptly cancelled—on the basis that the subject was "too political." Instead, I was invited to meet a few of the civil servants involved in policy development. "It'll be a very informal discussion," I was told. "There will just be a couple of us junior people there."

The Lester B. Pearson Building in Ottawa is a labyrinth of hallways and elevators, and I arrived at the designated meeting room five minutes late. "Not to worry," said my host and his two colleagues. "We're still waiting for a few people." At that moment, the door opened, and eight very senior bureaucrats walked in. Although missile defence had been deemed too politically sensitive for a public debate, there was no shortage of people willing to challenge my views. The senior bureaucrats fell into that camp, having already decided that Canada should join U.S. missile defence— because we had been asked to do so, and because the United States was going to construct the system regardless of what we did.

After our long, frank and occasionally heated discussion came to an end, I experienced a wave of despair. Since when had the Canadian foreign service stopped pursuing an independent, made-in-Canada foreign policy? Fortunately, one of the junior people rescued my optimism, whispering: "Thank you. Some of us agree with you. We just can't say so right now."

Around the same time, I hosted a visit to Duke University by General Raymond Rees, the American chief of staff of NORAD. The general's visit to North Carolina attracted some attention in Canada, for during an after-dinner speech he undercut one of the principal arguments advanced by proponents of Canadian participation in missile defence by asserting that NORAD would survive regardless of what Canada decided. The general's visit had another consequence for me, in the form of a reciprocal invitation to visit NORAD as his guest, coupled with an order—to the Canadian head of the Binational Planning Group—to be prepared to answer any questions that I had.

I learned many things during that trip to Colorado Springs, but none was more revealing than this: closer military co-operation between Canada and the United States is much more important to the Canadian Forces than to their American counterparts. Indeed, it seemed that a large part of the BPG's efforts was directed at making the Canadian military matter to the United States. During a group dinner at the end of my visit, I shared this impression with a French Canadian officer.

"You're absolutely right," he said, switching to French. "If you count the number of people actively involved in the BPG, three quarters of them are Canadian. It's a big deal for our generals, you see. They love hanging out with the Americans."

Many Canadians assume that the pressure for closer co-operation between Canada and the United States comes from south of the border. In fact, a great deal of the pressure comes from within this country, including our civil service. After decades of financial cutbacks and failures of political will, many of our bureaucrats have become jaded; others have been co-opted outright. An important part of rebuilding this country's independence and influence involves revitalizing Canada's civil service by encouraging those bureaucrats who still believe that we have a distinct and important role to play and providing them with the resources and political support they need. It is time to rebuild that sense of self-worth and identity. It is time to stop acting like a vassal state, and to start acting like a grown-up country.

− 9 −

DO WE NEED
A CONTINENTAL
ECONOMY?

A LIFE-SIZED carving of a bald eagle stands in the corner of my office, a beaver clasped in its talons. Cut out of a cedar block, it was commissioned by my grandfather from a travelling chainsaw artist three decades ago. For years, I saw the carving as most people did: the powerful, regal eagle dominating the weak, humble beaver. But after I inherited the carving, I began to wonder. Perhaps my grandfather, a keen observer of Canada's relationship with the United States, had intended a more optimistic message. The beaver, which is clearly still alive, is only thirty centimetres long. Now, an adult beaver can measure three times that at one metre, and it can weigh up to thirty-five kilograms, more than five times as much as a full-grown eagle. Sometimes, when I'm writing, I catch a glimpse of the carving out of the corner of my eye and can't help but think that the beaver, slowly but surely, is starting to grow up.

"FREE" TRADE

Every summer during the 1970s, my parents would drive from Ottawa to Stoughton, Saskatchewan, with my sister and me in the back seat of the car. My memories of those road trips include the vast forests and crystalline lakes of northern Ontario, the moose and bears we saw along the way and the red hats of the Voyager restaurants. I also remember the many semi-trailer trucks gaining on us when descending hills and slowing traffic on every uphill grade. During the summer of 2001, I did the drive again, this time with my wife and infant son. The Trans-Canada Highway seemed strangely quiet, for there were far fewer semi-trailers. Many of the eighteen-wheelers that had once plied east–west within a national economy were now on north–south highways, serving a continental economy instead.

Coincidentally, I had just finished teaching a course on international trade at Duke University. I had explained to my students how the term "free trade" refers to an absence of tariffs, quotas and other restrictions that make imports more expensive than domestically produced goods. I had taught them about David Ricardo's principle of "comparative advantage," whereby countries, by exporting those goods that they can produce most efficiently and importing those they cannot, can increase profits and therefore investment and tax revenue. I mentioned that my own country had long benefited from exports: from the fur trade between First Nations and Europeans, to our prairie farmers and their "breadbasket of the world," to the successes of Canadian companies such as Bombardier, Magna and Research in Motion. I also pointed out that totally unregulated trade can accelerate the loss of local traditions, family farms, small towns and mom-and-pop businesses. It can shift corporate and political power to other countries, creating problems of corporate and democratic accountability and even of health and public safety. I explained that balancing the costs and benefits of trade, and guarding against its excesses, are among the most important responsibilities of any national government as it negotiates, ratifies, oversees and sometimes renegotiates trade agreements.

In reality there is no such thing as totally free trade. When governments negotiate trade agreements, they always insist on exceptions. Indeed, a totally free trade agreement wouldn't require negotiation, since it would simply require the removal of every single barrier to trade. For this reason, when lawyers, economists and political scientists analyse free trade agreements, they focus on the exceptions: the many, often very technical ways by which a country tries to retain the right to protect part of its economy from foreign competition. It is the balance between retaining and surrendering these protections, and the number and importance of the concessions obtained from the other side, that determines whether a country's trade negotiators have succeeded or failed.

As Katharine, Cameron and I drove the Trans-Canada, I remembered Brian Mulroney's words during the 1983 Progressive Conservative Party leadership campaign: "That issue of free trade was decided in the election of 1911 and it affects Canada's sovereignty and we will have none of it, not during leadership campaigns or at any other time." I was only seventeen at the time, but I understood the historic reference: the Conservatives' Robert Borden had defeated Wilfrid Laurier in a campaign that focussed on the Liberal prime minister's attempt to implement a policy of "reciprocity"— as free trade was referred to then—with the United States. Canada's Tories, beginning with John A. Macdonald and his "national dream" of a trans-Canada railroad, had long resisted the pull of economic continentalism.

I voted for the Progressive Conservatives in 1984. For this reason, I was particularly upset when, just one year later, our new prime minister did a u-turn on free trade. Mulroney, who U.S. secretary of state George Schultz said was "ideologically on the same wavelength" as the Ronald Reagan administration, promised the Americans that he would pursue all options for reducing trade barriers between the two countries. The resulting negotiations on the Canada-U.S. Free Trade Agreement (FTA, later to become NAFTA, or North American Free Trade Agreement, when Mexico joined the economic partnership) were replete with drama and controversy. In September 1987, Canada's chief negotiator, the pugnacious Simon Reisman, stormed out of the talks in Washington, D.C. He complained that the Americans were not responding to "elements fundamental to Canada's position," by which he meant a binding dispute-settlement mechanism that would replace the use of U.S. domestic courts with respect to Canada-U.S. trade. Reisman flew to Ottawa to meet with Mulroney, only to be sent back to the negotiating table with his tail between his legs. Whatever the Canadian prime minister's motivations for initiating the negotiations, they had taken on a domestic political importance that, in his mind, overshadowed all other considerations. With the clock running down on his first term, and the New Democrats and Liberals vying for top place overall in the polls, Mulroney was intent on creating an election-defining wedge issue that would force the two opposition parties to share common campaigning ground.

In the end, the Reagan administration obliged by giving Mulroney something that he could claim as a victory. Canada obtained a binding dispute-settlement mechanism, but at a price, since U.S. domestic law would continue to apply to "dumping" (a technical term for the export of products at less than their alleged cost of production). As we later learned, this exception was nebulous enough, and the U.S. government ruthless enough, that Canada's interests rarely prevailed in disputes with our powerful neighbour. The decades-long battle over softwood lumber is a prominent example, for it revolves around the fact that most Canadian lumber is produced from public rather than private land and is, therefore, allegedly subsidized. The Canadian government has seized on every possible mechanism to resolve the dispute, from NAFTA panels to the World Trade Organization (WTO), but the U.S. government, instead of backing down when it loses, simply modifies its anti-dumping laws, forcing the Canadians to begin the dispute-settlement process all over again. When the Harper government agreed in April 2006 that U.S. forestry companies could keep $1 billion that had been taken from Canadian companies, we had Brian Mulroney to thank.

The end of the Cold War gave new impetus to international trade negotiations, with the United States seizing the moment to transform the relatively limited General Agreement on Tariffs and Trade into the far-reaching World Trade Organization. Eager to provide a model for that global agreement, Washington pushed hard for an expansion of the Canada-U.S. FTA to include more areas of economic activity and another country, Mexico. NAFTA was negotiated during Brian Mulroney's last months in office. But though the opposition parties objected to the deal, it attracted far less public attention than had the FTA six years earlier. Canadians seemed to feel that they had already had their election over free trade. The relative lack of attention was unfortunate, since no negotiator who was serious about defending the Canadian national interest would have accepted some of the new concessions set out in NAFTA, including two chapters that will have serious long-term consequences for the country's well-being.

Chapter 6 effectively mandates U.S. access to Canadian oil and gas supplies, and it requires that the prices charged for energy exports to the United States not exceed those charged to Canadians. Yet it is easy to imagine that the federal or Alberta government might one day wish to reduce the mining of the tar sands at Fort McMurray, which is this country's largest single source of carbon dioxide emissions and—in a staggering example of energy inefficiency—consumes massive quantities of natural gas.

It is also easy to imagine that a sovereign country whose citizens endure bitterly cold winters, and by necessity travel great distances, might one day wish to cap prices on domestically consumed energy; in 2001, an energy crisis in California convinced even the regulation-phobic George W. Bush to allow the introduction of price controls there. Is it naive to suggest that Canada should assert greater energy independence, given the importance that the U.S. government attaches to secure sources of oil and gas? Just consider the case of Mexico, which during the NAFTA negotiations secured a full exemption for its substantial oil and gas sector. If a developing country could do it, why couldn't we?

Chapter 11 is just as worrying. It was intended to protect American, Mexican or Canadian companies that invest in another NAFTA country, providing them with a mechanism whereby a company can initiate binding arbitration if it believes its investment has been harmed by governmental action. Designed to deal with overt acts of uncompensated expropriation, the provisions of Chapter 11 have been very broadly interpreted by some of the arbitration panels established to resolve particular disputes, especially in cases brought by U.S. companies. In one prominent case concerning a California-based waste management company operating in Mexico, the arbitration panel ruled that a municipal government had engaged in an expropriation when it refused to issue a permit for a hazardous-waste landfill.

Decisions like this have had a chilling effect on government regulators, who are increasingly choosing not to impose or enforce local environmental, health and safety standards on U.S. companies operating in either Canada or Mexico. In one particularly obnoxious case, Ethyl Corporation, a U.S. chemical company, challenged a Canadian ban on the importation and use of a gasoline additive and suspected neurotoxin called methylcyclopentadienyl manganese tricarbonyl (MMT). After losing a preliminary decision, the Canadian government repealed the ban, apologized to the company and paid US$13 million in an out-of-court settlement—at the same time that U.S. states were banning the use of MMT with impunity. Just think about it: Chapter 11 of NAFTA might be putting the healthy development of our children's brains at risk.

When particular provisions of NAFTA come under fire, supporters of the agreement respond that the overall benefits to Canada greatly outweigh any costs. The Canadian government claims that, in the first decade after NAFTA came into force, the economy grew by an average of 3.4 per cent annually and generated a total of 2.5 million jobs. However, opponents of the agreement come to quite different conclusions about the overall benefits, not because they're distorting the facts, but because they focus on different things. The Canadian Labour Congress points out that the number of high-quality manufacturing jobs today is below pre-NAFTA levels, and wages, measured in terms of purchasing power, have remained the same or declined. In short, more economic activity does not necessarily mean more good jobs and higher wages. Rather, the Canadian economy has become more stratified, with higher salaries and investment returns for the wealthy and lower wages, less job security, and a less secure social safety net for the middle class and the poor. According to Statistics Canada, the income of the top 20 per cent of Canadian families rose 16.8 per cent from 1989–2004, whereas the income of the bottom 20 per cent dropped 7.6 per cent. One of the costs of free trade is greater income inequality, as our increasingly Americanized economy leaves more and more of our fellow citizens behind.

That said, most claims about the effects of free trade are just educated guesses, since we cannot know what would have happened in the absence of the FTA and NAFTA. Would our economy have grown? Would more jobs have been created? The answer to both questions is undoubtedly yes, because Canada is a resource-rich country with a well-educated and growing population. Would we be witnessing the same amount of poverty, homelessness and hopelessness as we are today? Nobody knows for sure, but there is little doubt that aspects of NAFTA —such as chapters 6 and 11—are seriously flawed when viewed from the perspective of the Canadian national interest.

Canada's increasingly heavy reliance on the U.S. market also places our economy at considerable risk, particularly after years of gross fiscal mismanagement by the Bush administration. When former U.S. president Bill Clinton left office, Washington was running a record surplus; today, it has taken on a record deficit. Some of the red ink may have been unavoidable—the U.S. economy entered a recession in late 2000 when the dot.com bubble burst— but the situation was greatly exacerbated by massive tax cuts to the wealthiest Americans, new tax loopholes for large U.S.-based corporations and the squandering and corruption associated with the occupation of Iraq. The U.S. dollar has plummeted against

European and Asian currencies, real economic growth has slowed and millions of people have either lost their jobs or been forced to take lower-paying employment with fewer benefits. These developments have pushed the Canadian dollar higher against the greenback, hurting Canadian exporters and hindering the Canadian economy as a whole.

And the worst could still be to come. Today, the United States has a massive balance-of-payments problem, which includes hundreds of billions of dollars in U.S. government bonds held by the Chinese and other foreign governments. The U.S. economy is still standing only because other countries have chosen to prop it up. Should the worst come to pass, it might experience a massive "correction," with severe consequences for an increasingly dependent Canada.

During the 1988 election campaign, Brian Mulroney dismissed concerns about the FTA on the basis that either country was free to withdraw from the treaty, provided that it gave six months' notice. NAFTA includes a similar provision, creating a situation where Canada could apply real pressure for a renegotiation of the agreement. During the 1993 election campaign, Jean Chrétien said he would do just that, but as soon as he achieved power he reversed his stance and ratified NAFTA without seeking any changes.

It's time to return to that broken promise. It's time to stand up for Canada—by insisting that the energy provisions be removed from NAFTA, that international law rather than U.S. domestic law be applied to all trade disputes and that the protections for foreign investors be substantially revised. In the meantime, whenever our southern neighbour reneges or procrastinates on its promises, Canada should refuse to capitulate. We are, after all, the United States' largest trading partner and primary source of energy, making them as dependent on us as we are on them.

FOREIGN INVESTMENT: THE LAND OF ONE-NIGHT STANDS

I have a weakness for Canada's grand old railway hotels. Two drawings of the Château Frontenac in Quebec City have long adorned a wall in my parents' house. My favourite meeting place in Ottawa is the lobby of the Château Laurier, where I can almost feel the presence of Mackenzie King. In Montreal, it's the Queen Elizabeth, where Brian and Mila Mulroney once swept by me—a gawking law student—on their way to a campaign speech. In Victoria, it's the Empress, where the University of Victoria graciously houses visiting academics.

I was staying in the Empress in late January 2006 when my cell phone rang one evening. It was Mel Hurtig, calling to share his grief about the news that Fairmont Hotels, including the Empress, had been sold to a Saudi prince and an American private equity firm. Only four days earlier, another Canadian icon, Hudson's Bay Company, had been sold to a South Carolina businessman. "Mel," I said quietly, "you'll never guess where I am right now."

Mel Hurtig has been fighting for limits on foreign investment since the early 1970s, when he led a campaign to persuade Pierre Trudeau to create the Foreign Investment Review Agency (FIRA). At the time, foreign-owned companies accounted for 37.4 per cent of corporate revenues in this country; within ten years after the creation of FIRA, their share had been forced down to 21.4 per cent—still high compared with other industrialized countries, but a remarkable decrease nevertheless. The Foreign Investment Review Agency was shut down by Brian Mulroney in 1985, at the same time that he was doing his U-turn on free trade. He replaced it with Investment Canada, an agency charged with soliciting and facilitating foreign investment rather than constraining or regulating it. As a result, the past two decades have seen foreign ownership climb back to early 1970s levels, with little benefit to Canadians, as Hurtig has explained:

To the end of December 2005, there were 11,501 companies in Canada taken over by non-resident-controlled corporations. The total dollar amount monitored by Investment Canada was an enormous $620.7 billion. Of this amount, 97.1 percent was for takeovers, and only a pathetic 2.9 percent was for the hoped-for new business investment!

Since Investment Canada began keeping track (June 30, 1985), some 64 percent of these foreign direct investments have been attributed to American firms. Far behind in second place is the United Kingdom at just over 9 percent. So, essentially, when we talk about foreign ownership and control in Canada, it's predominantly American. And, contrary to all the nonsense in our newspapers about Canadian direct investment in the United States exceeding US direct investment in Canada, the American ownership of Canada was over $63.5 billion higher, and of course represented a much greater percentage of assets and GDP.

Indeed, over half of all manufacturing in Canada is foreign owned, a level more than three times higher than in any other major industrialized country. And in the first six months of 2006 alone, forty-nine major Canadian companies with a combined value of $93 billion were sold to foreign investors. The list of recent sell-offs is a roll call of leading Canadian brands. In addition to Fairmont Hotels and the Bay, two of Canada's largest mining companies are gone: Falconbridge to Switzerland's Xstrata; Inco to Brazil's CVRD. Hamilton-based steelmaker Dofasco was sold to Luxembourg's Arcelor SA; Guelph-based Sleeman Breweries to Japan's Sapporo Breweries. Vincor, our largest winemaker, went to New York-based Constellation Brands; Thornhill's ATI Technologies, a world leader in the production of graphics chips, to California-based Advanced Micro Devices; Montreal-based Domtar, the last large Canadian-owned producer of paper, to Weyerhaeuser, the U.S.-based forestry giant. In British Columbia, Intrawest, the proprietor of Whistler-Blackcomb ski resort, went to the New York-based Fortress Investment Group. Just think about it: even the principal site of the 2010 Winter Olympics now belongs to foreigners.

It's not as if other countries don't restrict foreign investment. In January 2006, the Bush administration gave permission for Dubai Ports World, the world's largest marine terminal operator, to purchase six major port operations in the United States. News of the deal sparked a firestorm of protest in Congress, where the fact that Dubai World Ports is based in the United Arab Emirates was cited as cause for concern about possible links with terrorism. As a result of the pressure, the company eventually agreed to sell the assets to a U.S.-based investment group. In 2005, China National Offshore Oil Corporation made a bid to purchase Unocal and was also blocked by Congress. The company was eventually sold to another U.S. oil company.

The potential pitfalls of foreign investment go far beyond security concerns. Such investment can erode a country's domestic tax base, as profits are shifted offshore through creative accounting, including by overpricing goods and services supplied by foreign companies that belong to the same proprietor. Foreign-owned companies are also less likely to act as good corporate citizens. They have less incentive to invest in the arts, sponsor local sports teams, fund scholarships and internships or encourage workers and managers to play active roles in the local community. Although some foreign-owned companies do make token gestures, they are unlikely to have the same loyalties as domestically owned firms. Being inherently mobile, they find it difficult to justify the kinds of long-term investments that would strengthen the societies in which they operate. For the same reason, foreign-owned companies are more likely to push for lower taxes and less stringent regulations, even if those taxes and regulations are a necessary part of maintaining the quality of life, education and health care that attracts and maintains high-quality jobs.

Today, when Canadian business leaders speak about issues of public policy, it is important to question whose interests they are serving. Many of them now work for foreign-owned companies whose presence in Canada is not unlike a one-night stand. If they can get a better deal elsewhere, they'll be gone tomorrow.

Other industrialized countries realize this. Most European countries have stringent procedures for reviewing foreign buyouts, ensuring that industries considered essential to their societies, such as utilities and transportation companies, remain under majority domestic control. Japan, the world's second-largest economy, is even more restrictive. Only in Britain is global capitalism as unrestrained as it is in Canada. To some degree, Canadian voters have themselves to blame. Following the sale of the Bay and Fairmont Hotels, the *Economist* said: "In many other countries, the sale of national heirlooms would spark fierce opposition. Not in Canada."

Well, not yet. But remember, it took just ten years for Pierre Trudeau to cut foreign control of the Canadian economy almost in half. All that is needed is for Canadians to realize the scope of the corporate sellout that's underway and the relative ease with which we could stop it. Ten years? When do we start?

FRESH WATER: ARE CANADA'S LAKES AND RIVERS FOR SALE?

In 2004, the Canadian actor Paul Gross starred in a made-for-TV drama entitled H_2O. Gross plays Tom McLaughlin, the charismatic son of a murdered Canadian prime minister, who takes over Canada at the behest of a group of international financiers eager to sell our fresh water to an increasingly thirsty United States. The film is a must-see for Canadians concerned about the independence of this country, for although the plot stretches the envelope of credibility—it is, after all, entertainment—it never leaves the envelope completely.

Climate change, the exhaustion of aquifers and an incessant and growing demand for fresh water in the United States are beginning to create pressure for bulk water (as opposed to bottled water) exports from Canada. In a debate on CBC Radio in December 2005, former U.S. ambassador Paul Cellucci said:

Canada has probably one of the largest resources of fresh water in the world. Water is going to be—already is—a very valuable commodity and I've always found it odd where Canada is so willing to sell oil and natural gas and uranium and coal, which are by their very nature finite. But talking about water is off the table, and [yet] water is renewable. It doesn't make any sense to me.

It might not make sense to a NAFTA tribunal, either. Indeed, when the day comes that an arbitration tribunal is asked to decide whether bulk water exports fall within the scope of NAFTA, it might well decide that they do. The negotiating history of the agreement could play an influential role, for although early drafts specified that water was not a "tradable good," this exemption—which protected the Canadian government's right to prevent or limit bulk water exports—was left out of the final version. In fact, removing the exemption may well have been one of the concessions that Simon Reisman made to obtain a binding dispute-settlement mechanism. Reisman was known to be a strong proponent of bulk water exports, which he believed "would be able to reap enormous economic benefits for this country."

Even if water does not currently fall within the scope of NAFTA, it could be drawn into the scope of the agreement quite quickly—if a bulk export of water were to take place. A single act of trading water on a bulk basis would arguably transform the resource into a tradable good that was legally indistinguishable from softwood lumber, potash or oil, rendering subsequent attempts to prevent or limit further exports illegal. Much like in the Northwest Passage, where even one non-consensual transit could fatally undermine Canada's claim, just a single instance of water being shipped in bulk could have a decisive legal impact. For this reason, it is imperative that Canada takes water off the free trade table, quickly and decisively—now, before it's too late.

Bulk water exports are contrary to Canada's interests for two related reasons. First, there is little surplus water close to the Canada-U.S. border. Climate change is shrinking the glaciers and snowpacks of the western mountains, leading to much lower river flows in British Columbia, Alberta, Saskatchewan and Manitoba, especially in late summer. Salmon runs on the west coast have been affected, and on the prairies irrigation farmers and municipalities are starting to feel the pinch. In central Canada, the level of the Great Lakes is dropping; in 2000, the International Joint Commission, a binational body established under the 1909 Boundary Waters

Treaty, determined that there was no surplus water in the lakes and warned against any new diversions. As for plans for diversions from farther north, the environmental consequences of moving large amounts of water between drainage basins and across thousands of kilometres are unpredictable and almost certainly extreme. The water shortage in the United States is largely the consequence of poor planning and overconsumption. The solution lies in conservation and legislated limits on growth in water-deficient regions, not grand engineering schemes that would disrupt and destroy natural ecosystems on a continental scale.

Peter Lougheed, the illustrious former premier of Alberta, understands the dangers. In a speech to the Calgary branch of the Canadian Club in December 2005, he said: "We should not export our fresh water—we need it and we should conserve it. And we should communicate to the United States very quickly how firm we are about it." Lougheed called for an all-party declaration in the House of Commons confirming Canada's refusal to allow bulk water transfers to the United States, in order to dissuade the U.S. government from even arguing that water is included in NAFTA.

A similar approach was proposed in 1999, as Tony Clarke of the Polaris Institute explains:

> On February 9, 1999, the House of Commons passed a motion (introduced by the NDP) calling on the federal government to ban the export of water. In response, however, the Liberal government of the day chose not to formally issue a ban on the export of water. The prime reason? A water export ban would contravene Canada's international trade obligations.

If the ambiguous position on the tradability of water wasn't bad enough, recent governments have also failed to stand up to the United States when it violates its obligations under the Boundary Waters Treaty. Most recently, Washington refused to accede to a request from Ottawa that the two national governments jointly submit the Devils Lake issue to the International Joint Commission for a full scientific review. The state government of North Dakota was building a diversion canal from Devils Lake—a large, stagnant, saline pothole—into the Red River drainage system, putting the large commercial fishery in Lake Winnipeg at potential risk from exotic fish parasites and toxic chemicals. At this stage, the Canadian government still had the option of making a unilateral request to the International Joint Commission for a review of the project, but it chose not to do so. Politicians and civil servants worried that, since all previous requests had been made jointly by both countries, a unilateral request might put established procedures for co-operation at risk; indeed, then Canadian ambassador to the United States Frank McKenna referred to this approach as the "nuclear option." Instead, Canada accepted that the construction of a gravel filter on the new canal would suffice, even though its efficacy is doubted by most experts.

The established procedures for co-operation are already in serious trouble. On water, as on so many other issues, our conciliatory, don't-rock-the-boat approach to Canada-U.S. relations has failed. Unless we stand up for our own interests, Canadian fresh water could soon be irrigating crops, watering golf courses and filling backyard swimming pools in the southwestern United States. It's time to dissuade Americans of the notion that we're going to rescue them from the consequences of their short-sighted, profligate ways by allowing them to mess with our environment, too. It's time to make it absolutely clear that bulk water exports are not covered by NAFTA.

SECURITY, PROSPERITY—BUT WHAT ABOUT SOVEREIGNTY?

The North American continent became a lot smaller in September 2006, when the governments of Canada, Mexico and the United States released the Security and Prosperity Partnership Report. The seventy-seven-page document details collaborative efforts to develop "compatible," "comparable" or "North American" standards on matters as diverse as railways, travel visas, air pollution and food safety.

Will this harmonization of standards affect Canadian sovereignty? Not according to the report, in which the partners vow to respect "the sovereignty and unique cultural and legal heritage of each country." Yet "sovereignty" means different things to different people. In Canada, since September 11, 2001, two distinct conceptions have competed with each other. The traditional notion holds that a country must have full independence in domestic and foreign policy. The other, more European approach maintains that sovereignty can be shared or delegated to other countries or organizations. Although the latter might sound appealing, it simply doesn't work well in the North American context, given the vast disparities in power between the United States and its neighbours. Take the debate on missile defence: For opponents of Canadian participation, sovereignty meant retaining independence in defence and foreign affairs. But proponents also claimed to be defending sovereignty, in the belief that participation would enhance the protection of Canadian lives and jobs. The Department of National Defence even argued that our sovereignty would not be diminished because any surrendering of it would, in itself, be an exercise of sovereignty.

When I told some of my students about this last argument, they laughed. One called it Orwellian. "Not so fast," I cautioned, quoting from a 2003 speech by Bill Graham, then foreign minister: "We know that co-operative ventures of many kinds involve giving up some degree of independence for the sake of greater benefits; that's what happens when couples get married, when athletes join sports teams... While this process is often portrayed... as a loss of sovereignty, in fact what we are seeking to achieve is 'pooled sovereignty'—in other words, increased effectiveness for all the participants."

"That's what we do in Europe," said a German exchange student. "I even have a European Union passport." She was right: the concept of pooled sovereignty is imported from western Europe, where the horrors of the Second World War convinced politicians of the need for a new approach to preventing armed conflict. They built continent-wide institutions and delegated components of their sovereignty to them. At the apex of the system, the European Commission was charged with setting economic policy for the new community of states.

For decades, Canadian politicians shied away from the concept of pooled sovereignty, knowing public suspicions of closer ties with the United States. But calculations changed after 9/11. Many of Canada's business leaders saw the new U.S. emphasis on "homeland" security as a threat to cross-border trade and their ongoing efforts to develop a continent-wide economy. They began pushing hard for legal and policy changes. David O'Brien, the CEO of Canadian Pacific (and now the chair of both EnCana and RBC) argued that Canada would have to adopt U.S.-style immigration policies to keep the border open. "We have to make North America secure from the outside," he said. "We're going to lose increasingly our sovereignty, but necessarily so."

Within months, Ottawa signed a Safe Third Country Agreement with Washington that requires people wishing to claim asylum in Canada or the United States to do so in whichever of the two countries they arrive in first. In the year prior to 9/11, more than eleven thousand asylum seekers arrived in Canada by way of the United States and had their claims processed here. Today, asylum seekers taking the same route are pushed back into the much harsher system south of the border, where they are often held in prisonlike conditions and denied legal representation. What is more, the Safe Third Country Agreement makes it impossible for anyone to obtain refugee status in Canada on the basis of persecution in the United States. This consequence is currently of greatest significance to U.S. military personnel disillusioned with the war in Iraq. But suppose the U.S. Supreme Court were to overturn *Roe v. Wade*, the 1973 judgment that prohibits bans or restrictions on abortions. If American women were then to seek asylum in

Canada, on the basis of having been denied access to abortions in the United States, they might be returned home.

Some business leaders also pushed for changes to criminal laws. As Nancy Hughes Anthony, the president of the Canadian Chamber of Commerce, explained: "We're not going to get anywhere with our American friends in terms of improving border security unless we can show we've got good, strong anti-terrorism legislation and that we intend to enforce it." The result was the 2001 Anti-Terrorism Act, which is modelled on the U.S. Patriot Act. The legislation defines terrorism in broad terms and authorizes the cabinet to arbitrarily designate any group as a terrorist organization. It gives police far-reaching surveillance powers, including tapping telephones and reading e-mails without judicial warrants. It provides far-reaching powers of preventive arrest and denies terrorist suspects their right to silence under questioning—though, as I write, the latter two provisions are about to lapse.

Big business even took aim at Canadian foreign policy. Patrick D. Daniel, the president of the Alberta-based energy company Enbridge, complained that Canada sometimes pushed its sovereignty "a little too far." In his view, "it would be realistic for the U.S. to expect us to either get onside with U.S. foreign policy or expect some change in our relationship."

I turned again to my students: "Does anyone see a problem with applying the concept of pooled sovereignty to Canada's relations with the United States?"

"There are many countries in Europe," a woman in a headscarf said.

"Why does that matter?"

"It's a more balanced situation. No single country can dominate the others. Here in North America, the U.S. is so much more powerful than Canada that it doesn't need to surrender any of its sovereignty to us."

Indeed, when Canada and the United States adopt common standards, they are usually those that are already being used in the U.S. From securities regulations to drug licences to rules of military engagement, convergence is a one-way street. Now, under the Security and Prosperity Partnership, the already heavy influence of the United States has been augmented by the fact that convergence is occurring through regulations rather than legislation. Transnational committees of unelected bureaucrats are making rules without direct parliamentary oversight. As a result, considerations that do not relate to economic or administrative efficiency, such as human rights and national identity, are less likely to be factored in.

Even when Canada surrenders some of its sovereignty, there's no guarantee that the United States will respect any of the conditions or procedures agreed upon. During the 1962 Cuban Missile Crisis, Canadian forces delegated to NORAD were raised to a heightened level of alert after consultation with U.S. political leaders only. More recently, the post-9/11 arguments of Canadian business leaders have been weakened by Washington's ongoing refusal to obey the applicable U.S. law concerning softwood lumber imports—notwithstanding Ottawa's eagerness to address its security concerns.

And when the United States takes Canada for granted, our standing in the international community suffers. The unique influence that we enjoyed in the past is compromised whenever doubts arise as to our status as an independent North American voice. The situation might be compared to that of the Ukraine and Belarus within the former Soviet Union: both countries had separate UN seats, but everyone knew who called the shots. Already, in Europe and elsewhere, Canadian foreign policy on some issues is seen as virtually inseparable from the United States'. In August 2006, I published an article on Israel, Lebanon and war crimes in the *London Review of Books*. My version of the piece began with quotes from Tony Blair, George W. Bush and Stephen Harper supporting Israel's strong—and, in my view, disproportionate—response to the capture of two of its soldiers by Hezbollah militants. Shortly before publication, an editor telephoned to verify a few facts. "By the way," he commented. "We took out the quote from that Canadian fellow. Nobody knows who he is, and it makes sense to focus on the chief perpetrators here."

When Canada allows itself to be pulled along in the slipstream of the United States, its international influence—and therefore its significance—might compare with California's or Michigan's, or, worse yet, Puerto Rico's. A Canadian prime minister taking an independent stand is news; one parroting the U.S. or British position isn't.

Yet the refrain of the integrationists continues, including in a column written by the *Globe and Mail's* John Ibbitson in August 2006, after twenty-four people were arrested in London on suspicion of plotting to destroy nine trans-Atlantic airliners in midflight:

> Our advantage over them lies in our unity. The various Muslim terrorist organizations would probably be fighting each other if they weren't fighting us. But Western nations see things the same way. We share our intelligence. We jointly preserve our liberties despite tough anti-terrorism legislation, and keep our borders open to each other despite all the new security measures.
>
> That is why those who accuse the Prime Minister of tying Canada too closely to the United States are so dangerously deluded. Winning the war on terror depends on solidarity among the allies.

One of the problems with advancing the threat of global terrorism as a justification for closer military, policing and intelligence co-operation between Canada and the U.S. should be obvious: it's simply not clear that closer co-operation would actually do much to protect Canadian citizens. Would it have prevented the attacks of September 11, 2001? Would the creation of a Fortress North America really improve Canadian security, when the greatest threats may well involve suicide hijackers, suitcase bombs or letters contaminated with anthrax or other pathogens or—even more likely—when the threat is climate change, pandemics and other non-violent challenges requiring truly global co-operation and goodwill?

"It's not just about power," said one of my students with a distinctly un-Canadian drawl. "Americans think of sovereignty differently."

Americans certainly feel more connected to their sovereignty than most contemporary Europeans do to theirs. As the nineteenth-century French historian Alexis de Tocqueville observed: "The people reign over the American political world as God rules over the universe." The U.S. Constitution is still regarded as the ultimate expression of the American people's consent to be governed. Any exercise of authority that is not expressly vested in that document is considered by most as illegitimate. Many international standards are regarded with suspicion. This populist and absolutist conception of U.S. sovereignty helps explain why NAFTA is only a treaty, rather than an international organization, and why cross-border disputes are usually adjudicated in U.S. rather than international courts.

Curiously, while Canadian integrationists advance a European conception of sovereignty, their opponents think in terms that are quite American. Although they might not like it, Americans understand the mindset of those who support a made-in-Canada approach. But what must they think, privately, about Canadians who actively seek to surrender this country's sovereignty to the institutions and interests of a foreign state? Do the Americans whom Thomas D'Aquino of the Canadian Council of Chief Executives so evidently admires have the same admiration for him?

At root, our conception of sovereignty depends on the value we ascribe to democracy. If we believe—as I do—that sovereignty resides in the people, the decisions that most affect us must be made by our own democratically elected representatives.

I surveyed my class one last time: "Has anyone heard of 'taxation without representation'?"

"That's what caused the American Revolution," a bearded young man replied. "King George was making rules for the colonists without giving them a say."

"Ah," I smiled. "Can you see any parallel today?"

BORDER SECURITY: FENCES BETWEEN FRIENDS

"I think we're back in Canada now," said Mark Kohls, craning his neck to look out the back window of my parents' car. My high school buddy and I had spent the night on top of the Sweetgrass Hills of northern Montana, sleeping under the stars. Two decades ago, it was still possible to drive across the Canada-U.S. border on gravel roads where the only indication that you were entering a different country would be a sign—asking you to check in at a customs office many kilometres away. On the prairies, few people bothered to do that. The "world's longest undefended border" was, for most of its nearly nine thousand kilometres, a marker rather than a barrier.

Today, if two teenagers from Lethbridge tried to cross the border without permission, a Blackhawk helicopter might swoop down to intercept them. Since September 11, 2001, the U.S. Department of Homeland Security has stationed five of these high-speed military aircraft along the Canadian frontier. It has tripled the number of agents assigned to that border, installed more than 350 video surveillance systems and awarded a US$2.5 billion contract to Boeing that could lead to the construction of up to 900 surveillance towers. The towers will be augmented by heat and motion detectors as well as unmanned aircraft.

Canada's largest corporations (foreign owned and domestic) are terrified that the new American obsession with homeland security might impede the free flow of goods across the border. In response, the Canadian government has spent almost $6 billion on border security since 2001. Part of the expenditure has involved the creation of twenty-three "integrated border enforcement teams" made up of RCMP, Canadian Border Services Agency and U.S. Department of Homeland Security personnel. In August 2006, Prime Minister Stephen Harper announced that Canadian border guards would be equipped with side arms. In truth, only the most amateur of illegal immigrants, drug smugglers and terrorists are likely to be caught as a result of these expensive measures. Consider the border between Mexico and the United States, which is only one-third as long as the Canada-U.S. border, and mostly desert, but patrolled by eight times as many U.S. border agents. In spite of all this, it is thought that one million illegal immigrants enter the United States from Mexico each year. More personnel and new technology can help to tighten a border, but it can do only so much. To give just one example, it's difficult to imagine heat and motion detectors working well in areas such as southern Alberta, populated by numerous deer, elk, coyotes, wolves and bears.

In addition to the major investments in border security, the Canadian government has changed our intelligence, criminal and refugee laws in an attempt to assuage American concerns. Yet none of these measures have satisfied the U.S. government which, for the first time ever, is requiring that Americans as well as Canadians present passports when entering the United States. At the same time, many of these changes have compromised the legal rights of Canadian citizens, as well as the rights of foreign nationals resident or visiting here. In the best of circumstances, the curtailment of rights for reasons of expediency is questionable. When we've received nothing in return, there is no room for argument: our new anti-terrorism and refugee laws are unjust and unnecessary and must be repealed.

The tighter border has at least one other consequence: it reduces the opportunities for contact between Canadians and Americans and thus exacerbates existing misunderstandings. During my five years in the United States, I was struck by how little most Americans know about Canada and how that lack of knowledge sometimes translates into disrespect. Fortunately, a bit of actual exposure to Canada could turn the situation around. I took a group of my American students to a conference in Ottawa in October 2000, and I remember how surprised they were with the beauty and sophistication of our capital city; several vowed to return. Now, as a result of our newly securitized border, fewer of their compatriots are likely to bother with the trek north.

Attempting to secure a frontier that is nearly nine thousand kilometres long is a fool's errand that will cost the American taxpayer dearly. But what the United States chooses to do with its land and money is beyond our control. Our task, as with the Iraq War and missile defence, is to avoid the mistake of thinking that the U.S. approach must be right for Canada, too. When it comes to border security, the better approach is one of restraint. Here in Canada, we should save our tax dollars for more important tasks, reinstate our rights and freedoms and keep our doors open—not just to Americans, but to people from around the world. Fences might make for good neighbours, but barriers are not good for making or keeping friends.

– 10 –

GLOBAL CITIZENSHIP

THE TERM "global citizenship" has been used with some frequency in Canada recently. In 2003, in an article in *Canadian Geographic*, Pico Iyer wrote that "Canada has become the spiritual home, you could say, of the very notion of an extended, emancipating global citizenship." In 2004, the Canadian Council for International Co-operation organized a round table on the promotion of an "active global citizenship." In Vancouver, Martha Piper, the former president of the University of British Columbia, emphasized: "As a major research-intensive public university, UBC has a responsibility to provide educational and research programs of the highest intellectual quality that will contribute to educating global citizens."

But is global citizenship a good way to define the kind of progressive, compassionate, collaborative leadership that Canada as a country could offer the world? What, indeed, does global citizenship mean? If there's one thing that millennia of philosophy and literature have taught us, it's that words—and our choice of words—matter. Words provoke and shape social, political and economic change. Words are complex, contingent and open to multiple meanings. If we're trying to frame a debate, we need to understand exactly what we're saying—and what listeners believe we are meaning to say.

Let's begin by asking what "citizenship" means. My Canadian citizenship gives me the right to reside, vote, express my opinion, associate with others, travel freely within and to leave and enter this country. It does *not* give me the right to reside, vote, express my opinion or associate with others outside this country; indeed, it does *not* give me the right to enter any other country. If such a thing as global citizenship exists, it clearly isn't equivalent to Canadian citizenship, transposed to the planetary level. There is no world government, since the United Nations is little more than a collection of member states, many of them non-democratic. And there are many parts of this world where the inhabitants have no right to reside, vote, express opinions, associate or travel, not even as part of a national citizenship.

Stateless persons provide the clearest demonstration of the absence of citizenship rights at the international level. Statelessness can arise in several ways. For example, a child with foreign parents might be born in a country that accords citizenship solely on the basis of parentage, and his or her parents' country of origin might accord citizenship solely on the basis of birth taking place on its soil. Or, to take another example, I once acted as an expert witness in a case involving a man, born in Montreal, who had surrendered his Canadian citizenship in the early 1970s to become a U.S. citizen. Decades later, the U.S. government discovered that he had lied in his application for U.S. citizenship. They stripped him of his citizenship and tried to deport him back to Canada, but the Government of Canada refused to let him in—on the basis that he was no longer a Canadian.

There are literally tens of millions of stateless persons in the world today, all of them lacking any right to reside, vote, express opinions, associate or travel. Their lack of national citizenship, and their consequential desperate need for governmental assistance and accountability, makes them the most obvious candidates for global citizenship. Yet they languish, many for their entire lives, in the worst of the third world's shantytowns and refugee camps, without work, education, medical care—without any legal rights or protections at all.

Citizenship could also be understood as being different from— or additional to—the ability to assert legal rights against institutions of power and governance. It might mean something as simple as engaging in the multiple spheres of community within which every individual lives. From this perspective, merely reading this book is an act of citizenship, and all the more so if you write a challenging letter to me—or even write your own book—afterwards. Engagement in community could also imply a certain concern for others, an awareness of our human commonality. Volunteering at a soup kitchen could be construed as an act of citizenship, as could a donation to a non-governmental organization (NGO) engaged in humanitarian relief. Such acts of citizenship exist on a broad spectrum, from Aung San Suu Kyi's choice—to spend her life under house arrest in Rangoon rather than concede her people's claim to democracy—to your choice of saying "thank you" to the next bus driver or janitor you see.

From at least one "communitarian" perspective, citizenship is as much about obligations as it is about rights, for example the obligation to pay taxes, to serve in the military, to obey laws and respect authority. The move to supplement the discourse of human rights with the language of obligations achieved prominence during the 1990s, with leadership from a mix of political figures including Helmut Kohl, Bill Clinton and Tony Blair. Today, curiously, one finds it in the mission statement of my university, which states that students "will acknowledge their obligations as global citizens." The mission statement makes no mention of rights. Nor does it recognize that the acknowledgement of at least some obligations might—perhaps should be—a matter of individual choice. Arguably, it seeks to turn citizens into subjects.

So what does the word "global" mean? I hold a research chair in global politics, and it was always my assumption that "global" means planetary, the entire world. I'm certainly biased about this, since the politics that I study involve interactions between and amongst nation-states, intergovernmental and non-governmental organizations, transnational corporations and even terrorist groups, quite literally around the world. But "global" could mean something much more local, even personal. "Global" could simply mean spherical, well rounded, so that describing someone as "global" would mean that they were widely read, holistic in their appreciation of the world around them and therefore understanding of the situations and perspectives of others. "Global" could even mean adaptable, like a travel plug for a hairdryer or electric razor. In this sense, a person who was "global" could readily fit into various positions, locations, even countries and cultures.

Things become even more complex when we join "citizenship" and "global" together. Those who invoke the term "global citizenship" could be thinking of very different things or combinations of different things. They could be thinking about people who are well read, generally aware, engaged in their communities and concerned and caring for others, the kinds of people that universities and colleges once claimed to produce through the provision of a good liberal-arts education. But it's just as likely that those who invoke the term "global citizenship" are thinking about the growth of exchanges and interdependencies—including shared economic, environmental and security vulnerabilities—among the political entities and peoples of planet Earth. As the result of low-cost airfares, the Internet, the hegemony of the English language and the rise of the transnational corporation, we're increasingly sharing social, cultural, identity-forming experiences. David Beckham is no longer British, Nicole Kidman is no longer Australian, McDonald's and Microsoft are no longer American. The searing memories of the collapse of the Twin Towers and the photos from Abu Ghraib are common to us all.

It's even possible that those who invoke or hear the term "global citizenship" are thinking about some sense of collective responsibility that unites the peoples of this planet. Such thinking is certainly manifested, sometimes quite powerfully: in the immediate aftermath of 9/11; in the first few weeks following the Boxing Day tsunami of 2004; and in the buildup to the G8 summit at Gleneagles, Scotland, in July 2005. But it's also true that such manifestations are episodic, as dependent on the fickle attention of the "global" media as on any genuine, sustained core of common concern. While Western governments obsessed about the threat of global terrorism, the concentration of carbon dioxide in our global atmosphere rapidly approached 375 parts per million, almost 35 per cent higher than pre-industrial levels. How many of us actually consider the cumulative impact of our daily habits on climate change? How many of us drove a car, truck or sport-utility vehicle to work or school today? How many of us fly regularly on business or vacation without giving a second thought to the acutely deleterious impact that burning jet fuel at altitude has on the atmosphere and, with time, the devastating effects it will have on those people who already live at or below sea level, from New Orleans to Richmond, from Bangladesh to Tuvalu? I find it ironic—and cautionary—that our country, in which the term "global citizenship" has become most prevalent, is also the country that produces more carbon dioxide, per capita, than all but a handful of other nation-states.

Early in 2005, while billions of dollars were being raised for tsunami relief, food shortages in Niger took 2.5 million people to the brink of starvation, with pleas from the United Nations being almost totally ignored. Without denigrating the importance of tsunami relief, it was for a few brief weeks the latest fad. And fads come and go. Two years after the tsunami in the Indian Ocean, data obtained by the BBC from the UN Department for Aid and Development indicated that of US$6.7 billion in pledges, only half ($3.4 billion) had been fulfilled. Of the $301 million pledged by China for relief in one of the countries affected, Sri Lanka, only $1 million was delivered. France pledged $79 million and delivered just over $1 million, while Spain pledged $60 million and delivered slightly less than $1 million. When it came to the devastation in Indonesia, the United States pledged $400 million and delivered less than $70 million. And then there was the Red Cross, which raised $2.2 billion for tsunami relief but two years later was still holding $1.3 billion of that in the bank. Millions of people still needed assistance, but they were yesterday's story.

In Darfur, Sudan, millions of people have been terrorized by their own national government and its surrogate mounted militia, the Janjaweed. More than 200,000 have been killed. Canada's response has been to send money and equipment to the African Union, an organization that will intervene only with the full consent and co-operation of the very same government that is responsible for the atrocities. In Zimbabwe, the average life expectancy is only thirty-four years, as a result of both HIV/AIDS and extraordinarily bad government. Yet Robert Mugabe, the tyrant who has turned one of Africa's most bountiful countries into a failed state, remains firmly in power. In 2005, he launched a slum-clearance program known as Operation Murambatsvina—which in the local language, Shona, means "drive out trash"—that destroyed the homes of 700,000 already impoverished people, many of them children. Yet nobody, anywhere, is even contemplating the option of using military force to achieve regime change in Harare.

How many of you—the readers of this book—have contacted your member of Parliament about these crises? It's not difficult. Ask him or her to explain the difference between Kosovo (where Canada participated in a humanitarian intervention in 1999) and Darfur, or between Kosovo and Zimbabwe. You might even ask about the purpose of this country's $16 billion annual military budget.

In Burma (now also known as Myanmar), a decade-long government campaign against minority ethnic groups has destroyed nearly three thousand villages and forced hundreds of thousands of people into internment camps where they are raped, tortured and forced to work as slaves—yes, slaves. Burma might seem like another planet to you, but it's a profitable source of revenue for Vancouver-based Ivanhoe Mines, thanks to a joint venture that Ivanhoe has with the Burmese military junta. But don't blame the directors and shareholders of Ivanhoe Mines, who are acting entirely within the law. Blame yourselves, as citizens of Canada, for doing nothing to prevent our democratically constituted laws from permitting such corporate behaviour. I wonder what the people of Burma would say if they heard that Canadians were describing themselves as "global citizens"?

Some readers might think I'm over-dramatizing the situation, and that our governments have made real progress towards implementing a form of global citizenship on our behalf. They might point to developments in international human rights and international criminal law or to the related concepts of "human security" and a "responsibility to protect." As one of the lawyers who worked for the human rights organizations in the *Pinochet* case, I'm not one to denigrate those developments. But I am acutely conscious that we've a long way to go. Amnesty International estimates that some 140 national governments are involved in torture. After the tragedies of Abu Ghraib Prison, Bagram Air Base, Guantanamo Bay and Canada's own Maher Arar, we know that the governments of the United States and Canada are not blameless. Two of the worst perpetrators of genocide in Bosnia-Herzegovina, Ratko Milosevic and Radovan Karadzic, remain at large fourteen years after the establishment of the International Criminal Tribunal for the Former Yugoslavia.

The International Criminal Court, created in 1998, is only now about to hear its first case. And in September 2005, the UN General Assembly endorsed a version of the "responsibility to protect" that is so tightly constrained that it precludes humanitarian interventions when the Security Council is unable or unwilling to act—which, if you recall Kosovo, was precisely why a previous Canadian government sought to develop the concept in the first place.

. Even if we've made some progress on some rights, how much good is that progress to the one billion people who live on less than one dollar per day, or the almost three billion who live on less than two dollars per day? Many of us will spend more today on coffee than half of humanity has to spend on food, accommodation, fuel, health care and education combined. Are those who invoke global citizenship even contemplating a system of economic redistribution that could eliminate global poverty? If not, why not?

In fact, the situation on the global citizenship front is even worse than I've described so far. Not only have we failed to live up to the benevolent vision of global citizenship described above, we might also be ignoring a potentially dark side to the term. For instance, it's entirely possible that some of those who invoke global citizenship are thinking of the ruthlessly capitalist economic system that now dominates the planet, where goods, capital and services move seamlessly across borders, where corporations have abdicated any fidelity to individual nation-states, where workers are abandoned whenever it makes cold economic sense to outsource their jobs overseas and where a small but growing cadre of lawyers, accountants and executives strides boldly from business-class lounge to business-class lounge, equipped with the *Economist*, a BlackBerry, and an LLM or MBA from an American, British or even a Canadian university. The world's largest transnational corporations are now more powerful than all but a handful of nation-states, and even those states are heavily influenced by powerful corporations—think of the White House's relationship with Exxon and Halliburton. Believe it or not, some of these corporations have explicitly branded themselves as "global citizens." That's right, these are economic entities that are required by law to focus upon profit making. Is this what global citizenship should be?

In September 2005, I hosted a symposium on the "meanings of global citizenship" at UBC. Eunice Sahle, a Kenyan-born Canadian who teaches at the University of North Carolina, argued that those who invoke global citizenship tend not to address deep power structures. Yet these structures constrain any potential for positive change, especially in terms of greater influence for civil society, concepts of redistributive justice and real attention to the voices and interests of those who live in our world's least developed states. If we're going to have a serious discussion of global citizenship, we need to be able to talk frankly about the "Washington consensus" that permeates the hugely influential policies of the World Bank, International Monetary Fund, World Trade Organization (WTO), Organization for Economic Co-operation and Development and G-8. We need to talk about TRIPS—the WTO Agreement on Trade-Related Intellectual Property Rights—and agricultural tariffs and subsidies and conditionality and the appallingly low levels of overseas development assistance. In that context, isn't it ironic that Canada, the country in which global citizenship is most often invoked, is the country most frequently derided for failing to exercise leadership on the target of 0.7 per cent of GDP for overseas development assistance, a target pioneered by one of own former prime ministers, Lester B. Pearson? If we're going to talk about global citizenship, let's talk frankly about how and where power vests and is wielded in today's world, about our own country's complicity in the global power game and about the hypocrisies and hollowness of lax and presumptively benevolent conceptions of global citizenship.

At the same symposium, Barbara Arneil, a political scientist from UBC, suggested that the term "global citizenship" could even be invoked deliberately and specifically in support of George W. Bush's foreign policy. The U.S. president, after all, professes to be seeking "democracy and freedom" for all, to be bringing at least some of the rights enjoyed by American citizens—to vote in national elections, to worship, to buy and sell—to all the people of this planet. As Arneil explained, the "aspiration to liberal empire" has, as one of its central features, a "civilizing mission"—a mission expressed by Bush in the following words in November 2003: "[T]he United States has adopted a new policy, a forward strategy of freedom in the Middle East... The advance of freedom is the calling of our time; it is the calling of our country."

Of course, it's easy to criticize George W. Bush. In doing so, we have to be careful not to become arrogant ourselves. Geographer David Ley has pointed out that those who invoke global citizenship risk isolation and hubris, since they typically do so from a position of class privilege, from the gentrified older neighbourhoods of Manhattan, North London, Sydney, and yes, the Annex and Point Grey. I sometimes write in a coffee shop on the west side of Vancouver that is frequented by white, thirty-something moms pushing five-hundred-dollar baby-joggers, most of whom undoubtedly think of themselves as progressive, cosmopolitan and environmentally friendly but who probably wouldn't dream of taking their babies for a stroll through the city's downtown east side, let alone the shantytowns of São Paulo, or even forgoing the annual midwinter vacation in Honolulu or Acapulco. As Radhika Desai of the University of Victoria has observed, the parochialism and paternalism associated with many invocations of global citizenship is the same parochialism and paternalism that skewed imperialism and colonialism.

The political philosopher James Tully has made the important point that one can conceive of democracy in narrow or broad terms. And of course democracy exists on a spectrum, from merely voting once every four or five years to playing an active, daily role in the political and social communities in which we live. Global citizens cannot be content to remain within the narrow, formal constraints of a voting democracy, since democracy of that kind simply doesn't exist on the global level. Whatever global citizens are, they must engage in other manners and forms of democracy, be activists of some kind.

It is this broad and proactive conception of global citizenship that, I believe, holds the most potential for Canada. For global citizenship is not only complex and contingent, it's also relatively new and therefore still open to appropriation. It's just sitting there, waiting for progressive, internationalist Canadians to seize upon it and make it their own. So here is what I think we should do: Just as women decided to "take back the night," we should "take back global citizenship" to make it what we want it to be, rather than what George W. Bush or some corporate advertising guru might wish to make it.

I cannot presume to speak for others, but here is a definition that appeals to me:

> Global citizenship empowers individuals to participate in decisions concerning their lives, including the political, economic, social, cultural and environmental conditions in which they live. It includes the right to vote, to express opinions and associate with others and to enjoy a decent and dignified quality of life. It is expressed through engagement in the communities of which the individual is a part, at the local, national and global level. And it includes the right to challenge authority and existing power structures—to think, argue and act—with the intent of changing the world.

Deciding whether you like this definition, and deciding how it should be replaced or improved, requires an honest and rigorous conversation, a debate, a straight-up intellectual argument of the kind that you can make happen, in kitchens, coffee shops, classrooms and chat rooms across the country and on the steps and in the corridors of political and economic power. What we must do is care about words and ideas, about the impact they're having on our world, and want to turn that caring into committed engagement and action. Global citizenship is a powerful term because those who invoke it do so to provoke and justify action. And understanding the power of words, and our own ability to appropriate and give them new meaning, is the first step towards acquiring power ourselves.

CANADIAN ROLE MODELS

We've all heard the refrain: Canadians are losing interest in politics; they no longer believe that it's worthwhile or necessary to be informed and active participants in the political process, even when it comes to something as fundamental as voting. The numbers would seem to bear this out: until the 1990s, voter turnouts in excess of 75 per cent were common for federal elections; since then, turnouts have declined steadily, reaching a nadir of 60.9 per cent in June 2004 before climbing back to 64.7 per cent in January 2006.

Now, if Canadians really have lost interest in politics, my suggestion that progressive, internationalist Canadians seize upon the term "global citizenship" is destined to fail. But I'm not convinced that Canadians are tuning out; rather, I believe that our conception of politics is changing. Since returning to this country, I've met thousands of people who are actively engaged in seeking change at the local, provincial, national and international levels. They're doing so in a variety of traditional and non-traditional ways, in many cases using the Internet as a mechanism for acquiring and transmitting information and connecting with others who share their concerns. Through their sustained efforts and personal sacrifices, they are having just as much influence on the direction of this country as previous generations did. Moreover, many of them are influencing developments outside of Canada—often bypassing the traditional institutions of political parties, government bureaucracies and state-to-state diplomacy. In this sense, they do represent a new kind of actor, the global citizen, for whom political engagement involves much more than casting a ballot every four or five years. In the following pages, I'd like to introduce you to just a few of these remarkable Canadians, as exemplars of what this country is—and could be.

SHEILA WATT-CLOUTIER was born in Kuujjuaq, in northern Quebec, in 1953. Her mother was Inuit, her absentee father was a white RCMP officer, and she spent the first decade of her life on "the land"—living in tents and travelling by dogsled. Today, Watt-Cloutier is one of Canada's most internationally influential politicians, having been elected president of the Canadian section of the Inuit Circumpolar Conference in 1995 and chair of the entire Inuit Circumpolar Conference in 2002. The Inuit Circumpolar Conference is an international organization that draws the Inuit of Alaska, Canada, Greenland and Russia together into a unified political force.

In the 1990s, Watt-Cloutier represented the Inuit during the negotiation of the Stockholm Convention on Persistent Organic Pollutants. These toxic chemicals, which include DDT and PCBS, are produced in the industrialized regions of the world. Disproportionate amounts are then carried to the Arctic by a process of global distillation involving evaporation at low latitudes and condensation at high latitudes, also known as the "grasshopper effect." After being deposited in the Arctic, they move up the food chain, accumulating in the fatty tissues of predators such as seals, walruses and ultimately humans.

Throughout the negotiations, Watt-Cloutier made a point of educating everyone involved about the fact that the Inuit are the world's most pronounced victims of persistent organic pollutants, to the point where Inuit women have to think twice about nursing their babies. During a particularly critical stage in the talks, Watt-Cloutier presented a soapstone carving of an Inuit woman and child to Klaus Topfer, the executive director of the United Nations Environmental Program. Her focussed yet impassioned efforts paid off: the Stockholm Convention, adopted in May 2001, requires states to take specific steps to reduce or eliminate the production of persistent organic pollutants and to dispose safely of existing stocks. So far, 128 countries have ratified the convention, including Canada, China, the European Community, India and Japan.

More recently, Watt-Cloutier turned her attention to climate change, the effects of which are particularly advanced in the Arctic. The traditional way of life of the Inuit has become more difficult, even dangerous to sustain, as temperatures rise, weather patterns change, snow and ice conditions become less predictable and populations of wild animals decline. In recent years, dozens of Inuit hunters have fallen through the unusually thin ice and perished, paying the ultimate price for humanity's greenhouse gas emissions. In the face of the cataclysm threatening her people, Watt-Cloutier has travelled like a woman possessed, challenging political and corporate leaders to act and delivering impassioned speeches at conferences, universities and think-tanks worldwide. In an awe-inspiring display of willpower, she has transformed the Inuit into the globally recognized human face of climate change.

Watt-Cloutier has even taken on George W. Bush, who for years denied that climate change was happening and still refuses to take meaningful action to stop it. In 2005, she and sixty-two other Inuit from Canada and Alaska filed a petition with the Inter-American Commission on Human Rights in Washington, D.C. They argue that the United States, by failing to reduce its massive emissions of carbon dioxide and other greenhouse gases, has violated the cultural and environmental rights of the Inuit. Regardless of the eventual legal outcome, the initiative is already having an important effect by raising media and public awareness about climate change in a country where such awareness is most desperately needed.

Watt-Cloutier is now a major international figure. Audiences at her speeches often number in the thousands, and she is sought out by scientists, activists and journalists worldwide. In March 2005, I stayed at a bed and breakfast just a few doors down from Watt-Cloutier's house in Iqaluit, and over the course of a single afternoon saw three foreign camera crews arrive to interview her—in a town of just seven thousand people located two thousand kilometres north of Montreal! In January 2007, Watt-Cloutier was nominated for the Nobel Peace Prize. Yet it's clear that she is motivated neither by fame nor by money. Her political and environmental work is driven by her concern for the future of her people, especially her grandson. She understands that a despoiled planet is the worst possible legacy that we can leave to our descendants. Watt-Cloutier is a great Canadian and a true global citizen, in the best sense of the term.

DAVID THOMAS is a journalist, author and technology entrepreneur from Montreal. A decade ago, he moved to the small town of Fernie, British Columbia, to escape the crowds and hassles of big-city life—only to discover that his new home was subject to some of the same problems and issues he was trying to flee.

The Flathead River valley in southeast B.C. is one of Canada's most pristine wilderness areas. Lynx, wolverines, grizzly bears and wolves roam the forests, while the river is home to rare populations of bull and cutthroat trout. But the valley also contains vast quantities of natural gas, trapped in coal seams just a few hundred metres below the surface. Extracting this kind of natural gas, commonly referred to as "coal-bed methane," requires closely spaced wells and thus considerable surface development, including access roads, power lines and compressor stations. The gas itself is trapped beneath large quantities of saline groundwater, which has to be pumped out and then disposed of, a process that has caused terrible soil and watercourse degradation in other places, such as Wyoming's Powder River basin.

The Government of British Columbia, intent on reaping billions of dollars in potential royalties, has energetically been promoting the development of coal-bed methane across the province. New wells are labelled as experimental for the first three years in order to exclude them from the usual regulatory framework, while the regulations themselves have been loosened to allow wells to be located closer together. Royalty rates are lower than for conventional oil and gas, and each new well receives a fifty-thousand-dollar credit.

By 2004, a handful of test wells had been drilled in the Flathead River valley. The activity attracted the attention of local residents, including Thomas, who by this point had been elected to Fernie City Council. Thomas persuaded his fellow councillors and a number of other local residents to ask the provincial government to conduct a full environmental-impact assessment before more drilling took place. The government promptly denied the request, and it announced that it would begin auctioning exploration rights for the area.

Thomas and his colleagues then appealed to the federal government for help, but Ottawa demurred, citing the fact that natural resources fall within provincial jurisdiction, which they normally do—unless there is an interprovincial or international dimension. The story might have ended there, were it not for the fact that the Flathead River flows south into the United States, where it forms the western border of Montana's Glacier National Park, a World Heritage Site. In a stroke of brilliance, Thomas contacted the governor of Montana and informed her that tainted water from Canada might soon be despoiling one of that state's most pristine and, because of tourism, economically important areas. Governor Judy Martz immediately appealed to the B.C. government to postpone the auction until a full environmental-impact assessment was conducted. When her request was denied, she contacted Ottawa, pointing out that Canada was obligated, under the 1909 Boundary Waters Treaty between Canada and the United States, to ensure that boundary waters "shall not be polluted on either side to the injury of health or property on the other." Martz also wrote to Colin Powell, the then U.S. secretary of state, and asked for his assistance.

The B.C. government was furious that Montana had involved itself in the matter. Richard Neufeld, the provincial minister of energy and mines, accused Martz of election grandstanding, despite the fact that she was not seeking re-election. In fact, if electoral considerations were affecting developments, they were doing so on the Canadian side of the border. Paul Martin's federal Liberals seemed reluctant to antagonize Gordon Campbell's provincial Liberals in the run-up to a federal election campaign in which B.C. seats would figure prominently.

But politicians in Victoria and Ottawa could do nothing about the fact that Montana's involvement was suddenly attracting national media attention. The day after the bidding for the exploration licences closed, a visibly disappointed Neufeld announced that no bids had been received. Rumour has it that Shell did in fact table a bid, only to withdraw it just hours before the auction closed. The company had experienced the effects of negative publicity before, first over its environmental and human rights record in Nigeria, then over plans to scuttle an old oil rig in the North Sea. It was not about to risk another highly visible environmental controversy.

David Thomas is another great Canadian who, through perseverance and imagination, has taken Canadian interests to the international level and prevailed.

MONIA MAZIGH was born in Tunisia and came to Canada in 1991 to study. At McGill University she met Maher Arar, her future husband, who was born in Syria and had moved to Canada with his family at the age of seventeen. Mazigh and Arar have both been Canadians for more than a decade, though Arar is also still a Syrian national—but only because that country refuses to accept renunciations of nationality.

Arar has experienced some of the very worst treatment that human beings are capable of inflicting on one another. His horrors began on September 26, 2002, when he was detained at New York's JFK Airport while returning to Canada from a family vacation in Tunisia. After twelve days of questioning, he was deported to Jordan and then Syria, where he was imprisoned for a year without charge. Stephen Toope, the independent fact-finder who was eventually appointed by a judicial inquiry, found that Arar was tortured in Syrian custody.

Were it not for Mazigh's determined efforts, her husband might still be in that tiny Syrian cell, or more likely dead. I vividly remember hearing Mazigh being interviewed by Anna Maria Tremonti on CBC Radio's *The Current* on February 12, 2003. By then, Arar had been imprisoned in Syria for 132 days. Mazigh's clearly articulated and controlled passion moved me and, as it turned out, tens of thousands of other Canadians. Although a transcript cannot convey the tone and tenor of a conversation, the following excerpt offers some sense of why that particular interview had such a powerful effect:

Mazigh: This is the way, how a citizen, a Canadian citizen is treated? It is nonsense. His life has been destroyed and the life of my kids and myself too.

Tremonti: Are you confident the Canadian government is doing everything it can do?

Mazigh: I don't think that they are doing whatever they can do, because if they are doing that, he should be here. It's now too much. It's now five months that he's not back. So, to my point of view, they are not doing everything that they can. They can bring him back and this will be a wonderful thing, and a wonderful gift for, not only me, for all Canadians.

Many Canadians joined Mazigh in pressing for government action, sending letters and e-mails to Ottawa, making phone calls and turning Arar into a *cause célèbre* that Jean Chrétien could not ignore. The Canadian government finally began to apply pressure on Syria and, on October 5, 2003, Arar was released and flown back to Ottawa.

Even then, the struggle was not over. As Toope explained, Arar's detention and torture had left deep psychological scars. One can only imagine the challenges faced by Mazigh in rehabilitating her husband and looking after their two children while working all the while to pay the bills. And then there was the issue of Arar's reputation and career. He is a highly trained computer engineer who specializes in wireless technology, but he found it impossible to secure employment after returning home. Many Canadians continued to regard him with suspicion, knowing that he had been detained and deported because of a suspicion that he was somehow linked with terrorism.

In response, Mazigh began a new advocacy effort, this time to pressure the Canadian government into establishing a judicial inquiry. Concerned that such an inquiry might reveal RCMP or CSIS involvement in Arar's detention and torture, the government resisted for over three months until announcing, in January 2004, that an inquiry would take place. The report of the Arar Commission was released in September 2006, four years after Arar's rendition to Syria. Although heavily censored, the report clearly and definitively cleared Arar's name. In January 2007, the Canadian government finally apologized to him and his wife and family, and agreed to provide $10.5 million in compensation.

Canadians still owe Arar and his family much, including our profound thanks. The attention that Mazigh brought to Arar's rendition and torture has been critically important in rallying support for civil liberties at a time when they've been threatened and compromised. We now know that Canada's police, security and intelligence services overstepped the mark after September 11, 2001, including by sharing incorrect or inconclusive "intelligence" with foreign governments. Thanks to Mazigh, the balance between security and individual freedoms in this country is much closer to where it should be. Some rights, such as the right not to be tortured, remain sacrosanct.

Today, Mazigh and Arar are putting their lives back together. In July 2006, Mazigh became a professor at Thompson Rivers University in Kamloops, B.C. The residents of that small city have embraced their new neighbours as remarkable Canadians and true global citizens. Toope concluded that Arar has moral courage. The same must be said of Monia Mazigh.

DOUGLAS ROCHE is a former member of Parliament from Edmonton who served as the Progressive Conservative Party's critic for external affairs during the late 1970s. In 1984, he was chosen by

Brian Mulroney to be Canada's ambassador for disarmament to the United Nations. There, Roche served as chair of the Disarmament Commission, a subsidiary body of the UN General Assembly that meets in New York City each spring. In 1998, Jean Chrétien appointed Roche to the Senate, where he chose to sit as an independent, on the basis that he'd be better able to express his values and views in the absence of party constraints.

Roche has spent a lifetime campaigning to eliminate nuclear weapons, which he describes as "the paramount moral and legal problem of our time." It's a daunting task, since there are more than twenty thousand nuclear weapons still in existence, enough to destroy life on Earth several times over. The weapons are held by a total of nine countries, five of which have ratified the 1968 Nuclear Non-Proliferation Treaty (NPT), three of which—India, Pakistan and Israel—have not, and one—North Korea—that ratified and then renounced the treaty. Of particular concern today is the possibility that a few nuclear weapons might fall into terrorist hands. Internationally, the high degree of concern about this issue was expressed in the first debate of the 2004 U.S. presidential campaign, when George Bush and rival John Kerry agreed that nuclear proliferation was the single most serious threat facing the United States.

In May 2005, the regular five-year review conference for the Nuclear Non-Proliferation Treaty took place in New York City. The 153 government delegations were seriously polarized. On one side, the United States wanted the conference to deal exclusively with the nuclear potential of countries such as Iran. On the other side, many developing countries were equally concerned about the thousands of nuclear arms still in existence and about plans by the United States to develop new kinds of nuclear weapons. They wanted more attention to be paid to the obligation of nuclear weapons states, under Article 6 of the NPT, to take steps to disarm. With neither side prepared to compromise, the conference collapsed after a month of procedural haggling.

Douglas Roche has been spearheading a global effort to save the NPT. He's the force behind the Middle Powers Initiative, an attempt to forge a new coalition between NGOs and "middle power" countries such as Canada, Brazil, South Africa and Sweden that have chosen not to acquire nuclear arms. The idea is that this coalition would be able to apply more pressure on the nuclear weapons states to begin serious negotiations on the reduction and eventual elimination of their nuclear arsenals. This, in turn, would provide the impetus for co-operation between developed and developing countries on other proliferation issues.

Roche speaks frequently and forcefully at international conferences. He has written eighteen books, countless newspaper articles and a series of influential policy papers. He lobbies politicians and bureaucrats incessantly, and not just in Canada. In 2004, he drafted an open letter to then prime minister Paul Martin opposing Canadian participation in U.S. missile defence. Thanks to Jillian Skeet, a Vancouver peace activist who can talk her way past any receptionist or agent, the letter was subsequently signed by a who's who of prominent Canadians, including Bryan Adams, Pierre Berton, Stompin' Tom Connors, Sarah McLachlan, David Suzuki and Sacha Trudeau. Other people played key roles in the campaign to keep Canada out of missile defence, but when Paul Martin finally announced his decision not to participate, nobody deserved more credit than Douglas Roche.

In June 2006, Roche persuaded former Canadian prime minister Kim Campbell to lead a "high-level" delegation from the Middle Powers Initiative to Ottawa. The delegation urged the Government of Canada to recommit to multilateral diplomacy in the aftermath of the failed NPT review conference. Although Roche, Campbell and their colleagues did not say so explicitly, they are increasingly concerned that Stephen Harper's government is realigning Canadian disarmament and non-proliferation policy to match that of the Bush administration. Since Bush took power in 2001, he has opposed a verifiable fissile material cut-off treaty, failed to seek

Senate consent for ratification of the 1996 Comprehensive Test Ban Treaty, renounced the 1972 Anti-Ballistic Missile Treaty, initiated the missile defence system and sought congressional funding for a new generation of tactical nuclear weapons. He also plans to put weapons systems in space.

But Bush and Harper will have to deal with Douglas Roche first. The last time I saw the seventy-seven-year-old, he was speaking at the University of British Columbia about his latest book, *Beyond Hiroshima*. One of my students made the mistake of asking when he was going to cease his efforts and retire. "When the last nuclear warhead is destroyed," he replied fiercely. "We must never, ever give up." What a Canadian! What a global citizen!

PEOPLE LIKE Sheila Watt-Cloutier, David Thomas, Monia Mazigh and Douglas Roche make me optimistic about Canada's future. They and thousands of other Canadians like them are actively and positively shaping this country and the wider world. They are global citizens seeking to improve the political, economic, social, cultural and environmental conditions of the communities in which they live, and not just for their own benefit.

Significantly, all four individuals have been prompted into action by government inertia or, in some cases, outright opposition. Sheila-Watt Cloutier might not have devoted herself to raising awareness of climate change had the Canadian government acted to address the threat. But since 1990, carbon dioxide emissions in this country have increased by 24 per cent, leaving us 30 per cent above our Kyoto Protocol commitment. The increase in Canadian emissions was neither inevitable nor economically necessary, since energy conservation and alternative technologies have proved successful and economically advantageous elsewhere. David Thomas needed to get help from a foreign government to save a nearly pristine Canadian river from the greed of the B.C. government and big oil. Again, Ottawa could have intervened, but it chose not to. Canadian officials were complicit in the rendition of Maher Arar, provided information to Syria about him despite knowing that he was probably being tortured there, did little to secure his release until Monia Mazigh generated an inconvenient amount of publicity and then resisted calls to establish a commission of inquiry. Douglas Roche, a former insider, now finds himself on the outside, organizing domestic and international coalitions of NGOs to apply pressure to reluctant governments—including the Government of Canada.

Many of my students at the University of British Columbia are also global citizens. They're remarkably international: roughly one in four was born outside Canada, and nearly everyone has at least one parent who was an immigrant. They're also incredibly engaged. Every fall, I teach a course called the Change the World Seminar, in which students strategically seek to influence public policy. Remarkably, more than half of them succeed in some discernible way. My most memorable experience from the seminar came courtesy of a young man from Newfoundland named Matthew Gillard. In September 2004, Gillard decided to investigate what the Government of Canada was doing to stop the many rapes, killings and displacements that were—and still are—taking place in Darfur. In the course of his research he came across a short report in the *Kelowna Daily Courier* about a federal cabinet meeting that had recently taken place there. According to the report, Paul Martin's Liberals were just days away from committing $20 million to the African Union (AU) peacekeeping mission in Darfur. But Matt was unable to find any further news reports on the $20 million, so he took it upon himself to track the money down.

I showed him how to use the Government of Canada online telephone book, and I lent him my telephone. He proceeded to call every civil servant in Ottawa who might conceivably have known about the $20 million. Most knew nothing; others were evasive; some clearly did not believe that Matt was just a student working on a class project. Finally, after dozens of calls, Matt turned to me and said: "I have to phone Africa. Someone just told me that the

Canadian High Commission in Addis Ababa might be able to help. Apparently they're responsible for Canadian interests in Sudan."

"Sure," I replied. "Go ahead."

"It's not that easy. Ethiopia is eleven hours ahead of Vancouver. I need to phone at 6 AM."

We met at my office the next morning. I well remember the walk to my office: it was dark and drizzly, and I nearly stepped on a skunk.

The first person to answer the phone didn't know anything about the $20 million, but he forwarded the call to someone else. The second person couldn't help either, but when she heard what Matt was asking, she cheerfully replied: "Okay, hang on a second. I'll put you through to the person who knows."

The "person who knows" was almost certainly the Canadian military attaché. He quizzed Matt at length. "You're phoning from where? Are you really a student?" After ten minutes, he chuckled, having convinced himself that Matt was harmless: "It's all very interesting, you know. Ottawa decided several weeks ago that it wasn't going to give the AU the $20 million. But they've been receiving so many telephone calls the last few days that, yesterday afternoon, they changed their minds."

CANADA AS A GLOBAL CITIZEN

When one reads the stories of these remarkable Canadians, the glass can seem either half empty or half full. On the negative side, Canadian governments seldom act boldly on the world stage, preferring instead to follow more powerful countries, most often the USA. Our political leaders are reluctant to advance bold ideas, take risks or inspire people to greatness. If Canada once punched above its weight, it now tends to pull its punches. On the positive side, Canada still has the vestiges of a good reputation and a huge potential to influence world events and thus define its own future. It also has millions of citizens who crave it to do just that.

Pierre Trudeau famously described living beside the United

States as "sleeping with an elephant." Even if the beast is friendly, there's always a danger that it will roll over on us in its sleep.

There is much that draws Canada and the United States together. Our two countries share one of the world's longest borders and have fully integrated air defences. We share a culture that is heavily influenced by Hollywood, Motown, Nashville and, yes, Toronto and Montreal. We also share a language—though many Canadians still spell "colour" thus, say "zed" rather than "zee" and speak French with varying degrees of fluency. Yet the values of most Canadians differ significantly from those of most Americans. In addition to universal public health care, same-sex marriage laws and (nearly) decriminalized marijuana, we take pride in our traditional contributions to UN peacekeeping, support for human rights, deliberate lack of nuclear weapons and our leadership in international law making. And these values are becoming more rather than less distinct. As pollster Michael Adams explained in his book *Fire and Ice*, Canadians have become more secular, tolerant of diversity and questioning of authority in recent years, while Americans have moved in the opposite direction.

Historically, our differing values led Canadian governments to adopt policies that regularly diverged from those of the United States. And they did so without paying any apparent price. In 1965, Lester B. Pearson publicly chided Lyndon Johnson about the bombing of North Vietnam; Pearson received a dressing-down for it, but a few months later, the two leaders signed the Canada–United States Auto Pact, a trade agreement on cars and automobile parts that benefited the Canadian economy. In 1985, Brian Mulroney declined an invitation to join Ronald Reagan's Strategic Defence Initiative, also known as Star Wars; two years later, the two men signed the Free Trade Agreement. In 2003, Jean Chrétien deftly avoided the Iraq debacle, then watched as trade with the United States continued to grow. In 2005, Paul Martin announced that Canada would not join U.S. missile defence, just before meeting George W. Bush and Mexican president Vicente Fox to initiate a broadening and deepening of trade relations. The United States, so heavily dependent on its northern neighbour, knows better than to allow differences of opinion to be blown out of proportion or to link a dispute on one issue to continued co-operation on another, unrelated issue.

It helps that successive Canadian governments have practised the art of the hidden compromise. No Canadian troops were sent to Iraq, but thousands served in Afghanistan. As American forces advanced on Baghdad, Canadian frigates patrolled the Arabian Sea, Canadian soldiers remained seconded to U.S. units and U.S. military aircraft passed freely through Canadian airspace en route to the Middle East. Thanks to this quiet assistance, the Bush administration's response to Canada's public abstention was limited to an equally public postponement of a planned presidential visit.

All countries feel the weight of American influence in their decision making, but few feel it as heavily and as often as Canada. Retaining a distinct political and cultural identity in the shadow of our powerful neighbour has both challenged and defined Canadians. It's time for Canadians to recognize our considerable strengths and past successes in promoting changes at the international level—even on matters, such as the International Criminal Court, where the U.S. government stands firmly opposed. Canada has used its still-strong reputation and middle-power status to help ban anti-personnel landmines, outlaw persistent organic pollutants and protect cultural diversity from the WTO. And it has done so not just in support of its own interests, but also for countries and people everywhere. This latter point is of key importance, for when Canada acts on behalf of the international community, it not only does good, it also bolsters its reputation, thus generating what Joseph Nye of Harvard University calls "soft power"—the capacity to persuade. This provides us with an advantage vis-à-vis the United States, which, by often acting in narrowly self-interested ways and favouring bullying over diplomacy, has squandered its soft power.

The benefits of being seen to seek the greater good leads to another key aspect of Canada's role in the world: the fact that this country achieves its greatest successes when it charts a path that is not determined solely by economic factors. We did so during the Iraq War and again on missile defence. From our incredibly multi-ethnic and livable cities to our friendly and cohesive rural communities and, occasionally, our foreign policies, this is a country that has rejected George Grant's thesis in *Lament for a Nation*. We are not destined to lose our identity and independence and be subsumed into the United States. We have a greater role to play, for a truly great country should be about more than a high GDP. It should be about maintaining and improving the quality of life of all its citizens, in terms of education, health care, social opportunity and a clean and sustainable environment. It should be about addressing global developments, such as climate change, that threaten the safety and well-being of all. And it should be about improving the lot of human beings everywhere, for the simple reason that doing so is right and just.

My mentor, the Cambridge international lawyer and social philosopher Philip Allott, opened my eyes to a simple but incredibly empowering fact: much of what human beings take to be immutable about political systems—traditions, norms, laws and constitutions; institutions and organizations; even the nation-state itself—exists principally at the level of human ideas. As a result, these seemingly immutable structures can in fact be changed. All we have to do is to imagine something different—better laws, a better country, even a better world—and then translate our ideas into action. Can we do it? Sheila Watt-Cloutier, David Thomas, Monia Mazigh, Douglas Roche, Matthew Gillard and thousands of other Canadians clearly think so. And what is a nation if not its people? Why can't an entire country be a "global citizen"? Why can't this be our "intent for a nation"? For this, I believe, is what Canada is for.